STEAM DRIFTERS

A BRIEF HISTORY

CONTENTS

Foreword

I regard it as a great privilege and an honour that Jim Tarvit has asked me to write the foreword for his new book on the history of British Herring Steam Drifters.

I think this is an extremely important book, and one which simply had to be written at this time before all of this valuable information might have been lost forever. Indeed, it comes as somewhat of a surprise to me that Jim has been able to collate all this information at all at this very late hour, and it was probably only his experience first as a fisherman, and then latterly as a fishery officer, that enabled him to do so.

In this book, along with many photographs, Jim has managed to record the history of every single one of the 1800 steam herring drifters that had ever been built in Scotland, England, Northern Ireland or the Isle of Man and this in itself must be no mean achievement. Jim also tells me, that although steam drifters had been owned in Wales, he believes that none had ever been built there.

The honour of being the very first steam drifters ever built, went to the "Onward" for Cellardyke owners, and the "Forward" for Aberdeen owners. They had been built together at Leith in the year 1878, and were simply just wooden Fifies powered by steam engine instead of sail. This great building period for these new type of boats was to last for almost 50 years, including the duration of the first world war when many drifters were built for war service. The very last steam drifter ever to be built, the "Wilson Line" for Cellardyke owners, was built of steel at Aberdeen and her completion in 1932 signalled the end of an era.

My own first association with the days of steam go back to 1947, when I served as a boy cook on the gas lit wooden steam drifter "Easter Rose" which sailed from Peterhead to attend the still very important herring fishery at Great Yarmouth in Norfolk. At that time, there were still literally hundreds of steam drifters fishing from all the principal herring ports around the coast, along with all the infrastructure connected with them. The end was getting very close though, and by 1960 almost every one of these beautiful boats had gone, replaced by modern diesel engined boats with their lower running costs.

David Smith M.B.E.

STEAM DRIFTERS - A BRIEF HISTORY

When I started this project, I thought it would be a relatively simple task to establish how steam drifters evolved. It seems, according to available evidence, that the transformation from sail to steam in the drift-net herring fishing was in some ways rather difficult; it was certainly not as easy as the transformation from sail to steam in the trawling and long-lining sections of the fishing industry. This transformation from sail to steam in the herring fishery took place over a period of 20 years from about 1880 to 1900 by which time the advantages of steam over sail were fully recognised and accepted by herring fishermen. It is apparent that the Scottish Industry led the way initially although the English owners were eventually the prime innovators from about 1900, probably because more capital was available via fishing companies.

PART 1

1. In order to understand the transition from sail to steam, it is necessary to recall the way in which drift-nets were operated by sailing drifters. I was brought up in the era when operating drift-nets by power had been refined to a fine art with hauling being done, "bow first and head to wind" whereas sailing drifters, with or without power assisted hauling, such as the Fifies or Zulus in particular, hauled drift-nets "stern first and not necessarily into the wind". This method is clearly illustrated in the following photograph of a contemporary painting ca 1900 held in the Scottish Fisheries Museum.

In the days before the advent of steam capstans, ca 1880, the only power available was man-power and fleets of herring drift-nets (in Scotland) consisted of about 20 to 30 nets per vessel. Herring drifters in Scotland were generally about 40' to 50' in length pre 1880 with the size being limited to what a man could handle in respect of sail handling and the operation of their fishing gear and were; as a result, restricted in their operations during bad weather. The use of a "messenger rope" (or bush rope) had been in existence since the middle of the 19th century albeit in an early form attached to the "cork line" on top of the net and this was eventually hauled by a manual capstan colloquially known in Scotland as the "Iron Man".

SAILING FIFIE ML 159 - Hauling Driftnets by the Stern.
From a contemporary painting held in Scottish Fisheries Museum, ca1903.

The advent of steam propulsion which had been gathering pace during the 19th century was noted by members of the herring industry and its advantages were recognised. During 1878 it was reported in the press (see note (1)) that D. Allan of Granton had built two steam drifters, "Forward" for Methven of Leith and "Onward" for Sharp and Murray, Fishcurers of Cellardyke.

This was four years before the first steam trawler fished from Aberdeen. Not much is known about these two drifters except that "Onward" could not obtain a crew from Cellardyke and fished mainly from Aberdeen. which incidentally was one of the main herring ports in Scotland at that time. By this period it was fairly well established that steam tugs were employed to tow sailing drifters to sea during calm conditions. As stated earlier, during and previous to the 1870s herring drifters around Scotland whilst fully decked, were generally no more than 50' in length and by the 1880s boats of up to 60' in length were beginning to appear. There seems no doubt that steam drifting started with the appearance of "Forward" and "Onward" in 1878 (2). This was followed by the "Cunliffe Fleet" early in the 1880s. From Ritchie's Article, reprinted at appendix I, these early drifters were of the Fifie hull form, fitted with small upright boilers and compound steam engines. The "Cunliffe Fleet" along with "Forward" and "Onward" were also used at the great line fishing from Aberdeen and played a considerable part in the introduction of steam fishing to Aberdeen. Also during this period it appears that experiments with steam power in herring drifters were being carried out along the Scottish East Coast by various people using Fifie or Zulu hulls."Rob Roy" LH 92 which is regarded by some as the first steam drifter, built 1882, certainly had a Fifie hull and was tiller steered (see photograph of model held in National Science Museum). A drawing of this model is illustrated in Peter Anson's book "Fishing Boats and Ports of East of Scotland" and the text states that this model is held in the National Science Museum, London. Progression took place in England in a similar manner although somewhat later. The first English steam drifter is generally recognised as "Consolation" LT 718, 72' long and built by "Chambers and Colby" of Lowestoft during 1897. Her hull form was very similar to the contemporary sailing smacks of that period with tiller steering.

Whole model of the line and net fishing boat 'Rob Roy', c 19th century built by Gifford and Co.
Courtesy of Science & Society Picture Library, Science Museum.

CONSOLATION LT 718 - First Steam Drifter to be built in England. Built by Chambers & Colby of Lowestoft 1897. Burnt 1908 after having been sold to Lerwick. Courtesy of Port of Lowestoft Research Society.

No wheelhouse or galley was fitted on deck and she was provided with a full set of sails, the only distinguishing feature being a boiler funnel.

2.   The introduction of a successful steam capstan and the use of the messenger rope (bush rope) as we now know it (i.e. underneath) the net probably provided the real push towards steam power. Steam capstans had been in use by sailing trawlers from English ports from about 1870, (4) but were not very satisfactory until William Garrood in 1884 invented a steam capstan with a hollow spine which allowed the delivery of steam to the two cylinder steam engine fitted on top of the capstan. This allowed the capstan to be turned without any interference to the hauling of ropes by steam pipes. This invention was quite revolutionary and it formed the basic design of steam capstan until the demise of steam in the 1950s. The advantages of a successful steam capstan were quickly recognised by herring fishermen and by the early 1890s they were fitting them into sailing drifters. This adoption of steam power allowed them to operate in much worse weather than previously when man-power was the order of the day. This change in operating led to a need for bigger and more powerful (in sailing terms) boats which were now feasible to operate with the availability of steam power to hoist and handle larger sails and to assist in the handling of nets via the messenger rope (bush rope).

The steam capstan was introduced into Scotland during the early 1890s and the first recorded installation in a East Fife sailing drifter was on board "Reliance" KY 312, 60' long, during 1894 although it is recorded that a sailing Fifie built at Pittenweem during 1893 was fitted with a capstan. No mention was made whether it was powered by hand or steam (1).

The use of steam capstans in sailing drifters in Scotland became general from about 1895 and resulted in an increase in the size of these vessels which ultimately led to the large Fifies and Zulus of 70' to 80' long. These larger sailing drifters were now capable of competing successfully with the early steam drifters principally because of their relatively low running costs compared with the steam drifters.

It should be noted at this point that sailing drifters continued to haul their nets stern first with the boilers and capstans being fitted in the after part of the vessel. This method of operation continued in sailing drifters until the introduction of internal combustion engines on board sailing drifters ca 1908 - 1915. These engines allowed the previously sailing drifters to operate in a similar manner to steam drifters i.e. by the bow and head to wind. It is perhaps worth noting at this point that a purely sailing large drifter, a Zulu named "Muirneag" SY 486 continued to operate from Stornoway with sails and a steam capstan until 1945 or so and was certainly the last large drifter to operate under sail.

3. We have seen the advent of steam drifters becoming established although not in the exact form which eventually evolved. During the late 1880s and early 1890s steam liners and trawlers made their appearance and their deck works and design were very similar to the ultimate design of steam drifters. I am firmly of the opinion that the configuration of steam drifters as we know them was very strongly influenced by early steam trawlers and liners. I am not referring to the very early steam trawlers which were, in effect, paddle driven tugs adapted to operate beam trawls but rather to the early screw driven vessels using the then relatively new (ca 1880 - 1890) trawl boards with "Granton" trawls.

The building of a fleet of steam liners was commenced during 1891 for the East Fife owners. The first one was launched at Anstruther by Jarvis during 1891 and named "Maggie Lauder" KY 499. She was 88' long and her design appeared to be based on earlier wooden liners of which three had been on hire to Cellardyke crews from 1890 and had operated very successfully with great lines.

WILLIAM TENNANT KY 472 - Built of wood by Wm. Jarvis of Anstruther during 1893. Shown as a liner - note no steam capstan, no galley and full set of sails. ca 1893. Lost off Humber 1918. Courtesy of Scottish Fisheries Museum.

This fleet was from 88' to 100' long and whilst most were built of wood at least seven were built of iron or steel mainly at Leith and Dundee. These vessels were very successful liners but proved to be too unwieldy to operate herring drift-nets. Steam capstans were not in general use until after 1894 and this is perhaps the reason why they couldn't successfully operate herring drift-nets.

The Cellardyke crews were content to fish from them with great lines and indeed were very successful but when the summer herring season came round, they deserted the liners in favour of drift-netting for herring and used their sailing drifters for this purpose (5). This naturally did not please the owners of these steam liners (mostly companies) and as a result all were disposed of by the early 1900s. Contemporary paintings of some of these vessels held in the Scottish Fisheries Museum clearly show that they were not fitted with steam capstans although some (perhaps all) did have steam winches. Most of these liners were converted to steam drifters during the early 1900s having been fitted with steam capstans by their new owners. The technology and expertise were now available for them to operate successfully as steam drifters. Indeed some were re-purchased by Cellardyke men and fished successfully with herring drift-nets. Most of these vessels when built were fitted with a wheelhouse in front of the funnel with a galley at the after end of the casing. Horizontal boilers were now well established in place of the earlier upright ones although it must be stated that upright boilers continued to be used on vessels which only required steam to drive capstans or line-haulers and not for propulsion. The first mention of a covered in wheelhouse as opposed to a "steering box" was made during 1892 in the East Fife Record report of the launch of the second "Anster" liner "Rob The Ranter" KY 458 (5).

ROB THE RANTER KY 458 - Built of wood by Wm. Jarvis of Anstruther 1892 as a liner. Shown after conversion to a Drifter and fitted with a steam capstan. ca 1909. Sold to Peterhead 1917 and became PD329, lost 1920. Courtesy of Scottish Fisheries Museum.

4. The popularity of steam drifters was slow to take hold in Scotland, most probably because of the introduction and general use of the steam capstan along with the use of the messenger rope (bush rope) which led to the increased size of the sailing Fifies and Zulus. These sailing drifters had very low running costs compared to the early steam drifters and of course were much cheaper to construct. Indeed the largest of these sailing drifters were built between 1900 and 1905. The last large Fifie to be built in East Fife was "True Vine" ML 20 and it is probable that she was the last large sailing drifter to be built in Scotland and was in effect obsolete before being completed.

As stated earlier most of the early steam liner/drifters were built of wood although iron and steel were the popular materials for trawler construction. However, in 1900, Smith Dock Limited of North Shields started to construct a fleet of steam drifters which was to be based at Great Yarmouth and owned by Smith Dock Trust Limited (6). This fleet, which was colloquially named the "Numerical Fleet," were all named with numbers i.e. One to Thirty Four. They were built by 1902 and this is most certainly the first real indication that the steam drifter had "arrived" and was accepted by fishermen as a suitable herring drifter. The technology and expertise was now fully established which enabled steam drifters to fish for herring successfully and out-perform sailing drifters despite the higher running costs. There was a considerable movement by the more progressive fishermen and fishing companies to convert from sailing drifters to steam powered ones with this momentum gathering pace from 1900 onwards to about 1905 when the building of the large sailing drifters finally ceased. It must be noted at this point that prior to 1905 most of the wooden boat builders around Scotland had been very busy building the large sailing drifters and these builders changed over to building wooden steam drifters overnight to meet the new and considerable demand for them.

FOUR PD 108 - Built of steel by Smith Dock Co. Ltd of North Shields as FOUR YH 480, 1901. Became SA 10 then PD 108. Sunk by submarine off Out Skerries June 1915, shown leaving Lowestoft ca1911. Courtesy of A. Durrant, Kessingland.

The initial building boom which basically started with the construction of the "Numerical Fleet" and the boat building firms at Lowestoft and Great Yarmouth led to the construction of 1727 steam drifters between 1900 and 1932 in the United Kingdom along with 12 being built in Holland (7). These figures, of course, exclude the Admiralty steel and wooden drifters built between 1917 and 1920. These "standard" drifters as they became known are dealt with in Part II. The period between 1906 and 1911 saw some 48% (829) of the above total being built with 15% (256) being completed during 1907 alone. The total of 100 drifters completed in one year was exceeded during 1907, 1908, 1910, 1911 and 1914 and it was not difficult to envisage the activity at boat building yards during these years - "boom-time indeed".

By 1904 the pattern, design and size of the steam drifter was firmly established and very few changes took place thereafter to the hull form and superstructures until the advent of pure motor drifters during the early 1930s. I use the words "pure motor drifters" to distinguish them from the large number of large sailing drifters which were fitted with internal combustion engines from about 1908 onwards. The installation of engines changed the sailing drifters to motor drifters which were colloquially known as "motor boats" thereafter. The capstans were moved from aft to forward during the installation of the engines thus the method of hauling was now the same on these ex-sailing drifters as that which took place on the steam drifters.

A total of 1852 steam drifters were built between 1890 and 1932 which included 125 built before 1900 mainly as liners or small trawlers which were converted to drifters at or about the turn of the century. This total includes 12 wooden vessels and 587 steel or iron drifters along with 6 wooden ones which were built as sailors but were converted to steam shortly after completion.

Wooden drifters were most popular as can be seen from the above figures and perhaps for three reasons:-
(a) Fisherman of that era were used to and comfortable with wooden vessels.
(b) There was considerable capacity and expertise around the coasts for building wooden vessels.
(c) It became well known that steel drifters and trawlers were inclined to ship fairly large amounts of water about midships where freeboard was low. Wooden drifters (and wooden boats in general) did not have this trait and on the whole were much drier.

LIZZIE WEST BF 213 - Built of wood by Herd & MacKenzie Ltd, Buckie during 1930. Became M 22 and shown as LT 495. Last wooden Drifter to be built in the U.K. Finished up as a "Barking Ship" at Fraserburgh and scrapped 1968. Courtesy of Scottish Fisheries Museum.

The popularity of wooden drifters waned almost at the same rate as steel ones with the last wooden one, "Lizzie West" BF 213, being built by Herd & MacKenzie of Buckie during 1930. She was certainly a fine looking vessel and after a spell under Lowestoft owners ended her days as a "barking vessel" at Fraserburgh. (8) She was eventually scrapped during 1968 and it was about that time that drift-netting went out of fashion having been ousted as a preferred method of catching herring by pair trawlers and purse seiners.

Steel drifters continued to be built until 1932 when the last one, "Wilson Line" KY 322 was completed by Alex Hall & Company of Aberdeen. Naturally the release of Admiralty standard drifters to fishermen during the early 1920s had a considerable adverse effect on the building of new drifters from 1920 onwards.

5. The early steam drifters were fitted with upright boilers and small compound engines (2 cylinders) but this soon changed with horizontal boilers being universally accepted. Compound steam engines continued to be popular particularly amongst the smaller wooden drifters but by 1907-08 were being ousted by "triple expansion engines" (3 cylinder) which became standard equipment for drifters.

Some owners mainly from Lowestoft built drifters fitted with a type of triple expansion engine which became known colloquially as a "Monkey Triple" because the high pressure chamber was fitted on top of the intermediate chamber. This configuration was invented and made by the famous engineering firm of "Elliot and Garrood" based at Beccles near Lowestoft. (This is the same firm which invented the first successful steam capstan mentioned earlier). Although steam drifters fitted with "Monkey Triples" were generally very fast, this configuration did not really catch on. During my early days at sea (in a motor drifter) most of the crew had been steam drifter men for most of their career and it was not uncommon to be told "She's a fast ship and is fitted with a "Monkey Triple". I have never seen a "Monkey Triple" as all the drifters I boarded as a laddie were fitted with the normal three-in-line triple expansion engines. Although I was at sea in various steam drifters (mainly standards) as a young teenager, it was only for fun and not employment. By the time I started fishing after leaving school, steam drifters were on the wane and mostly nearing the end of their useful life. Steam drifters generally had a life-span of up to 50-60 years at the most and the best continued until the mid to late 1950s when economics and age caught up with them. The oldest steam drifter operating during 1948, as far as I'm aware was "North Briton" A 746 then latterly PD 487, which was built during 1894 of iron by Hall Russell of Aberdeen as a trawler. She did not trawl for long and was converted to a drifter early in her career approximately about 1900. I can remember her clearly as she was operating from Peterhead for some years after I had started fishing. As far as I am aware she was sold for scrap ca 1952 along with many other much younger drifters.

NORTH BRITON PD487 - Built of Iron by Hall Russell Ltd of Aberdeen during 1894 as a Trawler, was converted to Drift Netting ca 1900. Shown here leaving Peterhead ca1948. Courtesy of Aberdeen Libraries - Benzie Collection.

Steam drifters were certainly durable and versatile fishing vessels and were employed variously at trawling, early seine-netting and great lining for white fish particularly when herring were out of season or catches were un-economic. It is somewhat ironic that latterly Cellardyke fishermen fished with great lines in their steam drifters for most of the year and only fished for herring during the Autumn East Anglian fishing, bearing in mind the earlier attitude prevalent in the East Fife area towards the early steam liner/drifters which incidentally were mostly converted to drifting by 1904 or a little earlier.

Some of the steam drifters built for Lowestoft and Great Yarmouth after about 1910 were really drifter/trawlers and operated as trawlers during the winter months from the end of the East Anglian fishing until the start of the Spring or Summer season depending, of course, on prevailing economic factors such as price and availability of white fish and prospects for the coming herring season.

English drifters started what became known as "boxing" from March onwards mainly based at Aberdeen during the early 1930s. This involved drift-netting for herring on grounds up to 200 miles ENE or E by N from Aberdeen, landing herrings iced and stowed in boxes which measured 6 to the cran i.e. approximately 4.5 stone (28.6 Kilos). It must be noted that whilst a cran of herrings was a volumetric measure of 37.5 gallons, it was accepted for statistical purposes as equivalent to 3.5 cwts (28 stones). It had long been known by Cellardyke fishermen that these distant grounds (from East Coast of Scotland) contained shoals of herring during the early Spring months, as these were favourite great line grounds and produced herring bait caught by drift nets. No doubt they were at least partly instrumental in the establishment of the "boxing" fishing by

English vessels as Ronnie Balls MBE (a prominent Great Yarmouth Skipper) stated that he had personally received information regarding the availability of herring on these distant grounds from KY skippers (article from World Fishing).

As trawlers they were most successful fishing the shallower waters of the Southern North Sea, English Channel and Irish Sea with flatfish being the main target species. Some of drifter/trawlers were longer than the average drifter and reached up to 100' to 120' in length. The normal drifter including standards had their stokeholds in the engine-room ie, fires were at the afterend of the boiler, but the longer drifter/trawlers such as "Margaret Hide" LT 746 and the "Sarah Hide" LT 1157 were fitted with a separate stokehold at the forward end of the boilers. They were known colloquially as "fore enders" and were easily recognisable by the placement of ventilators in front of the funnel whereas normal steam drifters had ventilators slightly aft of the funnel.

SARAH HIDE LT 1157 - Leaving Lowestoft ca 1948. Built of steel by J. Duthie (Torry shipbuilding Co. Torry) as ARTHUR GOULBY LT 1215 during 1921. Note ventilator foreside of funnel indicating furnaces at fore-end of boiler. Scrapped 1955. Courtesy of Port of Lowestoft Research Society.

Steam Drifters were amongst the earliest of vessels to operate seine-nets from Scottish ports particularly in and around the Moray Firth. Indeed the method of "fly dragging" with a seine net as opposed to then normal Danish method of anchor seining was originally developed by a Wick steam drifter "Zoe" WK 653 skippered by the late William Thain (9).

The Moray Firth fishermen especially those from Lossiemouth's area, realising the potential of the seine net, largely changed from steam to motor seines circa 1930, partly for economic reasons and the need to fish inside the three-miles fishery limit (this area was available for small boats to fish legally).

6. At the start of World War I, the Royal Navy was extremely short of small vessels for minor war duties and found it necessary to look to the fishing fleet for such vessels. This need resulted in 1371 steam drifters (10) being taken over under hiring arrangements along with most of the crews in addition to numerous steam trawlers and motor drifters. Steam drifters served all round the British Isles engaged in duties ranging from mine-sweeping to patrol duties and boom defence net attendance. These duties were too numerous to mention here and were extremely varied - "real maids of all work". A number of steam drifters served in the Mediterranean, mainly in the Dardanelles and Adriatic areas. The first drifters were hired early in the war during August 1914 with most being in service by the end of 1915. They proved so useful that a number were taken whilst still on the stocks being completed. All which survived served until 1919 with a few not being released until 1920. It is worth noting at this point that the hired steam drifters' usefulness was recognised by the Admiralty when they decided to build their own fleet of drifters i.e. "standards" (see Part II). It is also worthy of note that of the 1371 steam drifters which served in World War I some 300 of them also served during World War II. (11)

Unknown Wooden Drifter during World War I, 1914-1918, note small gun on foredeck.
Courtesy of Scottish Fisheries Museum.

Most steam drifters during World War I were fitted with either a 3-pounder gun or a 6-pounder one as a main armament, in the bows of the vessel. These vessels had not been built with a view to being fitted with such guns and had to be strengthened to cope with such armament.

Although very minor warships, some steam drifters saw action against enemy ships, aircraft and submarines. As early as 2nd September 1914, the first steam drifter casualty whilst on active service was "Eyrie" LT 1121 which was sunk by a mine whilst minesweeping in the vicinity of the "Outer Dowsing" Light-vessel. During the following day "Linsdell" LT 322 also minesweeping was sunk in the same area. The last steam drifter to be lost during that war was "Calceolaria" KY 267 being mined off Elbow Light Bay in the "Downs" during 27th October 1918.

In all 130 steam drifters were lost during World War I with 32 being lost in action, 32 by mines, 3 by submarines, 33 during collisions, 8 by disappearance and the remainder by other causes. (10) Perhaps the most famous action, although not well known outside of fishing circles, took place during 15th May 1917 when a fleet of drifters on patrol were attacked by Austrian cruisers off the Fano Islands in the Adriatic, resulting in 14 drifters being sunk during one afternoon in this rather one-sided action. It was because of the bravery of the skipper and crew of "Gowan Lea" FR 105, that skipper Joe Watt of Fraserburgh was awarded the VICTORIA CROSS for facing up to these Austrian cruisers with only a 6 pounder gun.

Steam drifters were, of course, part of the famous Dover Patrol of World War I. During the night of 27th October 1916, 6 drifters were sunk by German torpedo boats in one action and another 7 were sunk during the night of 15th February 1918 by German Destroyers (see Annex II). Both actions took place off Dover. 1916 and 1917 were the worst years for losses when 40 and 42 steam drifters respectively were lost (10).

During World War II (1939 - 1945) 356 steam drifters were commandeered (excluding standard drifters) and were employed much the same as during World War I. Although there were no losses by direct actions similar to those shown above in World War I, 73 steam drifters were lost in total with the first being "Ray of Hope" LT 280 which was mined in the Thames Estuary during 10th December 1939.

Steam drifters took part in the Dunkirk evacuation and 6 were lost during that operation. Causes of losses were as follows:- 12 by aircraft, 6 at Dunkirk, 20 by mines, 4 by bad weather, 3 by unknown causes, 19 by collision, 8 by grounding and 1 by enemy gunfire in Dover Harbour. The last one to be lost was "Broadland" YH 718 during bad weather in the North Atlantic on 6th June 1945. The worst years were 1940 and 1941 when 30 and 24 respectively were lost (11). Most served from 1939 until mid 1946 when the survivors were returned to their owners.

5. Steam drifters, which had been the mainstay of herring fishing from about 1904, continued in this role as they were released from active service, during 1946. However a number of them were rather elderly and although refitted after war service, were showing signs of their age and scrapping began during 1947. Numbers gradually increased until by 1955 very few steam drifters were fishing. Most fished successfully until the early 1950s but a number had been replaced by 75' Admiralty Motor Fishing Vessels (MFVs) which had been built to a standard design during World War II and were being released by the Admiralty for sale to the fishing industry. Most, if not all, of the World War I standard steam drifters which had been retained by the Royal Navy between the Wars were also released from active service and were sold to the fishing industry. By 1951 coal prices had risen considerably and steam drifters were finding it difficult to remain economical and compete financially with the new generation of motor drifters which were now being built by most boat building yards particularly in Scotland. As a result the remaining steam drifter fleet became concentrated in a few ports such as Fraserburgh, Peterhead, Lowestoft and Great Yarmouth. By 1952 most of the steam drifters in operation were either "standards" or those built after 1920. By 1955 steam drifters in general had been replaced by motor drifters which were proving much more economical and more easily converted to other methods. This process had actually started, in Scotland, during the 1930s but did not really gather momentum until after 1947 when diesel engines and wood became more readily available after the war had finished.

As I mentioned earlier, the last steel steam drifter was built during 1932 and along with those built after 1920 had a very sound hull and only became un-economical because it was a coal-burner. Converting these vessels to oil burning was not perceived as an option but converting them to diesel power was deemed to be more acceptable and most of the late builds were refitted with diesel engines and fully converted to the new method of propulsion. Although these conversations were satisfactory, drift-netting was on the wane by 1960 and most ended their fishing days as trawlers. Thus it seems that the circle had been completed and steam drifting was no more. Fortunately one steam drifter "Lydia Eva" YH 89 has been preserved and restored to her original form by the Maritime Trust. She was built during 1930 at King's Lynn Slipway and is 95' long.

7. We have seen that the building of steam drifters most probably started with D. Allan of Granton and that the early drifters were in reality, Fifie hulls (i.e. sailing boats) with a boiler and a steam engine installed. The ultimate design was very similar to and strongly influenced by early steam trawler design. A study of the list of builders shows quite clearly that many shipyards or boat building firms were involved all round the coast of the United Kingdom including the Clyde which was, in its heyday, the most famous ship building area in the world. Some of the yards which built steam drifters are or were until recently in operation and, of course, proved to be very versatile by changing designs and building programmes to suit demand from fishermen and fishing companies.

The builders listed in Annex III had all, as far as is known, been in business in some form or another prior to the boom in regard to the building of steam drifters and all showed considerable versatility and adaptability in taking full advantage of the demand for such ships.

The most prolific builder was undoubtedly J. Chambers & Co. Limited of Lowestoft who built a total of 211 wooden drifters and 9 steel ones between 1904 and 1927. This shows an average of 9 per year over the 24 year period. The peak year was 1911 when this firm built 28 steam drifters in the one year.

These figures exclude the 18 wooden standard drifters ordered by the Admiralty and built between 1918 and 1920. Only 2 other builders achieved totals of over 100 steam drifters namely Smith Dock Limited of North Shields and Middlesborough with 102 and Richard's Ironworks of Lowestoft with 118.

In Scotland most of the wooden boat builders had, prior to 1904 or so, been very busy building the large sailing Fifies and Zulus and when the demand for sailing craft faded, turned over to building wooden steam drifters and subsequently to building wooden motor drifters and seiners. Firms like Herd & MacKenzie of Buckie, J. & G. Forbes of Sandhaven, J. Miller of St. Monans, Wilson Noble of Fraserburgh etc. all went on to be successful motor boat builders. The firms which concentrated in building in steel such as Alex Hall and Hall Russell of Aberdeen, Cochrane of Selby, Cook, Welton & Gemmell of Hull & Beverley, Smith Dock Limited, and Richard's Ironworks were heavily engaged in steam trawler building in addition to producing other steel craft. Indeed some became quite famous for their motor trawlers and drifters.

Twelve steel drifters were built in Holland although only three were built for U.K. owners and the remaining nine were built for Dutch owners and subsequently sold to Lowestoft. Seven of the nine were large drifters in excess of 100' long and were generally recognised as drifter/trawlers.

PATRIA LT 178 - Built at Lieddordorp, Holland by Gebroders Boot. 1916, entering Lowestoft ca1947. Was originally named "ATLANTIC, then IRMA before being sold to Lowestoft. Scrapped 1954. Courtesty of Port of Lowestoft Research Society.

8.   The change over to steam drifters meant a drastic change in working practices in respect of catching herring by drift-nets and it is to fishermen's credit that the change from sail to steam was carried out successfully. It certainly illustrates clearly the professionalism and versatility of fishermen over the years which is still evident to this day. Indeed as one Peterhead skipper used to say to me

"A fisherman can turn his hand to anything if he sets his mind to it". This was said to me while he was showing me his display of prize dahlias and I realised the truth of his remark by recalling that prior to retirement, he hardly knew the difference between flowers and weeds.

Steam drifters required a crew of 10 men, namely Skipper, Mate, 5 Deckhands, 1 Engineer, 1 Fireman and 1 Cook whereas the larger sailing drifters generally had a crew of 8 men and a boy (who was generally employed as a cook). A minimum of 8 men were required to haul drift nets on board a steam drifter i.e. four men in the fish hold hauling and shaking herring from the nets, 1 man at the cork rope on deck, 1 man on the foot or sole rope on deck, 1 man releasing stoppers (short pieces of rope which fastened the nets to the messenger (bush) rope and 1 man (fireman or cook) coiling the messenger rope in the rope locker below decks, situated almost underneath the capstan forward of the fish hold. The engineer was in the engine room tending to the engine and boiler. The skipper would be in the wheelhouse until hauling was established and the messenger rope could be left to pull the drifter slowly ahead at the same speed as the nets were being hauled. In times of bad weather it would be necessary to use the engine to move the drifter slowly ahead thus the skipper and engineer were required to remain in the wheelhouse and engine room respectively. During periods when hauling did not require engine or helm movements, the skipper would assist in hauling the nets. It can been seen that every man on board was fully occupied. Indeed it has been said that to see a drifter crew hauling drift nets was to see team-work par excellence. All forms of fishing requires first class team-work mainly because crews are kept to the minimum required with each man having his own duties.

JEAN BAIRD PD 1. Steel Standard Drifter built by J.W. Brooke & Co. Ltd, Lowestoft 1919 for Admiralty as BLUE HAZE, became BLUE HAZE LT 564, JEAN BAIRD PD 1. Scrapped 1954. Shown hauling drift nets off Gt. Yarmouth ca 1950. Courtesy of Scottish Fisheries Museum.

The engineer and fireman, colloquially known as the "Black Squad" or "Below-Men", attended to all duties connected with the engine room and the boiler including coal trimming in the bunkers to ensure a regular supply of coal being kept at hand for the stokehold. In addition to those duties they were required to assist in the hauling of the nets along with keeping watch whilst steaming to and from the fishing grounds. The cook was required to provide all meals, keep the galley and cabin clean along with assisting the hauling, generally hauling the foot-rope of the nets or coiling the messenger rope but did not keep deck watches while the vessel was steaming to and from the fishing grounds. The mate and the deckhands looked after all the fishing gear and kept all deck watches, steaming or otherwise.

The skipper, in addition to being responsible for navigation and the general welfare of the crew and the vessel, took part in the watch-keeping system generally and of course was responsible for catching the herring by ensuring the vessel was in the proper place at the proper time. Thus it can be seen that all were kept busy and if a lot of herring were being caught regularly, sleep was hard to come by with the week-ends being welcomed to recharge physical batteries.

9.   Steam drifters, whilst being first class ships for the task, could be very uncomfortable for crews because of dampness, particularly during bad weather when fairly large amounts of sea-water could be shipped. Although not enough to do damage, this meant that the crew were often uncomfortably damp despite protective clothing being worn. The modern motor drifter did not have this problem and whilst steam drifters are remembered fondly, their demise was perhaps really welcomed. They had certainly fulfilled their purpose and like many things had outlived their usefulness and became obsolete, as indeed happened to drift-netting for herrings and mackerel, by the late 1960s.

NOTES

(1)   East of Fife Record and "The Lammas Drave & The Winter Herring" By Peter Smith.

(2)   James Ritchie - Article in Fishing News 1914 - see Annex I.

(3)   Page 34 - "Fishing Boats and Ports of East of Scotland" By Peter Anson 1929.

(4)   Page 94 - "Sailing Drifters" By Edgar J. March.

(5)   "Steam Fishing in the East Neuk" By Peter Smith.

(6)   "Numerical Fleet" By Hawkins.

(7)   See Builders Lists - Annex III

(8)   The boiler was used solely to produce steam to heat the "Barking" solution to boiling point as modern motor drifters did not have boilers.

(9)   "From Herring to Seine Net Fishing" By Ian Sutherland.

(10) "British Warships 1914 -1919" By Dithar and Colledge.

(11) "British Warships 1939 - 1945" By Lenton & Colledge.

Article in Fishing News. June 4th, 1914.

**Herring Drifters
The Story of their Progress.**

The question of the application of the steam vessel to the pursuit of the herring fishing and the development of the steam drifter has recently been commanding the attention of several writers and it appears that none of the persons dealing with the matter has given a full account of the history of that craft. That, I do intend to aim at here, but would like to connect a few lines in the chain that appear to be wanting, and to show that steam was successfully applied to herring 36 years ago.

Few people seem to be aware of the fact that Mr David Allan, shipbuilder, Granton took in what I consider were really the first successful steam drifters that operated on the Scottish coast. In the year 1878 that gentleman built and equipped two very tidy steam drifters purposely for the prosecution of the herring fishing. During the fishing season of that year both of these craft fished at Aberdeen and engaged to work at that port for the whole season. They were named the "Forward" and the "Onward". The former fished for the firm of Messrs James Methven & Co. of Leith and the latter for Messrs Sharp and Murray, Cellardyke. For a number of years afterwards the "Onward" continued to fish at Aberdeen for the Cellardyke firm. These craft appeared at Aberdeen four years before steam trawling was commenced at that port and there is little doubt but what they were the first steam craft that operated there. A few years later a number of other vessels intended for the catching of herrings were built by Mr Allan some of which would compare favourably with the drifters of today. There was the "Gannet" of Leith which afterwards carried mails for some time from Oban to the Outer Hebrides also the sister ship "Green Castle" that was built to the order of James Wood, Cullen.

Lossiemouth Enterprise.

About the same time, a compact little steam vessel owned at Glasgow wrought at the herring fishing at Aberdeen.

The once well known Mr. James Moss of Great Yarmouth was for some time in charge of that craft. Lossiemouth one of the homes of new ideas in the fishing industry also attempted the adoption of steam at an early stage of the movement when the Zulu boat "Flying Fish" was converted into a steamer. This scheme, however, proved an unfortunate one for the owner as the engineering work did not give satisfaction. Previous to the year first referred to, one attempt to utilise steam power for the prosecution of the herring fishing was made at Wick with the "George Loch", an ordinary Fifie boat. From information obtainable it appears that the venture did not work out successfully owing to defective machinery. At Aberdeen I can remember seeing another Fifie boat that had been fitted by Mr. Alexander Gauld with an upright engine and boiler. That so far as I can recollect was in the late seventies. Unfortunately the promoter was not enriched by his enterprise.

Early in the eighties the Cunliffe fleet appeared, all bearing the names of well known birds. Some of the names were "Merlin", "Fulmar", "Osprey and "Cygnet". Wick was early in the field with the small craft "Alpha", which wrought at the port of Wick in 1879 and was seen by the writer in Wick Harbour at the end of that season. When the Cunliffe fleet was built it was the intention of the owners that they should be exclusively employed at the net fishing and he therefore provided them with fleets of herring and mackerel netting. It was with the Cunliffe boats that Aberdeen fishermen commenced steam lining so that they ultimately played no mean part to the introduction of steam fishing at Aberdeen.

Introduction of the Bush Rope.

From the forgoing remarks it will be seen that the problem of applying steam power to the propelling of the herring boat occupied the minds of men on various parts of the coast its success and development since the year 1899 is well known to all interested in the industry. At the time when these early ventures were made the "Bush Rope" now in use had not been introduced. It was after its adoption that the rapid advance in the size and construction of the herring boat took place. Fishing in rough weather then became a possibility, hence the necessity and scope for the enlargement of boats. At quite an early period various Leith craft of the Fifie build were fitted with steam. It was also where the Cunliffe fleet was turned out.

The question might arise - How did Leith builders come to take such an interest in the applying of steam power to fishing craft? it may be explained by the fact that the two interested builders were North countrymen Mr. Allan being an Orcadian and Mr. McKenzie a native of Wick. It may not be out of place to mention that Mr. Allan also produced some of the first wooden steam trawlers built in Scotland. There was little or nothing done at premier herring ports of Fraserburgh and Peterhead in what may be termed the experimental days of steam drifting. Fraserburgh's first move for steam was in 1892 when the steam liner "Philorth" was built. In the following year the "Pioneer" was built by a Peterhead Company for steam lining. Peterhead, however, now leads with steam drifters and Fraserburgh is hard in chase. Sometime in the seventies, the acquiring of a steam propelled herring boat was the ambition of the late William Strachan of Cairnbulg.

A Wonderful Development

There is one experiment in the application of steam-power to the propelling of the herring drifter that I almost omitted. Mr. William Reid of Lossiemouth was one of the most ingenious fishermen I have ever known and one who was never happy treading the beaten path. In the early eighties he had a "smack" equipped with a steam capstan long before they were adapted by Scottish fishermen The mode of propulsion was portable paddles driven by an arrangement of cranks and shafts connected with his capstan. I had the pleasure of seeing him doing his trial run in the Albert Basin in Aberdeen. Having been brought closely in contact with the "Forward" in 1878 as I was then in the employment of Methven & Co., I have watched with interest the development of the steam drifter. When I compare the "Forward" with the "R.R.S. of Yarmouth" (owned by Mr. Richard Sutton) the latest in drifters, a wonderful development has been effected. In the accomplishment of that task practical fishermen and shipbuilders have not been idle.

James Ritchie
Fishing News.

CHANNEL RAID ON DRIFTERS

14th February, 1918

Composed by Skipper David Parker

The sun was setting in the west, on a February's winter night,
As the boys in blue, so staunch and true, carried on with all their might.
From the Varne to the French coast, the drifter line abreast.
Were keeping station faithfully, submarines their quest.

But sad to say ere break of day, those men who ploughed the deep
had fought and fallen, heroes all, now their's the last long sleep.
Their memory we'll ne'er forget, for us they gave their all.
Fighting for their country, they answered heaven's call.

'Twas wearing on to midnight, and the stars were shining bright,
As the trawlers with their "flare ups" turned the darkness into light.
Everything so peaceful, the sea as calm could be;
But ere the morning dawn appeared, seven ships no more we'd see.

'Twas on the stroke of half past twelve, as the tide began to rise
When the guns roared forth, with shot and shell, that flashed across the skies
besides the gates of Folkestone, where the salvos burst and spread,
The drifters there 'gainst fearful odds, lost ninety-eight in dead.

The German ships with four inch guns, regardless of the lives,
Poured salvo after salvo into the drifters sides.
But British pluck was there that night, what did the drifters do ?
They manned their guns till every man was riddled through and through.

The leading drifter "Clover Bank", which was the first to go,
With decks awash, fired to the last, against the fiendish foe.
The "Jeannie Murray", next in turn, with decks a mass of flame,
Went to her doom, with every man, the sea its toil to claim.

The "Cosmos" now is under fire, her bridge is swept away,
But she carries on while every man the sacrifice would pay.
The "Silver Queen", with fearless scorn, to the "Cosmos" help did go,
But sad to say, while on her way, she met the cowardly foe.

On her they trained with every gun, her time is drawing neigh,
But she died for Britain's honour as she lighted up the sky.
Everything is quiet again, the fighting seems to be o'er
But hark the quiet is broken again as the guns begin to roar.

The "William Elliot", next in turn is driving for the shore,
But ah! his days are numbered as the shells into him pour.
he's sinking fast, but till the last his rockets lit the sky.
When from the smoke the "Courage" broke to save him or to die.

The "Courage" now is closing in before the final plunge
Just in time to save the lives of the wounded British sons.
The guns again begin to roar, the "Veracity" is doomed,
but she carries on until the last, a watery grave entombed.

The "Christina Craig" a target made, is now amongst the slain,
As she faced the foe, gave blow for blow, was there a man dismayed ?
True British sons until the last, carry on as she smokes and reels,
But her time had come as a German ram, her doom did quickly seal.

The "Violet May", bridge swept away, is battered shelled and torn,
But her enginemen two, all that's left of her crew,
back to haven they bring her for-lorn.
The "Golden Rule", decks all strewn with splinters of shot and shell,
Ship all alight she emerged from fight, three parts of her crew had fell.

Still the murderous work goes on, the Germans laugh and jest
As the "Golden Gain" with might and main, returns the fire with zest.
her chances are but little, she does her little bit.
When a salvo from the German, her starboard bow did hit.

She trembles, rolls and shivers, but recovers from the blow,
And as the gloom goes o'er the moon, she is hidden from the foe.
Full speed ahead the drifter sped into the dark of night,
The ocean ploughs with shattered bows, she's safely through the fight.

The "Treasurer" now is under fire, her quarter shot away,
The German ships with laughing scorn, her crew intent to slay,
They now have smashed her broadsides, but still she keeps afloat
When a salvo from the brutal Hun, takes away her little boat.

They leave her now, from bridge to bow is shattered torn and smashed,
But her crew will keep pumping till the shore is reached at last
Everything is quiet again, morning drawing neigh,
But jolly tars have paid the price, their souls have soared on high.
The deeds and works of valour, inscribed in honour's roll,
Shall carry on through ages of the Dover Drifter Patrol.

ANNEX III

NUMBERS OF STEAM DRIFTERS BY BUILDERS (EXCLUDING STANDARD DRIFTERS)

Annex II Page		WOODEN		STEEL OR IRON	
		PRE 1900	1900 +	PRE 1900	1900 +
73	W. Alexander and Co., Govan	1	-	-	-
31	D. Allan and Co., Granton	1	-	-	-
78	Ardrossan Shipbuilding Company, Ardrossan	-	-	-	2
45	Beeching & Co. Ltd., Great Yarmouth	5	88	-	-
80	G. Brown & Co. Ltd., Greenock	-	-	-	5
87	Caledon Shipbuilding & Engineering Co. Ltd., Dundee	-	-	-	6
39	Carnegie & Matthews & Co. Ltd., Peterhead	-	13	-	-
78	Wm. Chalmers and Co., Rutherglen	-	-	-	1
56,81	J. Chambers & Co. Ltd., Lowestoft	-	211	-	9
54	Chambers & Colby Ltd., Lowestoft	10	47	-	-
80	Charlton & Doughty Ltd., Grimsby	-	-	1	10
95	Cochrane & Sons Ltd., Selby	-	-	-	69
100,102	Cochrane & Cooper Ltd., Beverley	-	-	3	4
41,93	R. Cock, Appledore	-	2	-	2
50	Colby Bros. Ltd., South Yard, Lowestoft	-	6	-	-
41	Colby Bros. Ltd., Oulton Broad, Lowestoft	-	34	-	-
94	Cook, Welton & Gemmell Ltd., Hull	-	-	3	2
82	Cook, Welton & Gemmell Ltd., Beverley	-	-	-	7
94	George Cooper, Hull	-	-	-	2
99	Crabtree & Co. Ltd., Great Yarmouth	-	-	-	41
25	A. Dryburgh, Patent Slip Dysart	-	1	-	-
63	T. Duncan and Son, Garmouth	-	2	-	-
93	Dundee Shipbuilding Co. Ltd., Dundee	-	-	-	14
28	Dunston Shipbuilding Co., Dunston on Tyne	1	-	-	-
94	J. Duthie & Co. Ltd., Montrose	-	-	2	2
88	J. Duthie, Torry Shipbuilding Co., Torry, Aberdeen	-	-	-	82
102	Earles Shipbuilding & Engineering Co.Ltd., Hull	-	-	2	-
102	Edwards, North Shields	-	-	2	-
90, 102	J. T. Eltringham and Co., South Shields	-	-	5	6
43,98	Fellows & Co. Ltd., Great Yarmouth	-	63	1	8
34	J. & G. Forbes Ltd., Sandhaven, Fraserburgh	-	28	-	-
39	Forbes and Birnie, Peterhead then	4	11	-	-
39	R. Irvin and Sons, Peterhead	-	3	-	-
25	W. Fulton, Pittenweem	3	4	-	-
54	Gardiner, Cullen	-	7	-	-
26	W. Geddes & Co. Ltd., Portgordon	-	55	-	-
94	Goole Shipbuilding & Repairing Co. Ltd., Goole	-	-	-	4
41	J. Grigor, Portgordon	-	1	-	-
84	A. Hall & Co. Ltd., Aberdeen	-	-	5	45
91	Hall Russell & Co. Ltd., Aberdeen	-	-	7	16
47	Henry Reynolds Ltd., Oulton Broad, Lowestoft	2	87	-	-
73	Hawthorn & Co. Ltd., Granton	2	1	-	-
77	Hawthorn & Co. Ltd., Leith	-	-	3	2
63	J. Hay, Garmouth	-	3	-	-
93	R. & W. Hawthorn Leslie & Co Ltd., Hepburn on Tyne	-	-	4	-
37	Herd & Mackenzie, Findochty & Buckie	-	35	-	-
40	G. Innes & Son, Portknockie	-	5	-	-
42	G. Innes & Co., Macduff	-	14	-	-
22	Wm. Jarvis, Anstruther	13	-	-	-
101	King's Lynn Shipbuilding Co. Ltd., King's Lynn	-	-	-	1
66	Kitto & Sons & J Bowden, Porthleven	1	27		

ANNEX III

NUMBERS OF STEAM DRIFTERS BY BUILDERS (EXCLUDING STANDARD DRIFTERS)

Page		WOODEN		STEEL OR IRON	
		PRE 1900	1900 +	PRE 1900	1900 +
93	Larne Shipbuilding Co. Ltd., Larne	-	-	-	1
25	Launcelot & Liddle, Wallsend on Tyne	1	-	-	-
70	Lee & Wight Ltd., Tweedmouth	3	-	-	-
25	J. Lindsay, St. Anthony's, Newcastle	1	-	-	-
81	Livingstone & Cooper Ltd., Hessle	-	-	-	3
69	MacIntosh, Portessie, Buckie	-	21	-	-
69	Mackenzie, Thurso	1	-	-	-
77	Mackay Bros., Alloa	-	-	-	4
78	Mackie & Thomson Ltd., Govan	-	-	-	49
72	D. Main, Hopeman	-	1	-	-
22	James Miller, Anstruther	-	19	-	-
23	James Miller, St. Monans	8	2	-	-
80	Montrose Shipbuilding Co. Ltd., Montrose	-	-	-	15
29	Morton & Co., Marr Bros., A & G Gifford, J. McKenzie & Co., all Leith	11	8	-	-
39	Noble & Co. then Wilson Noble, Fraserburgh	-	4	-	-
91	Phillips & Son, Dartmouth	-	-	-	6
50,100	S. Richards & Co., Then Richards Ironworks Ltd., Lowestoft	2	115	-	1
93	Ritchie, Graham & Milne Ltd., Whiteinch, Glasgow	-	-	-	1
24	Robertson, St. Monans	-	5	-	-
29	Rose Street Foundry & Engineering Co., & J. Macdonald & Co. both Inverness.	-	24	-	-
63, 95	Sanders Ltd., Gibb Ltd., both Galmpton, Devon	-	33	-	2
93	Scott & Sons Ltd., Bowling	-	-	-	1
36	Scott & Yule, Fraserburgh.	-	18	-	-
99	Selby Shipbuilding & Repairing Co. Ltd., Selby	-	-	-	8
72	Slater Bros., Lossiemouth	-	14	-	-
68	George Smith Jr., Buckie	-	19	-	-
74	Smith Dock Trust & Co. Ltd., North Shields and Middlesborough	-	-	-	102
67	F. W. Stanger, Stromness	-	2	-	-
31	W. G. Stephen & Stevenson and Asher, both Banff	-	91	-	-
67	G. Thomson, Buckie	-	10	-	-
73	J. Tyrrell & Sons, Arklow	-	1	-	-
40	Union Co-operative Shipbuilding Soc., Blyth	7	5	-	-
70	Upham & Co., Brixham	-	3	-	-
25	Watterson & Neakle Ltd., Peel	-	2	-	-
72	G. Walker, Nairn	-	1	-	-
26	J. Weatherhead, Eyemouth	3	3	-	-
37	Wm. Weatherhead Ltd., Cockenzie	-	3	-	-
29	Wm. White & Sons, Cowes	2	-	-	-
101	Wood Skinner & Co., Bill Quay on Tyne	-	-	4	-
71	W. Wood & Co., Lossiemouth	-	20	-	-
73	Yare Dry Dock Co. Ltd., Great Yarmouth	-	1	-	-
	ONLY PLACE OF BUILD HAS BEEN ESTABLISHED				
69	**at Shandwick, Shetland**	-	1	-	-
28	at Shoreham	1	-	-	-
67	at - Wick	-	8	-	-
	Built in Holland				
83	at - Ambach	-	-	-	1
83	at - Leiderdorp - Gebroders Boot.	-	-	-	8
83	at - Rotterdam - M. & S. Burgerhouts	-	-	-	1
83	at - Zalt Bommel - J. Meier	-	-	-	2
	Totals	**83**	**1182**	**42**	**545**
	GRAND TOTAL	**1852**			

Wm. JARVIS - ANSTRUTHER

WOODEN

Reg No	NAME	G.R.T.	N.T.	H.P.	LENGTH	YR BUILT	HISTORY
DE 528	DEWDROP	70	36	32	86. 6'	1888	A 11, STRANDED 1899, SALVAGED THEN DEWDROP, ACACIA WK 561, LT 984
KY 449	MAGGIE LAUDER	82	46	35	82. 8'	1891	1ST "ANSTER LINER" - AD 1 HERRING CARRIER ON CLYDE - BF 745 - BURNT EAST ANGLIA 1903
KY 461	ANSTER FAIR	88	32	32	89'	1892	SCRAPPED 1922
KY 458	ROB THE RANTER	90	33	34	89'	1892	SOLD TO PETERHEAD 1917, PD 329 - LOST 1920
KY 472	WILLIAM TENNANT	93	34	34	89. 1'	1883	LOST OFF HUMBER 1918
KY 493	GLENOGIL	95	34	34	89. 6'	1894	TO DUNDEE 1899 - TO COCKENZIE 1920'S - SUNK 1938
KY 546	EAST NEUK	118	44	50	91'	1895	A 37, KY 176, TO ABERDEEN 1920 AS CARGO BOAT - SUNK 1923
KY 536	COPLEY	96	36	34	90'	1895	ALNWICK CASTLE SN 24, KY 120 - SCRAPPED 1922
KY 571	WHITE CROSS	101	38	38	90. 2'	1896	SCRAPPED 1935
KY 604	INVERGELLIE	100	37	38	91. 3'	1897	BCK 232, YH 715, LT 1091 - SCRAPPED 1925
KY 594	KILRENNY	97	36	38	90. 2'	1897	A 388 - SANK IN HUMBER 1911
KY 16	ROTHESAY BAY	101	37	38	91. 6'	1897	A 885, KY 97, TO COCKENZIE - SCRAPPED 1935
A 89	CRUDEN BAY	125	50	47	96. 6'	1899	TO FALMOUTH AS SALVAGE VESSEL 1912

BUSINESS SOLD TO J. MILLER & COMPANY, ST MONANS

J. MILLER - ANSTRUTHER 1900 - 1912

WOODEN

Reg No	NAME	G.R.T.	N.T.	H.P.	LENGTH	YR BUILT	HISTORY
SN 268	BADEN POWELL	93	35	32	90'	1900	LT 152
PD 397	SHAMROCK	77	29	18	76. 1'	1900	SCRAPPED 1924
SN 275	LILY	72	34	20	74'	1900	YH 502
SN 295	EDITH	67	28	20	76.3'	1901	PD99 SCRAPPED 1930
SN 297	REDVERS BULLER	99	34	33	91'	1901	
SN 300	RANTER	99	37	33	91.4'	1901	
SN 308	KITTY	56	27	20	76'	1901	PD 103 - SOLD TO BELGIUM 1919
SN 303	MINNIE	62	29	20	77. 5'	1901	FR 210 - SCRAPPED 1924
KY 122	ST. AYLES	78	32	33	84. 1'	1906	SCRAPPED 1935
KY 199	VENUS	87	30	33	86. 6'	1907	SUNK OFF SCARBOROUGH 1934
KY 163	PRIMROSE	87	31	33	86. 6'	1907	SOLD TO CLYDE AS HERRING CARRIER 1933 - WRECKED SOUTH KINTYRE 1933
KY 138	MAGGIES	85	31	33	85. 7'	1907	SCRAPPED 1936
KY 134	CAMELIA	85	30	33	86. 3'	1907	SCRAPPED 1937
KY 253	BREADWINNER	88	31	36	86. 5'	1907	SCRAPPED AT FRASERBURGH 1946
KY 189	EVENING STAR	87	30	35	86. 6'	1907	SCRAPPED 1936
KY 178	INTEGRITY	86	31	33	86. 1'	1907	SOLD TO NORTH SHIELDS THEN EYEMOUTH BK 28 - SCRAPPED 1937
ML 122	LIZZIE HUTT	82	27	33	87'	1908	SCRAPPED AT CAIPLIE 1935
ML123	CHRISTINA MAYES	82	26	27	86.6'	1908	MARE VIVIMUS KY 98, SUNK OFF ELIE NESS 12.12.25
ML 126	JANET REEKIE	81	26	27	86.8'	1908	ABDIEL KY 95 - SCRAPPED 1938
SN 150	HIBERNIA	94	35	30	85. 2'	1892	LK 257
A 716	OSSIFRAGE	86	36	30	86.1'	1893	CEASED FISHING 1920, TO CARGO, SCRAPPED 1924
A 740	MERGANSER	86	36	30	85. 1'	1893	SCRAPPED 1923

LILY SN 275 - Built of wood 1900 by J. Miller at Anstruther, became YH 502.
Courtesy of Scottish Fisheries Museum.

BREADWINNER KY 253 - Built of wood by J. Miller at Anstruther 1907. Shown leaving
Anstruther ca 1910. Scrapped 1946 at Fraserburgh. Courtesy of Scottish Fisheries Museum.

ANNEX IV JAMES MILLER - ST. MONANS WOODEN

REG. NO.	NAME	G.R.T.	N.T.	H.P.	LENGTH	YR BUILT	HISTORY
SN 157	GLENAVON	90	34	35	90'	1893	WRECKED AT BOULMER, 1895
SN 196	GLENCONA	78	29	32	88'	1894	LT 179 SCRAPPED 1924
SN 212	SAPPHIRE	77	29	32	88'	1895	FOUNDERED OFF WHITBURN, 1909
KY 601	NEWARK CASTLE	85	30	32	87. 1'	1897	M 7, SN 229, SUNK BY U. BOAT OFF TYNE, 1916
SN 35	NORHAM CASTLE	93	41	31	92'	1899	PD 102, SN 3, SUNK OFF STORNOWAY, 1920
SN 89	LANGLEY CASTLE	96	35	35	92'	1900	SUNK BY U-BOAT OFF TYNE, 1916
SN 188	LUCANIA	92	34	35	92'	1900	SUNK BY U. BOAT OFF COQUET, 1916

NEWARK CASTLE KY 601 - Built of wood by J. Miller at St Monans 1897 as a Liner. Shown dried out at St Monans ca 1897. Note full set of Sails and no Capstan, became M7 SN 229 and was sunk by U.Boat off Tyne 1916. Courtesy of Scottish Fisheries Museum.

ANNEX IV   **ROBERTSON - ST. MONANS**   **WOODEN**

REG NO	NAME	G.R.T.	N.T.	H.P.	LENGTH	YR BUILT	HISTORY
KY 152	PURSUIT	79	30	25	85. 3'	1907	SUNK OFF PENZANCE 22.4.1918
KY 162	UNITY	80	30	24	86'	1907	SCRAPPED 1936
KY 220	OLIVE LEAF	82	32	25	86. 3'	1907	CASIMER ML 42 - SUNK OFF GREAT YARMOUTH 1931
ML 125	MACKAYS	83	30	23	88. 7'	1908	SEA LAVENDER KY 148, EVENTIDE - WRECKED AT ELIE NESS
ML 337	REJOICE	83	35	36	86. 7'	1915	SN 8 - SUNK OFF TYNE 1927

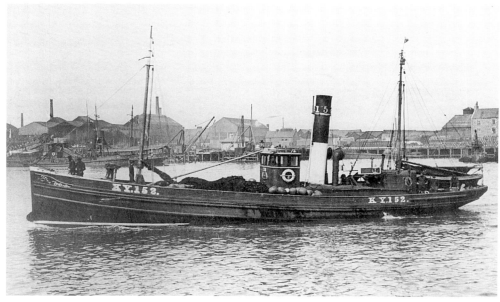

PURSUIT KY152 - Built of wood by Robertson of St Monans during 1907, shown at Aberdeen ca 1910. Note carrying full set of sails. Sunk off Penzance, April 1918. Courtesy of Scottish Fisheries Museum.

WM. FULTON - PITTENWEEM WOODEN

REG NO	NAME	G.R.T.	N.T.	H.P.	LENGTH	YR BUILT	HISTORY
SN 148	TEAL DUCK	64	49	26	81'	1892	
SN 171	SHELLDRAKE	95	46	32	91'	1893	LOST 1904
KY 544	ST. ADRIAN	89	32	33	86. 4'	1895	SOLD TO ABERDEEN 1901, A 253 THEN KY 103 SOLD TO SUNDERLAND 1920
PD 133	VIOLET	88	33	33	85. 1'	1906	SCRAPPED 1930
KY 121	PRESTON	84	31	33	83. 8'	1906	SCRAPPED 1930
KY 201	TULIP	88	31	33	85. 1'	1907	SUNK OFF ST. ANTHONY'S HEAD 25.8.1918
KY 148	GOLDEN SUNRISE	87	33	33	87. 5'	1907	SUNK OFF PETERHEAD

A. DRYBURGH - PATENT SLIP, DYSART, FIFE WOODEN

REG NO	NAME	G.R.T.	N.T.	H.P.	LENGTH	YR BUILT	HISTORY
FR 236	THISTLE	87	31	21	87. 7'	1907	SUNK MORAY FIRTH 1927

WATERSON & NEAKLE - PEEL, ISLE OF MAN WOODEN

REG NO	NAME	G.R.T.	N.T.	H.P.	LENGTH	YR BUILT	HISTORY
PL 29	MANX PRINCESS	89	28	24	88. 8'	1908	SY . . . SUNK OFF RATTRAY HEAD 1917 BY U. BOAT.
PL 53	MANX BRIDE	61	24	14	74. 7'	1910	SY 328, P. A. G. YH 237

LANCELOT & LIDDLE LIMITED - WALLSEND ON TYNE WOODEN

REG NO	NAME	G.R.T.	N.T.	H.P.	LENGTH	YR BUILT	HISTORY
SN 518	SCOTIA	55	30	17	71. 5'	1886	GK 122 , YH 597

LINDSAY - ST. ANTHONY, NEWCASTLE ON TYNE WOODEN

REG NO	NAME	G.R.T.	N.T.	H.P.	LENGTH	YR BUILT	HISTORY
SN 174	ORCADIA	89	30	30	86.7'	1893	A 67 - SCRAPPED 26.8.11

ORCADIA SN 174 - Built of wood by J. Lindsay of St. Anthony, Newcastle on Tyne as a Liner, 1893. Shown as a Drifter, A 67, ca 1902. Scrapped 1911. Courtesy of Scottish Fisheries Museum.

REG NO	NAME	G.R.T.	N.T.	H.P.	LENGTH	YR BUILT	HISTORY
SN 88	LILLIAN MAUD	57	21	25	79	1890	PD 372, WK 687 - SCRAPPED 16.11.1924
SN 154	NANCY HUNNAM	58	20	25	80'	1892	SUNK OFF TYNE 1916
SN 198	SCOTIA	92	11	34	86.8'	1894	SUNK 1907
BK 246	FAITHFUL	86	31	31	87. 7'	1907	SUNK - RIVER YARE 1924
BK 260	EXCEL III	86	31	20	87. 1'	1907	BROKEN UP 1938
BK 269	MARY MALTMAN	79	26	20	85. 3'	1908	LOST 1932

EXCEL III BK 260 - Built of wood by J. Weatherhead & Sons, Eyemouth 1907. Shown entering Gt. Yarmouth with 249¹/₂ crans of herring, Oct. 1937 - runner up for Purnier Trophy. Scrapped 1938. Courtesy of Scottish Fisheries Museum.

REG NO	NAME	G.R.T.	N.T.	H.P.	LENGTH	YR BUILT	HISTORY
BF 1338	LEADER	72	26	20	81. 7'	1903	SUNK MORAY FIRTH 1930
BF 1301	PEARL	65	38		81. 4'	1903	SAILING ZULU CONVERTED TO STEAM - BURNT 1921
BF 1580	DAISY	77	27	25	83.8'	1904	KY 105, BK 66 - SCRAPPED 1937
BF 1447	HONEYSUCKLE	73	25	21	82. 1'	1904	BCK 37 - SCRAPPED 1935
BF 1551	SUNBEAM	72	30	24	81. 6'	1904	BCK 376 - SUNK NORTH SEA 1923
BF 1805	WINNER	75	25	24	82. 1'	1904	SCRAPPED 1.1952
BF 1463	DAFFODIL	74	31	24	82. 2'	1904	SCRAPPED 1937
BF 34	SNOWDROP	68	23	17	81'	1905	SCRAPPED 1939
KY 128	MORNING STAR	84	36	30	87. 2'	1906	SCRAPPED 1937
BF 306	DAISY	85	31	34	88. 1'	1906	LOST 1919
INS 209	HERO	84	37	34	86. 4'	1906	SY 42 - SCRAPPED 12.1950
BF 182	INDUSTRY	80	28	24	83. 5'	1906	SCRAPPED 1936
BF 208	CORONA	76	27	30	83. 5'	1906	SCRAPPED 1934
BF 386	ECONOMY	95	35	34	86. 7'	1906	BCK 173 - SANK WEST COAST 1923
BF 305	LEAD ME	71	24	17	80. 4'	1906	FR 23 - SCRAPPED 1937
BF 214	STRATHLENE	81	29	27	85. 7'	1906	BCK 372 - SCRAPPED 1936

HERO INS 209 - Built of wood by Wm. Geddes, Portgordon 1906. Pictured leaving Peterhead, became SY 40 and was scrapped 1950. Courtesy of Scottish Fisheries Museum.

	ANNEX IV		WILLIAM GEDDES - PORTGORDON - CONTINUED					WOODEN
REG NO	**NAME**	**G.R.T.**	**N.T.**	**H.P.**	**LENGTH**	**YR BUILT**	**HISTORY**	
BF 347	GOWAN	86	37	34	87. 1'	1906	SCRAPPED 1939	
KY 210	ALICES	84	35	21	85. 7'	1907	DAWNAWAY KY 210 - SCRAPPED 1937	
KY 251	VIOLET	84	35	21	85. 6'	1907	SCRAPPED AT NORTH QUEENSFERRY ca 1938	
KY 218	PRIDE OF FIFE	83	35	24	85. 7'	1907	SCRAPPED 1947	
KY 149	RESTLESS WAVE	84	35	35	85. 6'	1907	SCRAPPED 1937	
YH 227	PLEIADES	90	39	21	90'	1907	FR 489, BF 155 - SCRAPPED 1937	
BF 471	OBERON	86	38	21	88. 2'	1907	TO NORWAY 1947	
BF 671	SUBLIME	84	36	21	87. 4'	1907	BCK 74 - SUNK BY AUSTRIAN CRUISER ADRIATIC 5.1917	

OBERON BF 471 - Built of wood by Wm. Geddes of Portgordon 1907. Shown proceeding down Gt. Yarmouth River ca 1930s. Courtesy of Scottish Fisheries Museum.

REG NO	NAME	G.R.T.	N.T.	H.P.	LENGTH	YR BUILT	HISTORY
BF 631	TRIUMPH	90	38	21	88'	1907	SCRAPPED 1936
BF 1002	JEANNIE	83	35	24	85. 1'	1907	BCK 101 - SCRAPPED 1948
BF 618	VALOROUS	84	35	25	83. 6'	1907	BCK 203 - SCRAPPED 1939
KY 276	HIEDRA	78	32	25	86. 2'	1908	BCK 348 - SCRAPPED 1937
KY 279	CRAIGNOON	77	32	25	86'	1908	SUNK BY AUSTRIAN CRUISER IN ADRIATIC 5.1917
INS 609	BON AMI	76	32	25	86'	1908	BCK 377 - SCRAPPED 1936
A 217	HAZELBANK	77	32	25	86. 3'	1908	LH 13, LK 271
YH 289	LAUREL BANK	84	35	20	85'	1908	A 213, BCK 178 - TO SALVAGE WORK 1941
BCK 7	PRESS HOME	77	32	24	85'	1908	WRECKED AT PORTLETHEN 28.11 1924
BCK 24	LETTERFOURIE	77	32	25	85. 1'	1908	SANK NORTH SEA 1932
A 227	J. M. S.	78	33	30	87. 4'	1908	AGNES DICKSON PD 191 - SUNK 1915
A 261	WILLOW BANK	80	33	27	87. 1'	1909	FR 518 - WRECKED AT ABERDEEN 1938
BCK 43	BARBARA COWIE	82	34	26	88. 3'	1909	FR 265 - SCRAPPED 1950
A 258	HOLLYBANK	78	33	30	86. 4'	1909	YH 147, LT 35 - SCRAPPED 1940
BCK 78	PRIDE OF BUCKIE	79	33	27	87. 4'	1910	SCRAPPED 1937
BCK 75	FELICITAS	67	27	20	81'	1910	SUNK BY AUSTRIAN CRUISERS ADRIATIC 5.1917
BCK 59	LUCANIA II	78	33	30	87. 4'	1910	SANK OF GREAT YARMOUTH 1932
LT 1130	OCEAN ANGLER	84	35	29	88. 2'	1911	YH 725, KY 208 - SCRAPPED 1938
YH 788	OCEAN REWARD	85	35	28	88. 3'	1911	GIRL LILY BCK 115 - SCRAPPED 1932
BCK 93	CLAVIS	87	36	28	88. 1'	1911	SUNK BY AUSTRIAN CRUISERS BRINDISI 9.7.1916
KY 107	GOLDEN STRAND	69	32	26	79.5'	1911	TO EYEMOUTH 1920, BK 212, SANK NORTH SEA.
FR 511	GEORGE HAY	83	34	35	88. 4'	1912	R 51, REUNITED LT 68 - SUNK OF LOWESTOFT 1938
YH 278	OCEAN SEARCHER	83	34	29	88'	1912	FR 75 - SCRAPPED 12.1948
FR 544	PITTENDRUM	84	35	35	87. 3'	1913	SY 700 - SCRAPPED 1951
FR 550	BOY JOE	85	36	27	88'	1913	HEADWAY - WRECKED AT SCALPAY 1941
BCK 162	PAX VOBISCUM	84	35	35	88'	1913	SCOTCH THISTLE PD 48 - SUNK THAMES ESTUARY 7.10.1940
BK 5	BORDER LADS	86	36	27	88. 8 '	1914	SUNK OFF TYNE 3.1918
A 31	COMELY BANK	85	36	27	88. 8 '	1914	YH 202 - SCRAPPED 1949
A 48	CORAL BANK	85	36	27	88. 5'	1914	YH 134, FR 12 - SCRAPPED 1948
BCK 183	THAINS	87	37	35	88. 4'	1914	AURILIA BF 89 - SCRAPPED 1948
BCK 207	BRAES O' ENZIE	87	37	26	90'	1915	LEWS SY 111 - SCRAPPED 10.1952

REG NO	NAME	G.R.T.	N.T.	H.P.	LENGTH	YR BUILT	HISTORY
NN 18	FREEWILL	50	31	7	55. 7'	1888	LT 178

REG NO	NAME	G.R.T.	N.T.	H.P.	LENGTH	YR BUILT	HISTORY
SN 95	GANNET	63	25	23	75'	1890	YH 450

ROSE STREET FOUNDRY & ENGINEERING Co.
AND J. MacDONALD & Co. - INVERNESS   WOODEN

REG NO	NAME	G.R.T.	N.T.	H.P.	LENGTH	YR BUILT	HISTORY
INS 172	CASTLE STEWART	77	31	23	82. 5'	1910	BF 501 - SCRAPPED 1946
INS 143	HIGHLAND LASSIE (A)	78	25	23	82'	1910	SCRAPPED AT PETERHEAD 1938
INS 117	MOY HALL	71	27	23	82. 5'	1910	SCRAPPED AT ORKNEY 1939
BCK 79	SCOTTISH CHIEF (A)	78	33	23	86. 5'	1910	SUNK OFF GREAT YARMOUTH 1922
INS 220	CRAIG CONIS	78	32	30	85.9'	1911	BURNT 1911
INS 254	BROCH HEAD	85	36	38	86'	1911	SILVERY SEA BF 400 - BURNT GAIRLOCH 1943
INS 233	GREATHEART	76	33	35	84. 5'	1911	MINED OFF DOVER 9.1915
INS 239	STRENUOUS	77	32	35	84. 5'	1911	FR 118, SCRAPPED 4.1951
INS 237	INVERNAIRNE	78	32	35	84. 5'	1911	SY 764, SCRAPPED 10.1952
INS 261	TROPHY	83	32	36	86'	1911	BCK 25, FR 25 - SCRAPPED 3.1950
LY 872	FINROSS	78	32	30	82. 4'	1911	SUNK AT GALLIPOLI 11.1916
BCK 94	MAGGIE BRUCE (A)	76	32	30	82. 4'	1911	SUNK OFF GREAT YARMOUTH 1924
INS 311	MONADLIATH	85	37	30	87. 6'	1912	FR 107 - SCRAPPED 1945
INS 313	HIGHLAND LEADER (A)	82	31	30	83. 1'	1912	SCRAPPED 1937
INS 296	NAIRNSIDE	84	33	27	88. 1'	1912	BCK 155 - SCRAPPED 1946
LY921	CARRIGART	84	33	30	87. 4'	1912	
INS 303	RAIT CASTLE	87	37	27	88'	1912	BF 486, SCRAPPED 1951
LY 937	GWEEDORE		32	27		1913	D. . ., GW 8 AS HERRING CARRIER CLYDE ESTUARY - SOLD TO ICELAND 1939
INS 367	J.E.C.M.	84	33	27	87. 1'	1913	KINCRAIG KY 23, PD 70 - SCRAPPED 1950
BCK 164	FAIRY KNOWE	87	34	28	89. 5'	1913	PD 106
INS 61	BRAEHEAD	85	34	27	87. 1'	1914	SCRAPPED 1938
INS 66	LUCRATIVE	87	34	28	87. 1'	1914	EASTER ROSE FR 29, PD 191, SCRAPPED 1950
INS 399	MISTRESS ISA	99	40	36	89. 5'	1915	PD 71 - SCRAPPED 11.1950
BCK 235	GOLDEN GRAIN	94	40	40	86. 1'	1918	DARNAWAY INS 171 - SCRAPPED 1949
THOSE MARKED (A) WERE BUILT BY J.MacDONALD AND Co. INVERNESS							

WM. WHITE & SONS - COWES, ISLE OF WIGHT   WOODEN

REG NO	NAME	G.R.T.	N.T.	H.P.	LENGTH	YR BUILT	HISTORY
NN 36	NICK OF TIME	41	26	6	60'	1886	LT 115
LT 247	LILLITH	34	15	9	54. 3'	1883	SOLD AS A HOUSE BOAT

A. G. GIFFORD & Co., J. MacKENZIE & Co.,
MORTON & COMPANY, MARR BROTHERS - LEITH   WOODEN

REG NO	NAME	G.R.T.	N.T.	H.P.	LENGTH	YR BUILT	HISTORY
A 669	ABERDEEN	49		10	64	1881	K 486, SONNET, WK 650 - WRECKED AT ORKNEY
LH 92	ROB ROY				56'	1882	
GN 15	PUFFIN		23			1884	YH 414
LH 1088	EARNEST	38	23	10	62. 1'	1884	M 141, A 615
LH 1140	EVELYN	47	20	11	67. 2'	1885	SOLD TO IRELAND
LH 2	PERSEVERANCE	48	20	9	67. 4'	1886	YH 429 - CONVERTED TO COAL LIGHTER
LH 3	RESOLUTE	48	19	10	67. 4'	1886	LT 960 - CONVERTED TO HOUSE BOAT, NORFOLK BROADS
LH 18	EDITH	49	19	17	69'	1886	KY 460, A 780 - WRECKED ISLE OF MAY 8.9.1924

A. G. GIFFORD & Co., J. MacKENZIE & Co., MORTON & COMPANY, MARR BROTHERS - LEITH (CONTINUED)   WOODEN

REG NO	NAME	G.R.T.	N.T.	H.P.	LENGTH	YR BUILT	HISTORY
SN 25	KITTIWAKE (A)	49	19	17. 6	72. 5'	1887	A 187, BF 72, SH 209, YH 472, LT 964 - SCRAPPED 1924
SN 61	EMERALD (C)	47	20	18	71. 5'	1889	KY 522, YH 437, BOY THOMAS YH 162, LT 1133 - SUNK 28.10.1913
SN 175	MAYFLOWER (C)	85	38	31	86. 4'	1893	PD 298 - SOLD TO SPAIN 1920
SN 208	ST. ABBS (C)	92	34	30	90. 2'	1895	LT 798
BF 713	SPEEDWELL (B)	68	27	18	77. 7'	1901	SY 221 - WRECKED OFF LEWIS 1924
BF 655	FAME (B)	68	28	18	77. 1'	1901	WY 71 - LOST W.W.I. OFF POOLE 10 1916
BF 1036	PROGRESSIVE (B)	68	26	20	77. 1'	1902	PD 276 - SCRAPPED 1934
BF 946	SHIELA (B)	83	27	31	84. 3'	1907	SCRAPPED 1937
BF 973	GRACIE (B)	83	27	23	84. 3'	1907	LOST W.W.I. OFF TONGUE LIGHT VESSEL 2.1917
BF 897	VIOLA (B)	83	26	31	84. 5'	1907	WRECKED OFF GREAT YARMOUTH 1934
BF 872	HOPE (B)	79	28	31	84. 7'	1907	SCRAPPED 1929
BF 637	SUSANNA (B)	83	27	31	83. 6'	1907	LOST W.W.I. OFF MILFORD HAVEN 12.1915

THOSE MARKED (A) WERE BUILT BY J.MacKENZIE & Co.

(B) WERE BUILT BY MORTON & Co.

(C) WERE BUILT BY MARR BROS.

RESOLUTE LH 3 - Built of wood by J. McKenzie & Co. of Leith 1886. One of the earliest Steam Drifters. Shown entering Lowestoft ca 1900. Became WK 45 then LT 960, believed to be converted to House-boat, Norfolk Broads ca 1920. Courtesy of Scottish Fisheries Museum.

VIOLA BF 897 - Built of wood by Morton & Co. of Leith 1907. Wrecked off Gt. Yarmouth 1934.
Courtesy of Scottish Fisheries Museum.

ANNEX IV — D. ALLAN & COMPANY - GRANTON — WOODEN

REG NO	NAME	G.R.T.	N.T.	H.P.	LENGTH	YR BUILT	HISTORY
BF 1356	GREEN CASTLE	83		30	90'	1884	CEASED FISHING 1899

ANNEX IV — W. & G. STEPHEN & STEVENSON & ASHER - BANFF — WOODEN

REG NO	NAME	G.R.T.	N.T.	H.P.	LENGTH	YR BUILT	HISTORY
BF 1411	NORSEMAN (A)	75	29	16	81. 1'	1903	SANK OFF FRASERBURGH 1912
BF 1524	RELIANCE (B)	75	32	28	83. 4'	1904	SCRAPPED 1930
BF 260	LILY (B)	74	27	30	80'	1906	FR 487 - SCRAPPED 1936
BF 257	PRODUCTIVE (B)	73	26	20	78. 7'	1906	SOLD TO SWANSEA AS TRADER WILD GOOSE 1922, TO PORTUGAL 1923
BF 415	JOSEPHINE (B)	85	31	33	84. 3'	1906	YH 978 - SUNK OFF SHETLAND 1915
BF 434	SPEEDWELL IV (A)	73	35	30	81. 5'	1906	LOST IN COLLISION 1910
SN 66	IRENE (B)	85	37	25	84. 1'	1907	BK 23, BCK 341 - SCRAPPED 1937
BK 247	GUIDE ME III	87	31	26	83. 8'	1907	WY 85
BF 687	LIVELYHOOD (A)	84	35	30	86. 5'	1907	FR 549 SCRAPPED 1934
BF 991	CEDRON (B)	84	35	32	86. 1'	1907	SANK OFF TOD HEAD 1932
BF 968	VIOLA (B)	86	36	30	86. 1'	1907	SCRAPPED 1934
BF 611	JASPER (A)	84	32	30	86. 8'	1907	SCRAPPED 1938
BF 679	FERN (A)	85	33	30	87'	1907	CORAL CLUSTER FR 64 - SCRAPPED 1945
BF 528	CONDOR (A)	84	29	30	87'	1907	LOST 1932
BF 922	BLOSSOM (B)	86	36	30	86'	1907	SCRAPPED 1934
BF 905	LUFRA (A)	84	29	30	86. 1'	1907	SCRAPPED 1932
BF 526	LUSTRE GEM (B)	82	32	30	85. 7'	1907	SANK OFF PORTLEITHEN ABERDEEN 31.7.24
BF 1145	TARLAIR (A)	80	33	28	86. 6'	1908	LH 1, SH 130, BF 617 - SCRAPPED 1934
BF 1140	THE COLONEL (B)	80	34	40	86. 8'	1908	TO BOSTON 1921 THEN TO SPAIN
BF 1136	GELLYBURN (A)	86	36	30	86'	1908	SCRAPPED 1947
INS 71	PRIDE OF MORAY	50	19	14	76. 5'	1909	LK 95 - SCRAPPED 1947

REG NO	NAME	G.R.T.	N.T.	H.P.	LENGTH	YR BUILT	HISTORY
BF 85	MONTCOFFER (A)	53	22	14	76. 5'	1909	SCRAPPED 1936
BF 59	BRIGHTER HOPE (A)	53	22	14	76. 5'	1909	SCRAPPED 1937
BF 45	CRAIGALVAH (A)	80	33	30	85. 8'	1909	TRUST ON - SCRAPPED 1950
BF 81	FORGLEN (B)	80	33	30	87. 7'	1909	SCRAPPED 1938
BF 122	CULLYKHAN (A)	75	33	30	82. 7'	1910	SCRAPPED 1936
BF 205	WHEATSTALK (A)	72	31	16	81. 6'	1910	BCK 133 - SCRAPPED 1952
BF 271	WHITE DAISY (A)	79	32	30	89'	1910	LK 304 - SUNK 25.9.40
BF 136	MONTBLETTON (B)	76	32	32	86. 5'	1910	SCRAPPED 1938
BF 247	PROSPECTIVE (A)	75	31	20	82. 1'	1910	SCRAPPED 1938
BF 195	LUSTRING (B)	73	30	30	83. 5'	1910	LOST OFF HELLIER HOLM 10.18
BF 175	DUNEDIN (A)	78	32	30	86. 5'	1910	SCRAPPED 1949
BF 144	GAVENEY BRAE (A)	54	23	30	77'	1910	SCRAPPED 1935
BF 149	FRAGRANCE (B)	72	30	30	83. 5'	1910	SCRAPPED 1936
BF 193	GOWANBANK (A)	78	32	27	86. 2'	1910	SCRAPPED 1938
BF 231	BOYNDIE BURN (B)	73	30	30	84. 1'	1910	SCRAPPED 1948
BF 169	CONVALLARIA (A)	77	32	34	86. 7'	1910	LOST 1924
INS 230	CORAL HILL	56	26	26	78. 6'	1911	SY 48 - SCRAPPED 1938
INS 229	CUDWEED	68	32	26	80'	1911	SANK OFF WICK 1923
BF 326	PRESSING ON (B)	72	30	30	86.7'	1911	SUNK 1912
BF 350	GIRL EVELYN (A)	85	35	35	86. 6'	1911	FR 519 - SCRAPPED 23.9.36
BF 393	DAISY BANK (A)	84	37	28	85'	1911	LOST 1949
BF 395	UNIFLOROUS (A)	76	33	28	85'	1911	FLOWING STREAM, BF 395 - SCRAPPED 1938
BF 364	RUBY GEM (B)	76	32	30	84. 7'	1911	BURNT 1924
BF 353	SILVER FORD (A)	85	35	30	86. 3'	1911	LOST 1921
BF 330	TEA ROSE (A)	84	35	25	86'	1911	LK 87, PD 188 - SCRAPPED 1945
BF 327	SILVER PEARL (B)	71	30	26	81. 3'	1911	AR 2
BF 345	LILYBANK (A)	83	35	25	86. 5'	1911	BRAES O'GAMRIE, BF 345 - SCRAPPED 1938
BF 394	ROYAL BURGH (B)	78	33	20	84. 6'	1911	JOHN ROBERT, BF 394 - SCRAPPED 1938
BF 397	CORONARIA (A)	81	34	28	86'	1911	MHOR HEAD - LOST 16.7.29
BF 303	ELEGANT (A)	84	35	35	86. 4'	1911	FR 179 - SCRAPPED 1938

FORGLEN BF 81 - Built of wood by Stevenson & Asher of Banff during 1909. Seen leaving Lowestoft 1911.
Scrapped 1938. Courtesy of A. Durrant, Kessingland.

JOHN ROBERT BF 394 - Built of wood by Stephenson & Asher of Banff 1911 as Royal Burgh BF 394.
Shown entering Gt. Yarmouth ca 1936. Scrapped 1938. Courtesy of Scottish Fisheries Museum.

ANNEX IV   W. & G. STEPHEN & STEVENSON & ASHER - BANFF (CONTINUED)   WOODEN

REG NO	NAME	G.R.T.	N.T.	H.P.	LENGTH	YR BUILT	HISTORY
BF 286	IVY LEAF (A)	87	39	25	87. 6'	1911	RESTORE - SCRAPPED 1947
BF 323	CLOVER (B)	83	35	20	87. 6'	1911	SCRAPPED 1932
BF 325	CINCERIA (B)	75	31	30	86. 7'	1911	LOST 1920
BF 445	LILACINA (A)	83	35	25	87. 5'	1912	SCRAPPED 1939
BF 465	CORONATA (A)	81	35	29	86. 1'	1912	SY 310 - SCRAPPED 10.52
BF 428	PERILIA (A)	83	35	25	86. 4'	1912	FR 295 - LOST IN LOCH RYAN 1930
BF 449	COURAGE (A)	88	37	29	87. 5'	1912	SCRAPPED 1938
SN 227	ETHNEE	86	37	25	88. 2'	1913	LOST ON GOODWIN SAND 1.18
BF 536	FORETHOUGHT (A)	86	36	35	88. 2'	1913	FR 186 - WRECKED YORKSHIRE 1921
FR 559	TROUP HEAD (A)	86	36	35	88. 2'	1913	SCRAPPED 1947
A 559	GOLDEN DAWN	79	33	30	87'	1913	PD 46, YH 49, PD 239, BK 129 - LOST
A 579	GREY DAWN	84	35	30	87. 4'	1913	SUNNY VALE, PD 44 - SCRAPPED 1948
FR 586	ALEX WATT (A)	86	37	25	87. 7'	1913	SCRAPPED 1950
BF 93	CRAIGNEEN (B)	90	38	26	88. 5'	1913	WRECKED 1940
BF 614	GOLDEN FEATHER (A)	88	37	30	87. 8'	1913	LOST OFF EAST ANGLIA 1923
BF 615	CONCORDIA (A)	91	36	26	88. 7'	1913	SCRAPPED 1947
BF 545	BRITISH CROWN (A)	85	35	27	88. 3'	1913	FR 69 - SCRAPPED 1949
BF 620	THERMOPYLAE (A)	84	35	28	87. 4'	1913	PD 233 - SCRAPPED 1950
BF 508	PROFICENCY (B)	82	34	27	85. 4'	1913	SCRAPPED 1938
BF 652	LAVATERA (A)	84	37	30	87'	1913	SCRAPPED 1948
BF 600	OCEAN GLEANER (A)	86	36	35	88. 2'	1913	FR 274 - SCRAPPED 3.51
BF 544	GEORGE A. WEST (A)	86	36	25	87'	1913	LOST 1928
BF 640	FLOWING TIDE (A)	83	35	25	86'	1913	SCRAPPED 1950
BF 105	GOLDEN EFFORT (A)	87	36	28	88. 7'	1914	FR 408 - LOST ON WAR SERVICE 1943, CLYDE
BF 57	ASTRUM SPEI (B)	82	35	20	85. 4'	1914	SUNK BY AUSTRIAN CRUISERS OFF BRINDISI 7.16
BF662	HELENORA (B)	88	37	25	89. 7'	1914	SUNK BY AUSTRIAN CRUISERS OFF FANO ISLANDS 5.17
BF 39	BUDDING ROSE (A)	88	38	26	90'	1914	SCRAPPED 1936
BK 334	MAGGIE COWE (B)	91	38	27	89. 5'	1914	RACHEL FLETT, BCK 434 - SCRAPPED 1949
BF 96	KILNBURN (A)	88	37	27	89. 7'	1914	SCRAPPED 1936
BF 82	DEVERONSIDE (A)	89	38	28	90'	1914	PD 169 - SCRAPPED 1946
BF 103	TOKEN (A)	89	37	26	89. 6'	1914	LOST SKERRY SOUND 23.12.43
BF 92	GAVENWOOD (A)	88	37	28	89'	1914	MINED OFF BRINDISI 2.16
BF 115	GAMRIE BAY (A)	87	35	27	88. 8'	1914	SCRAPPED 1950
FR 293	I. & J. (A)	95	40	36		1916	LOST OFF NEWHAVEN ENGLAND 1.19

THERMOPYLAE BF 620 - Built of wood by W. & G. Stephen of Banff 1913. Shown as PD 233 entering Peterhead ca 1938. Scrapped 1950. Courtesy of Scottish Fisheries Museum.

ANNEX IV   W. & G. STEPHEN & STEVENSON & ASHER - BANFF (CONTINUED)   WOODEN

REG NO	NAME	G.R.T.	N.T.	H.P.	LENGTH	YR BUILT	HISTORY
BF 284	CLARA WOOD (A)	88	37	30	85. 7'	1916	GILT EDGE, BCK 121, BF 61 - SCRAPPED 1950
A 665	YOUNG DAWN	86	36	38	88'	1916	LT 1294, PD 178 - SCRAPPED 1950
BF 365	BARLEY STALK (A)	91	38	36	88. 3'	1917	SCRAPPED 1938
A 731	CLOVERBANK	92	39	37	85.4'	1917	SUNK DOVER STRAITS 15.2.18
LK 682	MAID OF THULE (B)	97	41	40	88. 6'	1917	CLINGS WATER, LK 240 - SCRAPPED 5.52
PD 325	M.H.BUCHAN	101	42	37	88. 3'	1917	SCRAPPED

THOSE MARKED (A) WERE BUILT BY W. & G. STEPHEN, BANFF

THOSE MARKED (B) WERE BUILT BY STEVENSON AND ASHER, BANFF

ANNEX IV   J. & G. FORBES - SANDHAVEN AND FRASERBURGH   WOODEN

REG NO	NAME	G.R.T.	N.T.	H.P.	LENGTH	YR BUILT	HISTORY
	WILLIAM PECK	60	26	11	64. 8'	1905	BUILT AS MOTOR CONVERTED TO STEAM 1912 - WILLIAM BEARDMORE, BCK 77, CROY, FR 129 - SCRAPPED 1944
KY 169	AZARAEL	94	40	35	90'	1907	PD 76 - SUNK OFF BELL ROCK - 2.10.38
PD 523	J. T. STEPHEN	82	28	27	87. 1'	1907	SCRAPPED 1936
BF 957	CAMPANIA	90	35	21	89. 5'	1907	BCK 98 - LOST OFF ST. ABBS HEAD 3.17
BF 923	HAWTHORNE	93	34	35	89. 4'	1907	SCRAPPED 1934
FR 212	TAITS	93	36	28	89. 7'	1907	SUNK BY AUSTRIAN CRUISERS OFF FANO ISLANDS 7.5.17

TAITS FR 212 - Built of wood by J & G Forbes of Sandhaven 1907. Sunk by Austrian Cruisers off Fano Islands 7 May 1917. Courtesy of A. Durrant, Kessingland.

ANNEX IV J. & G. FORBES - SANDHAVEN AND FRASERBURGH (CONTINUED) WOODEN

REG NO	NAME	G.R.T.	N.T.	H.P.	LENGTH	YR BUILT	HISTORY
FR 214	ANCHOR OF HOPE	95	36	32	89. 6'	1907	SCRAPPED 1936
A 216	HEATHBANK	75	25	25	87'	1908	BCK 176 - HERRING CARRIER - SUNK AT BOWLING 1946
FR 254	BUCHAN	81	34	30	87. 5'	1908	BCK 123 - SCRAPPED 1949
FR 286	BOY ALEX	75	31	28	87. 3'	1908	SCRAPPED 1947
INS 158	BEN BUI	73	30	30	84. 2'	1910	SCRAPPED 1936
BCK 61	OLYMPUS	58	24	26	76. 3'	1910	SCRAPPED 1936
FR 432	MELINKA	77	32	27	86. 5'	1911	GOLDENLEA, BF 499 - SCRAPPED 1947
INS 214	DO WELL	71	29	20	85. 3'	1911	ELOQUENT, BCK 26 - TO NORWAY 1945
YH 732	OCEAN HOPE	81	34	29	88. 1'	1912	BF 29 - LOST AT SEA 1936
A 739	CLOVER BANK	78	33	29	88'	1912	MINED OFF ZEEBRUGGE 4.16
FR 566	CORAL HAVEN	82	34	35	86. 5'	1913	SUNK BY AUSTRIAN CRUISERS OFF FANO ISLS 7.5.17
FR 561	SHEPHERD BOY	81	34	35	86. 5'	1913	SCRAPPED 1938
FR 536	ANNIE CUMINE	80	30	35	87'	1913	MARY J. MASSON, FR 536 - REGISTRY CANCELLED 1947
FR 582	ACQUISITION	83	34	27	87. 8'	1913	SCRAPPED 1949
BK 328	AGNES AND JANET	91	38	40	89. 3'	1914	LAUREL CROWN FR 121, BF 236, SY 708 - SCRAPPED 1951
BF 63	GOLDEN WEST	88	37	27	89'	1914	FR 59 - SCRAPPED 1952
FR 81	ST. COMBS HAVEN	89	37	27	88. 6'	1914	SOLD TO ITALY 1919
FR 95	CRAIGHAUGH	89	38	27	88. 7'	1914	SCRAPPED 1950
FR 106	DUTHIES	89	38	27	88. 6'	1914	BOMBED AND LOST OFF MONTROSE 25.10.40
FR 72	MILLBURN	85	36	27	87. 8'	1914	SUNK 1938
PD 231	UGIEBRAE	88	37	27	88. 2'	1915	SCRAPPED 1950
PD 232	WHITEHILL	90	37	27	88. 5'	1915	SCRAPPED AT PETERHEAD 1944

CRAIGHAUGH FR 95 - Built of wood by J. & G. Forbes of Sandhaven 1914. Shown leaving Fraserburgh ca 1949. Scrapped 1950. Courtesy of Scottish Fisheries Museum.

ANNEX IV SCOTT & YULE, NOBLE & Co THEN WILSON, NOBLE & Co. - FRASERBURGH WOODEN

REG NO	NAME	G.R.T.	N.T.	H.P.	LENGTH	YR BUILT	HISTORY
FR 245	LAUREL (A)	97	33	25	88'	1907	LY 31
FR 232	GOWAN (B)	97	41	31	90'	1907	LY 49, FR 99 - IDENT, PD 47 - SCRAPPED 1937
FR 201	SPEEDWELL (A)	96	33	35	90. 6'	1907	SCRAPPED 1932
FR 226	ALBATROSS (A)	86	31	25	87. 6'	1907	SCRAPPED 1936
FR 205	KINNAIRD (B)	94	32	22	85. 4'	1907	MYSEAL A 145, INS 125 - LOST AT LOCH EPORT 1930
FR 260	LIGHT (A)	81	34	25	87. 1'	1908	SCRAPPED 1936
FR 401	PENNAN (A)	64	26	33	80. 2'	1910	SOLD TO GREECE 1947
A 373	LIZZIE BROWN (A)	76	32	29	88. 3'	1911	CLARA CHAPMAN GY 377, MORNING GLORIES FR 79 - SCRAPPED 1936
FR 415	GEORGE WALKER (A)	65	27	27	81'	1911	SCRAPPED 1936
FR 459	WESTS (A)	78	33	29	88. 1'	1911	BF 212 - SCRAPPED 1937
FR 439	CITRON (A)	78	33	29	88. 7'	1911	SCRAPPED 1947
FR 491	BRACODEN (A)	81	33	29	88'5"	1912	SCRAPPED 1936
FR 496	DENNYDUFF (A)	80	33	29	87. 5'	1912	SCRAPPED 1938
FR 506	LAUREL CROWN (A)	81	34	35	88. 7'	1912	MINED WEST COAT OF ORKNEY 6.1916
FR 558	WHITE OAK (B)	75	31	35	84. 4'	1913	BF 523 - SCRAPPED 1934
FR 534	STAR OF BUCHAN (A)	81	34	34	88. 7'	1913	MINED OFF NAB BUOY 10.15
FR 565	ROSEHEARTY (A)	82	34	35	88. 5'	1913	SCRAPPED 1949
PD 118	LILLIUM (A)	83	35	27	88. 7'	1913	SOLD TO MINISTRY OF WAR TRANSPORT 1942 - REGESTRY CANCELLED 1946
PD 148	VIOLET FLOWER (B)	87	38	27	91. 5'	1914	SCRAPPED 1947
FR 105	GOWAN LEA (A)	84	35	27	89'	1914	INS 168 - SCRAPPED 1937
FR 74	AUCHMEDDEN (A)	82	34	27	88. 7'	1914	SCRAPPED 1947
FR 148	JESSIE TAIT (A)	84	35	30	89'	1915	SCRAPPED 1947
THOSE MARKED (A) WERE BUILT BY SCOTT AND YULE							
THOSE MARKED (B) WERE BUILT BY NOBLE & Co., LATER WILSON, NOBLE & Co.							

REG NO	NAME	G.R.T.	N.T.	H.P.	LENGTH	YR BUILT	HISTORY
LH 250	MORNING STAR	89	37	30	86. 8'	1907	BF 625 - SCRAPPED 1937
LH 183	VIOLET	90	34	34	86. 9'	1907	BROKEN UP 1935
ME 203	PANSY	91	32	33	86. 8'	1907	ML 69, COREGA KY 101 - SOLD TO FORTH COMMISSION AS BUOY TENDER

VIOLET LH 183 - Built of wood by Wm Weatherhead of Cockenzie. Shown at Port Seton fitted for trawling ca 1930. Broken up 1935. Courtesy of Scottish Fisheries Museum.

REG NO	NAME	G.R.T.	N.T.	H.P.	LENGTH	YR BUILT	HISTORY
BF 218	BLOOMFIELD	83	29	27	83. 6'	1906	GY 343 - SANK 1936
BF 249	VALLAR CROWN	78	27	26	82. 3'	1906	SCRAPPED 1938
BF 324	ENERGY	79	27	20	85'	1906	SCRAPPED 1950
BF 683	EXCELSIOR	85	30	30	86'	1907	BCK 53 - SCRAPPED 1933
BF 831	ROXANNA	86	30	25	87.75'	1907	NEXUS BCK 159 - MINED THAMES EST. 13.3.18
BF 497	TRANSIT	83	29	31	85. 1'	1907	SUNK BY AUSTRIAN CRUISERS OFF FANO ISLS 7.5.17
BF 914	PETREL	86	29	30	85. 2'	1907	SCRAPPED 1936
BF 937	CONIE	85	30	30	85. 2'	1908	SCRAPPED 1937
BCK 17	BON CHIEF	83	35	28	86. 5'	1908	SCRAPPED 1949
BCK 27	DESIRE	83	34	30	86. 6'	1908	SCRAPPED 1944
BCK 53	GLENALBYN	82	34	28	86'	1909	FR 57 - MINED IN LOCH EWE - 23.12.39
BCK 65	STERLOCHY	78	33	27	83. 2'	1910	PD 384 - SCRAPPED 1948
BCK 70	DOCILE III	82	34	27	86. 1'	1910	SCRAPPED 1937
BCK 89	HOME FRIEND	89	38	24	87. 7'	1911	BF 257 - SCRAPPED 1939
BCK 90	HARVEST HOPE	91	39	28	89'	1911	BF 106 - SCRAPPED 1937
BCK 126	SUMMERSTON	83	35	29	87. 3'	1912	SCRAPPED 10.1951
BCK 112	DAVID FLETT	84	35	29	87. 7'	1912	STAR OF LIGHT PD 167, FR 221 - SCRAPPED 1950
BCK 110	G. S. L.	85	36	29	87'	1912	TO SPAIN 1921

REG NO	NAME	G.R.T.	N.T.	H.P.	LENGTH	YR BUILT	HISTORY
BK 271	CHRISTINA CRAIG	86	37	35	87'	1912	SUNK BY GERMAN DESTROYER DOVER STRAITS 15.2.18
PD 92	MONARDA	87	37	29	89. 8'	1913	SUNK BY SUBMARINE OFF OUTER SKERRIES 24.6.15
BCK 145	BARLEY RIG	86	37	36	87'	1913	MINED OFF TYNE 27.8.14
BCK 153	HEATHER SPRIG	83	34	35	88. 2'	1913	SCRAPPED 10.51
BCK 163	LIZZIE BIRRELL	92	39	35	87'	1913	SOLD TO NORWAY 1946
BCK 180	EGLISE	99	42	30	92. 5'	1914	FR 102 - SCRAPPED 1938
BCK 187	ENTERPRISING	98	41	36	92. 3'	1914	INS 3, BK 63, FR 26, SA 8 - SCRAPPED 1950
BK 72	BORDER KING	92	39	41	90. 5'	1914	PD 159 - SCRAPPED 1945
BK 304	J. AND A.	98	43	27	92'	1915	SUNK OFF SCARBOROUGH 4.4.18
BCK 210	ELIBANK	96	43	35	90. 5'	1915	GINA RITCHIE PD 126, ABIDE - SOLD TO R. A. F. 1942
PD 266	MONARDA	108	43	36	91'	1916	LOST THAMES ESTUARY 8.11.41
BK 357	MARY SWANSTON	109	46	44	93. 1'	1916	DEWEY EVE BF 215 - LOST AT SCAPA FLOW 9.6.40
BCK 355	OBTAIN	105	45	37	90. 7'	1917	ROSE VALLEY BF 80, PD 22 - SCRAPPED 25.10.50
BCK 128	HARVEST REAPER	92	40	29	87'	1925	FR 34 - SCRAPPED 1950
BCK 3	LORANTHUS	95	40	26	86.5'	1929	BF 58 - SCRAPPED 1951
FR 149	JOHN HERD	103	44	43	91.9'	1930	BF 94 - SCRAPPED 1951
BF 213	LIZZIE WEST	103	44	34	90.6'	1930	M 22, LT 495 - ENDED AS A "BARKING" SHIP AT FRASERBURGH - SCRAPPED 1968 LAST WOODEN DRIFTER TO BE BUILT IN THE U.K.

EXCELSIOR BF 683 - Built of wood by Herd & MacKenzie Ltd of Findochty & Buckie 1907. Became BCK 53, shown leaving Gt. Yarmouth, ca 1920s. Scrapped 1933. Courtesy of Scottish Fisheries Museum.

CARNEGIE & MATTHEWS - PETERHEAD **WOODEN**

REG NO	NAME	G.R.T.	N.T.	H.P.	LENGTH	YR BUILT	HISTORY
BF 282	OLIVE	83	29	22	84'	1906	LOST OFF GREAT YARMOUTH 1933
BF 369	TRUSTFUL	87	31	32	84'	1906	PD 366, DO 27 - TO PLEASURE 1927
PD 356	ENDEAVOUR	89	32	31	86. 3'	1907	SCRAPPED 1936
BF 854	FERTILITY	86	32	31	86'	1907	SCRAPPED 1936
PD 510	ASPIRANT	81	28	27	84. 5'	1908	SCRAPPED 1937
PD 352	SLAINS CASTLE	81	28	27	84. 6'	1908	BF 7
PD 560	VETERAN	73	30	33	80. 1'	1910	SCRAPPED 1936
BF 332	DAISY WOOD	72	30	30	80'	1911	SCRAPPED 1937
PD 50	DIRECT ME	71	31	32	80. 2'	1912	FR 157 - SCRAPPED 1938
SN 222	HONOR	72	30	24	80. 4'	1913	BK 22, FR 131, PD 331 - SCRAPPED 2.9.52
BF 54	GOLDEN RAY	79	34	35	83. 8'	1914	TO ICELAND 1932
PD 210	PETERUGIE	81	34	36	84. 7'	1915	SCRAPPED 1938
PD 352	BYDAND	90	37	37	82. 1'	1917	FR 139 - SANK IN PENTLAND FIRTH 1936

STEPHEN & FORBES, THEN FORBES & BIRNIE, **WOODEN**
THEN RICHARD IRVIN & SONS LTD 1915 - PETERHEAD

REG NO	NAME	G.R.T.	N.T.	H.P.	LENGTH	YR BUILT	HISTORY
A 370	PALESTINE	69	40	25	76.7'	1889	TO MILFORD HAVEN 1901
A 693	CALEDONIA	82	31	27	81. 7'	1892	PD 438 - SCRAPPED 1926
A 708	BRITANNIA	75	34	28	81. 5'	1893	
PD 54	PIONEER	95	35	32	87. 6'	1893	SOLD TO GUERNSEY 1921
A 279	VINE	110	42	27	97'	1900	LOST OFF SHETLAND 1915
PD 398	LILY	74	25	18	77. 8'	1900	BCK 218 - SCRAPPED 1927
PD 402	IRIS	74	26	23	82.1'	1901	SCRAPPED 1927
PD 414	STATELY	75	26	23	81'	1901	LT 279
PD 406	JOHANNA PETRIE	75	25	30	86.1'	1901	FAIR CHANCE, WILLIAM REAICH, BCK 123, PD 393 - SCRAPPED 1936
PD 415	GUIDE ME	79	28	30	86' 1"	1901	INS 251, PD 469 - WRECKED PENTLAND FIRTH, 1928
FR 972	CONCORD				77.9'	1903	TO MOTOR 1904, PD 507, TO STEAM 1917, A 870. BUILT AS SAIL, SCRAPPED 1936
PD 156	JENNY LIND	89	33	30	90. 1'	1907	LOST IN COLLISION 1910
PD 360	ERA	94	39	35	91.5'	1907	SOLD TO SPAIN 1920
PD 529	PRIDE OF BUCHAN	86	29	29	88. 7'	1908	KY4 MARGARET MAIR, BF 160 - BURNT 1931
KY 267	CALCEOLARIA	92	36	23	88.4	1908	MINED OFF ELBOW BUOY 27.10.18
SN 80	JOCELYN	94	40	45	88. 1'	1915	PD 154 - SCRAPPED 1947
SN 287	LORRAINE	96	42	39	86.1'	1916	
SN 23	MAUVEEN	95	40	40	90'	1918	GOLDEN EMBLEM, BF 232 - SCRAPPED 1947
JOCELYN, LORRAINE & MAUVEEN WERE BUILT BY RICHARD IRVIN AND Co Ltd							

PRIDE OF BUCHAN PD 259 - Built of wood by Forbes & Birnie of Peterhead 1908.
Became KY 4, MARGARET MAIR BF 160, shown as KY 4 entering Gt. Yarmouth ca 1920s. Burnt
1931. Courtesy of Scottish Fisheries Museum.

ANNEX IV   G. INNES & SONS - PORTNOCKIE   WOODEN

REG NO	NAME	G.R.T.	N.T.	H.P.	LENGTH	YR BUILT	HISTORY
BF 403	PARVAIM	87. 05	29. 48	30	83. 7'	1906	SUNK 1907
BF 888	LAPWING	89	37	30	85. 5'	1907	SH 170 - SCRAPPED 1929
BF 510	SUNSHINE	89	30	30	84'	1907	
BF 641	EMULATOR	82	30	25	84. 8'	1907	PRIDE OF FILEY, SH 215, CUHONA H 307 NO LONGER FISHING 1928
BF 1114	BERRIE BRAES	87	27	27	85. 8'	1908	SCRAPPED 1936

UNION CO-OPERATIVE SHIPBUILDING SOCIETY - BLYTH, NORTHUMBERLAND
ANNEX IV   WOODEN

REG NO	NAME	G.R.T.	N.T.	H.P.	LENGTH	YR BUILT	HISTORY
SN 64	MORNING STAR	63	17	19	76'	1889	
SN 153	COQUET	76	33	32	85. 4'	1892	
SN 178	TWEEDSIDE	79	34	32	87. 2'	1893	
SN 190	SCOTS GREYS	76	33	32	84. 5'	1894	KY 52, BF 360 - SUNK NORTH SEA 19.11.13
SN 261	PRUDHOE CASTLE	84	40	33	91'	1898	INS 35 - WRECKED OFF DONEGAL 1911
SN 247	RAMBLER	92	35	33	90. 4'	1898	MINED OFF BLYTH 26.2.18
SN 2	REAPER	91	35	33	90' 8"	1899	MINED OFF TYNE 21.1.18
SN 47	ROAMER	93	36	33	91. 3'	1900	
SN 163	NANCY	59	26	20	74'	1900	SUNK OF GREAT YARMOUTH 1919
SN 272	ETHEL	58	25	20	74. 5'	1900	
SN 309	ETHELBERT	92	26	33	91' 4"	1901	LH 24 - SUNK 27.6.1911
SN 323	ETHELBALD	92	36	34	91. 3'	1902	SUNK OFF FRASERBURGH AFTER COLLISION August 1916

ANNEX IV   J. GRIGOR - PORTGORDON   WOODEN

REG NO	NAME	G.R.T.	N.T.	H.P.	LENGTH	YR BUILT	HISTORY
BF 1502	BALM	62	18	18	70. 2'	1904	SAILING ZULU CONVERTED TO STEAM - SOLD TO FRANCE 20.9.05

ANNEX IV   R. COCK - APPLEDORE, DEVON   WOODEN

REG NO	NAME	G.R.T.	N.T.	H.P.	LENGTH	YR BUILT	HISTORY
YH 843	LUDHAM CASTLE	66	33	25	80. 4'	1904	TO FRANCE - LOST 1921
YH 850	BOY BILLY	70	36	20	83. 4'	1904	SCRAPPED 1928

ANNEX IV   COLBY BROTHERS - OULTON BROAD, LOWESTOFT   WOODEN

REG NO	NAME	G.R.T.	N.T.	H.P.	LENGTH	YR BUILT	HISTORY
LT 1197	LORD CARNARVON	50	36	28	80'	1912	MINED OFF GREAT YARMOUTH 20.11.14
LT 373	GOLDEN NEWS	95	44	32	87. 3'	1914	SCRAPPED 1951
LT 477	COSMOS	91	43	20	86. 5'	1914	SUNK BY GERMAN DESTROYERS DOVER STRAITS 15.1.18
SH 103	ZUBULON	94	43	20	86. 7'	1914	
YH 45	NORFORD SURFFLING	86	40	24	83. 6'	1914	LT 685 - LOST 1946
LT 119	SUPPORTER	88	43	20	84. 5'	1914	YH 74 - WRECKED OFF NEWHAVEN 5.11.44
LT 777	LORD ZETLAND	89	44	20	85. 1'	1914	SCRAPPED 1951
LT 507	SILVERY WAVE	96	43	37	88'	1915	LOST IN CROW SOUND 13.11.15
BCK 214	B.SUTHERLAND	96	45	33	86. 4'	1915	LORD CAVEN LT 680 - LOST AT DUNKIRK 1.6.40
PD 222	STAR OF FAITH	94	46	37	88'	1915	REGISTRY CANCELLED 1946
VH 312	OCEAN TOILER	102	47	26	88. 2'	1915	SCRAPPED 1949
LT 711	LORD FISHER	89	44	30	85. 5'	1916	SCRAPPED 1951
YH 279	SUNBEAM II	85	39	24	83. 3'	1916	LT 304 - SCRAPPED 1954
LT 705	INFINITIVE	103	49	26	88. 6'	1916	SCRAPPED 1937
LT 671	JAMES AND WALTER	96	46	37	86. 7	1916	SCRAPPED 1938
SH 253	DIXON	104	44	31	88. 5'	1916	LT 1287 - SCRAPPED 1937
HL 85	KATREEN	104	45	33	88. 2'	1916	GY 404 - TO BELGIUM 1949
LT 914	QUEEN MOTHER	126	54	29	93.5'	1916	SOLD TO BRISTOL AS PILOT CUTTER
LT 678	COLEUS	102	43	35	88. 5'	1916	MINED OFF DOVER 4.10.18
LT 487	G. S. P.	100	43	29	88. 6'	1916	SUNK OFF OWERS LT VESSEL 2.12.17
YH 579	CHEERIO LADS	103	51	28	89. 3'	1917	SCRAPPED 1938
YH 610	NULLI SECUNDUS	104	50	28	89. 3'	1917	SCRAPPED 1938
YH 667	BOY BOB	101	46	40	88'	1917	ELSIE AND NELLIE BF 531, SCRAPPED 1946
SH 325	FLO JOHNSTON	117	52	46	93. 7'	1917	ABIDING STAR LT 451, SCRAPPED 1947
YH 273	HERRING GULL	93	42	33	83. 6'	1917	LT 330 SCRAPPED 1937
YH 247	LA MASCOT	83	37	33	85. 4'	1917	LT 970
WY 226	LISBURN	102	48	29	88. 5'	1917	LT 1262, SCRAPPED 1937
HL 88	CLARA SUTTON	102	43	35	88. 8'	1917	SOLD TO FAEROES 1946
WY 187	JESBURN	99	41	44	88. 5'	1917	
LT 7	LORD CURZON	88	43	30	85. 2'	1917	LK 374 - SCRAPPED 1947
LT 1174	GIRL GLADYS	115	56	40	88. 4'	1917	SCRAPPED 1947
YH 593	HERRING HO	85	42	33	83. 5'	1917	SH 220, LT 1063 - LOST OFF SMITHS KNOLL 1932
YH 277	CAPTAIN FRYATT	87	39	33	84'	1917	DUNDEE PILOT CUTTER 1922 - 1947
LT 1201	WILMINGTON	111	54	28	90'	1920	YORKSHIRE LASS - SCRAPPED 1948

REG NO	NAME	G.R.T.	N.T.	H.P.	LENGTH	YR BUILT	HISTORY
BF 77	ROSIEBURN	56	26	17	72'	1909	SCRAPPED 1947
BF 179	AIVERN	72	30	30	84'	1910	INS 325 - SANK ENGLISH CHANNEL 2.17
BF 108	ROSE O'DOUNE	64	28	23	77'6"	1910	LK 397 - SCRAPPED 1948
BF 253	CEDAR LEAF	76	31	24	84'	1910	SCRAPPED 1938
BF 359	JOHN WATT	84	35	28	86'	1911	SANK OFF GRIMSBY 1921
BF 301	LONICERA	78	32	29	84. 3'	1911	TO DENMARK 1924, TO A91 1925 - WRECKED
BF 311	AVONDALE	80	33	29	85'	1911	SUNK BY AUSTRIAN CRUISERS OFF FANO ISLANDS
BF 407	LOOK SHARP	83	34	26	86. 1'	1912	SCRAPPED 1932
BF 568	VIGOROUS	81	34	26	86. 4'	1913	SCRAPPED 1938
BF 530	REPLENISH	83	34	35	86. 4'	1913	SANK OFF ABERDEEN 1931
BF 75	SPRIG O'HEATHER	86	36	36	87. 2'	1914	GY 1193, H 771, FR 127 - SCRAPPED 1947
BF 654	LOVEDALE	84	35	27	87. 4'	1914	SUNK OFF LOWESTOFF 1929
SN 105	ISA	87	36	27	87. 1'	1914	BOY JOHN FR 186 - SCRAPPED 1950
BF 309	CORNSTALK	73	30	32	79. 1'	1916	SCRAPPED 1936

AVONDALE BF 311 - Built of wood by G. Innes & Son, MacDuff during 1911. Seen leaving Lowestoft ca 1911. Sunk by Austrian cruisers off Fano Islands, 15 May 1917. Courtesy of A. Durrant, Kessingland.

REG NO	NAME	G.R.T.	N.T.	H.P.	LENGTH	YR BUILT	HISTORY
YH 481	LORD BOB'S	60	35	20	74.2'	1900	BF 163, BCK 71, VALKYRIE BF 223 - SOLD AS A HOUSE BOAT 1922
BF 410	PROMOTE	57	36	20	76.3'	1900	PD 136, FR 275 - SCRAPPED 23.3.22
BF 657	SIRIUS	60	34	18	79'	1901	FR 523, LT 317 - SCRAPPED 1925
YH 359	HARRY	60	32	20	74.1'	1901	FR 527 - LOST 1927
SN 327	MARY	61	39	20	78'	1902	PD 161 - SCRAPPED 1932
YH 735	SPRING FLOWER	59	36	28	78'	1902	SCRAPPED 1926
BF 994	MASCOT	66	33	18	81.5'	1902	SCRAPPED 1935
YH 763	FERN	59	34	20	79'	1902	LOST 1928
YH 839	RELIANCE	67	22	20	79.2'	1903	BF 1590 - LOST 1927
BF 1312	PANSY	67	22	20	79.2'	1903	SCRAPPED 1932
BF 1090	HEARTY	67	21	18	79.2'	1903	WK325 - WRECKED N. COAST 1932
BF 1263	HANDY	67	34	26	78.5'	1903	BCK 161, SY 2 - SCRAPPED 1939
BF 1340	GOLDEN HOPE	58	22	20	79.2'	1903	BCK 30 - SUNK BY SUBMARINE OFF KINNAIRD HD 7.6.17
YH 846	SEYMOLICUS	67	22	20	79.2'	1904	SUNK OFF SMITH'S KNOLL 11.14
YH 24	HOPE	67	22	25	79.2'	1904	INS 138 - SCRAPPED 1927
YH 397	MEG	82	32	24	82.5'	1906	LT 316
LT 516	NELSON	71	34	28	80'	1906	TO SPAIN 1925
BF 316	CELANDINE	73	32	30	82'	1906	SCRAPPED 1933
INS 194	BRIGHTON	75	31	30	82'	1906	BCK 120 - SCRAPPED 1936
BF 189	MONITOR	68	24	28	79.2'	1906	BCK 72 - SCRAPPED 1938
YH 313	ERIN	81	34	24	82'	1907	ASPIRATION - SCRAPPED 1941
BF 630	MARY'S	82	34	30	82.4'	1907	BCK 198 - SCRAPPED 1938
LT 3	GIRL ENA	89	30	32	85'	1907	BK 304, LT 1263, YH 464 - SCRAPPED 1947
BF 771	ACTIVE	81	23	34	82'	1907	MINED OFF MILFORD HAVEN 15.10.17
YH 407	MASTERPIECE	82	34	31	82.2'	1907	FR 222 - SCRAPPED 1936
INS 444	RESOLUTE	82	34	30	82'	1907	SCRAPPED 1938
YH 388	UFFA	89	33	26	83.1'	1908	PD 82 - SUNK OFF SHETLAND 23.6.17 BY U-BOAT
BCK 18	PANOPIA	77	25	31	82.7'	1908	SCRAPPED 1949
BCK 36	MARY REID	77	26	30	82.5'	1908	SCRAPPED 1938
INS 578	CLACHNACUDIN	78	32	31	83.6'	1908	BCK 152, YH 361, BCK 448 - SCRAPPED 1933
LT 456	CLARA & ALICE	79	27	31	83.5'	1909	SUNK OFF PALERMO 26.5.18
INS 27	GLENERNE	79	33	25	83.5'	1909	SCRAPPED 1938
LT 577	MADIS	79	27	30	83.2'	1909	FISHER PRINCE
LT 736	THREE BOYS	84	28	31	82.6'	1910	RAJAH OF MANDI, BOY RAY YH7 - SCRAPPED 1947
LT 526	SCADAUN	86	39	31	83.8'	1910	DEVON COUNTY - MINED THAMES ESTUARY 1.7.41
LT 686	LORD STRABROKE	79	38	28	79.6'	1910	OUR KATE YH 71 - SCRAPPED 1954
YH 702	EGBERT	84	28	24	82.7'	1910	FR 481, PD 72 - SANK OFF ULLAPOOL 1936
YH 766	GIRL EILEEN	82	39	25	82.1'	1910	FR579, LK579 - SOLD TO HERRING INDUSTRY BOARD 3.51
YH 94	FENNEW	77	29	24	83'	1911	YOUNG ALFRED
YH 786	GIRL ROSE	86	30	25	85'	1911	SUNK BY AUSTRIAN CRUISERS OFF FANO ISLANDS 15.5.17
YH 817	SPERANZA	86	30	33	83.5	1911	SCRAPPED 1951
YH 720	ARCHIMEDES	83	28	35	84'	1911	PD 208 - SCRAPPED 1952

REG NO	NAME	G.R.T.	N.T.	H.P.	LENGTH	YR BUILT	HISTORY
YH 93	HASTFEN	77	26	24	80.7'	1911	MINED OFF LONGSAND 24.9.17
LT 1153	B.T.B	89	31	25	87.5'	1911	SCRAPPED 1946
YH 977	GIRL WINIFRED	90	31	25	86.5'	1912	SCRAPPED 1951
YH 743	EVELYN JOYCE	93	32	25	90.5'	1912	SN 198
YH 866	GIRL MARJORIE	92	32	25	88.5'	1912	SCRAPPED 1938
YH 209	CENWULF	93	32	33	90.7'	1912	LT 49, OLYMPIAN
YH 851	COVENT GARDEN	84	30	32	84.7'	1912	LT 1258, YH 851 - SCRAPPED 1956
YH 363	KITTY GEORGE	87	30	32	85.3'	1913	SCRAPPED 1954
YH 350	PLEASANTS	86	30	24	85'	1913	JOHN & ALFRED LT 340 - SCRAPPED 1946
INS 2	J. & M. MAIN	89	31	26	87'	1913	BF 148 SCRAPPED 1951
LT 56	LORD LOVAT	79	36	28	80'	1913	
YH 396	FRIENDLY GIRLS	90	31	25	87.2'	1913	LK 401, LT 214 - SCRAPPED 1953
SN 83	QUINTIA	90	31	30	87.4'	1914	FR 205, MAYFIELD BCK 130 - SCRAPPED 1950
SN 51	RENE	89	40	26	87.1'	1914	FR 220 - SCRAPPED 1947
YH 479	YOUNG JOHN	100	43	28	88.2'	1914	ENDED AS A BARKING SHIP AT PETERHEAD 1950
YH 228	EADWINE	96	44	26	87'	1914	SCRAPPED 1951
YH 189	OCEAN PIONEER	90	40	27	87.4'	1915	SCRAPPED 1954
YH 217	FRONS OLIVAE II	93	43	39	87.7'	1916	SCRAPPED 1954
YH 34	OSWY	95	44	28	88.1'	1916	RE-ENGINED 1924 LOST OFF TYNE 1937
YH 578	PHYLLIS MARY	94	40	28	88.1'	1917	SCRAPPED 1953
LT 288	RENASCENT	100	43	29	85.6'	1926	LOST ON PASSAGE TO NORWAY 1946

DEVON COUNTY LT 256 - Built of wood by Fellows of Gt. Yarmouth 1910 as Scadaun LT 526.
Was lost after striking a mine in the Thames Estuary during July 1941. Courtesy of Scottish Fisheries Museum.

BEECHING BROS. LTD - GREAT YARMOUTH

REG NO	NAME	G.R.T.	N.T.	H.P.	LENGTH	YR BUILT	HISTORY
YH 550	MAGGIE MAY	40	21	33	79'	1894	LOST HOLME SANDS 1908
YH 238	QUEEN BOROUGH	51	22	15	68'	1895	SCRAPPED 1926
YH 236	MILTON	50	22	15	67.4'	1896	SY 443 - WRECKED 1922
YH 106	PETUNIA	56	34	15	75'	1899	PD 396 - SCRAPPED 21.9.16
YH 105	PISCATOR	53	31	20	72'	1899	BF 462, YH 603, SH188, SALVAGE VESSEL AT TEES - SCRAPPED 1927
YH 460	GLEN ROSA	59	36	20	75'	1900	LOST ENGLISH CHANNEL 1902
YH 617	GIRL DAISY	58	35	20	75'	1900	BF 607 - SCRAPPED 1927
YH 502	LILY	61	39	20	77.2'	1900	K 81
BF 479	BLOSSOM	58	32	18	75.2'	1900	D 233 - SCRAPPED 1936
YH 517	BOY FRED	58	30	20	75'	1900	INS 311 - SCRAPPED 1932
YH 494	MISHE NAHMA	58	35	20	75'	1900	SCRAPPED 1931
YH 309	VIKING	62	32	20	77.2'	1900	INS 318 - SCRAPPED 1930
YH 567	SUNFLOWER	62	32	20	76'	1901	
BF 546	QUEEN ALEXANDRIA	63	36	25	79.5'	1901	LT 319, M74
YH 647	SNOWDROP	63	29	20	78.5'	1901	SCRAPPED 1929
YH 540	KING EDWARD	63	36	35	79.5'	1901	PD 168 - SCRAPPED 1929
BF 541	STAR OF THE SEA	61	36	20	76.7'	1901	SCRAPPED 1931
YH 737	GIRL KATHLEEN	58	31	25	79	1902	CHATTERENO - SOLD TO FRANCE
YH 752	BOY ERNEST	56	31	20	76'	1902	SN 34 - SCRAPPED 1936
YH 754	WENSUM	58	24	28	79'	1902	SCRAPPED 1927
YH 745	WAVENEY	58	24	28	79'	1902	SUNK BY GERMAN DESTROYERS DOVER STRAITS 27.10.16
YH 716	BURE	58	31	28	79'	1902	SY 167 - LOST 1920
YH 703	YARE	58	31	28	79'	1902	BF 99 - SCRAPPED 1923
YH 667	CORONATION	58	33	25	79'	1902	FR 472, BF 66, SY 483 - HERRING CARRIER - SCRAPPED 26.12.1935
BF 1122	MAGNET	60	34	25	79.1'	1902	SCRAPPED 1933
BF 1339	LIVELY HOPE	66	32	28	81'.1'	1903	SUNK MORAY FIRTH 1914
YH 797	BOY GEORGE	70	30	25	80'	1903	PD 146 - SCRAPPED 1934
BF 1121	ISABELLA FERGUSAN	60	32	25	79.1'	1903	BCK 346, WK 135 - SCRAPPED 1946
BF 1351	RUBICON	60	32	28	79.1'	1903	BCK 200 - SCRAPPED 1925
YH 816	ANT	61	33	28	79.1'	1903	BCK 124 - SCRAPPED 1937
YH 847	THURNE	60	33	26	79.1'	1903	BCK 149 - LOST 1931
BF 1362	ATALANTA	60	32	28	79'.1'	1903	BCK 165 - SCRAPPED 1934
BF 1484	EXCELLENT	60	32	28	79.1'	1904	BCK 95 - SCRAPPED 1945
BF 1531	LEBANON	60	22	21	79.1'	1904	BCK 437 - SCRAPPED 1936
BF 1554	OLIVE	60	31	28	79.2'	1904	WRECKED AT GREAT YARMOUTH 1934
BF 1473	ROSE	60	32	28	79.1'	1904	SY 112 - SCRAPPED 1936
YH 717	MARIE	60	32	20	79.1'	1905	BURNT 1921
YH 237	IRENE	66	30	18	78.1'	1906	BCK 196 - SCRAPPED 1934
BF 368	ORION	70	29	31	80'	1906	ESSIE BCK 208, SY 650 - SCRAPPED 2.51
LT 266	PREMIER	71	34	30	81'	1906	SH 152, BCK 145 - SCRAPPED 1945
INS 155	CHAMPION	71	32	31	81.1'	1906	WRECKED AT LOSSIEMOUTH 1931
BF 416	GLENAFTON	72	30	31	80.4'	1906	FR 767, SY 533 - SCRAPPED 1943
EXPERIMENTAL	NIKE	90	32	31	80.4'	1906	(1911) ROYAL BANK A 363, YH 209 - SCRAPPED 1920

BEECHING BROS. LTD - GREAT YARMOUTH (CONTINUED)

REG NO	NAME	G.R.T.	N.T.	H.P.	LENGTH	YR BUILT	HISTORY
BF 160	COMET STAR	60	32	30	80'	1906	LY 44, BCK 336 - SCRAPPED 1933
YH 117	SELINA	78	35	25	85.5'	1907	BCK 429 - SCRAPPED 1936
YH 475	SPHINX	77	32	24	81.1'	1907	SCRAPPED 1939
LT 1075	HOPE	92	33	20	82.4'	1907	ADEQUATE BCK 443 - SCRAPPED 1938
YH 568	TRIUMPH	90	15	24	83.7'	1907	
BF 929	AMITY	82	34	30	82'	1907	BCK 32, FR 7, ADFIN SY833 - SCRAPPED 12.50
INS 321	RADIANT	95	33	24	83.1'	1907	BCK 106 - SCRAPPED 1937
INS 285	ROSE	81	34	30	81.4'	1907	BCK 71 - SCRAPPED 1937
YH 917	FELICIA	90	32	24	83'	1907	LK 1
YH 241	BOY ARTHUR	90	31	24	83.5'	1907	PD 1 - SCRAPPED 1936
YH 973	INTERNOS	90	33	24	83'	1907	BCK 179, INS 32 - WRECKED 1924
YH 767	J. C. P.	73	24	24	80.3'	1908	SUNK OFF GREEN FLASH BUOY 22.3.18
YH 367	GIRL RHODA	86	31	24	83.2'	1908	PD 201, WY 78, ASPIRATION YH 313
YH 875	GLADYS & ROSE	72	24	20	80.1'	1908	BCK 192 SCRAPPED 1949
YH 331	BONO	70	24	19	78.6'	1908	SCRAPPED 1937
YH 747	LERWICK	86	28	20	83.4'	1908	WRECKED OFF GREAT YARMOUTH 27.3.16
YH 78	MORRISON	80	28	28	83'	1908	PD 580 SCRAPPED 1938
YH 390	PIMPERNEL	88	31	26	84.3'	1908	PHYLLIS ROSE - SCRAPPED 1951
YH 627	G. A. W.	73	24	20	80.2'	1909	ROSEHALL FR 71 - SCRAPPED 1936
YH 187	CALLISTOGA	72	25	25	80.4'	1910	LY 852 - SCRAPPED 1920
WY 59	E. J. M.	72	25	27.5	80.4'	1910	PD 97, BF 350, BCK 156 - TO NORWAY 13.3.47
YH 527	YOUNG HENRY	91	32	26	86'	1910	PD 124, INS 220, CHERISH BF 135, B 237 HERRING CARRIER - SCRAPPED 1937
YH 770	R. MACKAY	73	25	24	81'	1910	BECAME HERRING CARRIER - GK 29
YH 710	PARADOX II	73	24	24	80.8'	1910	SCRAPPED 1939
YH 544	AMIABLE	72	24	19	81'	1910	BK 206 - SCRAPPED 1946
INS 160	SKIBO CASTLE	81	28	31	82.4'	1910	SANK OFF GREAT YARMOUTH 1920
LT 1128	GALILEAN	72	24	30	80.6'	1911	FR 68 - SCRAPPED 28.12.36
YH 740	E. E. S.	91	31	26	87.2'	1911	H 473
YH 746	J. S.	90	31	26	86.7'	1911	GY 34
YH 970	OCEAN FOAM	90	32	26	86.2'	1911	SUNK OFF PENZANCE 7.10.18
YH 974	OCEAN WARRIOR	90	32	26	86.2'	1911	SCRAPPED 1938
YH 714	HERRING QUEEN	72	24	24	80.3'	1911	GY 27
YH 837	SANTORA	90	31	26	86.6'	1911	GY 440
YH 637	C. & E. W.	81	29	24	80.8'	1911	LOST OFF HUMBER 1922
YH 575	OCEAN SOUVENIR	99	34	28	89.7'	1912	JEANNIE HOWIE FR 122 - SCRAPPED 1948
YH 470	OCEAN REAPER	101	35	28	89.6'	1912	FR 366 - SCRAPPED 1945
YH 792	OCEAN PLOUGH	99	34	29	88.7'	1912	MINED OFF LOWESTOFT 27.8.16
YH 692	THOMAS BEECHING	99	35	28	88'	1912	LT 52, RISSA, BCK 103 - SUNK NORTH SEA 1933
WY 169	ALABURN	85	28	20	84.3'	1912	
WY 165	OBURN	93	32	26	84.1'	1912	GIRL PAMELA YH 17, LT 32 - LOST AT DUNKIRK 29.5.40
YH 239	OCEAN FAVOURITE	99	34	35	88.6'	1913	SCRAPPED 1949
YH 325	OCEAN PILOT	95	32	26	86.6'	1913	SOLD TO NORWAY 1946
YH 305	OCEAN HARVEST	95	32	35	86.6'	1913	WRECKED AT PETERHEAD 1939
WY 186	IBURN	90	30	26	86.7'	1913	RADIANT ROSE YH 11 - SCRAPPED 1937
YH 234	THE THRONE	99	33	24	88.4'	1913	GY 431

REG NO	NAME	G.R.T.	N.T.	H.P.	LENGTH	YR BUILT	HISTORY
YH 368	BOY CHARLES	86	29	25	85.7'	1913	PROVIDE PD 186 BURNT AS PART OF SILVER JUBILEE
							CELEBRATIONS 1935
YH 402	ARTHUR H. JOHNSTON	99	35	35	88.1'	1913	GY 425
YH 172	OCEAN EMPEROR	99	44	26	85.8'	1914	SCRAPPED 1948
WY 18	ESKBURN	90	41	26	87.4'	1914	SUNK OFF DOVER 30.11.16
YH 519	SELINA SALMON	96	40	44	88.5'	1917	REFLECTOR, GIRL VIOLET - SCRAPPED 1948

ALABURN WY 169 - Built of wood by Beeching & Co. Gt. Yarmouth during 1912. Became GY 456.
Courtesy of Scottish Fisheries Museum.

REG NO	NAME	G.R.T.	N.T.	H.P.	LENGTH	YR BUILT	HISTORY
YH 854	FAME	39	22	8	62'	1892	GY 352 SAILING VESSEL CONVERTED TO STEAM
LT 382	SPERANZA		40			1893	
A 203	GLENGAIRN	64	41	12	77'	1900	BURNT OFF ORKNEY 23.3.1901
A 207	GLENBARRY	64	41	12	77'	1900	LOST AT ABERDEEN BEACH 5.10.20
A 210	GLENLIVET	64	41	15	77'	1900	BCK 426 - SANK OFF GT. YARMOUTH 1926
A 346	GLENESK	67	38	20	79.3'	1901	BCK 425, SY 556 - SCRAPPED 1936
A 386	GLENSHEE	67	38	20	79.3'	1901	LOST AT ABERDEEN BEACH 5.10.20
A 396	GLENGARRY	67	38	17	79.3'	1901	FR 798 - SCRAPPED 1924
LT 257	PROCEED	64	39	15	79.3'	1901	TO BELGIUM 1920
LT 271	LEADER	64	36	20	79.4'	1901	BF 838 - SCRAPPED 31.12.25
LT 253	DIAMOND	64	40	15	79.4'	1901	BCK 73, BF 255 - SCRAPPED 1924
LT 368	PIONEER	63	37	38	64'	1901	CONVERTED TO MOTOR VESSEL SOLD TO LAS
							PALMAS 1913
BF 649	PROSPERITY	64	39	29	79.3'	1901	CEASED FISHING 1921

REG NO	NAME	G.R.T.	N.T.	H.P.	LENGTH	YR BUILT	HISTORY
LT 27	YOUNG CHARLES II	57	35	18	76'	1902	HERRING FINDER
LT 532	BRITANNIA	63	38	28	79.3'	1902	INS 47 - SCRAPPED 1923
LT 462	PRINCE ALBERT	64	39	20	79.3'	1902	INS 396, SY 157 - SCRAPPED 1935
LT 907	ONWARD	63	32	20	79.3'	1902	PD.40, INS351 -SUNK IN MORAY FIRTH 12.30
LT 937	MAJESTIC	63	31	20	78.7'	1902	INS 151, PD 141, STORNOWAY CASTLE SY 259, PD 233, H 83
YH 754	KERNOOZER	63	33	18	79.2'	1902	SOLD TO AIR MINISTRY - LOST 1943
YH 736	GOOD HOPE	63	38	18	79.3'	1902	
LT 259	RESULT	63	35	28	80.7'	1903	BCK 139, SY 25 - LOST 1920
H 723	SHETLAND	77	45	35	83.1'	1903	
LT 967	GRACE LILLIAN	69	33	32	83'	1903	LOST 1919 OFF HARTLEPOOL
LT 968	BOY HECTOR	81	34	29	82.4'	1903	SH 111 - SCRAPPED 1926
LT 985	INTEGRITY	67	41	26	80'	1903	YH 985, PD 51 - SCRAPPED 1935
LT 996	WHITE HEATHER	64	38	20	80'	1903	FR 387 - SCRAPPED 1926
YH 871	THE KING	58	33	28	81'	1903	BF 97 - LOST 1921
LT 974	HOPEFUL	67	41	20	80'	1903	SY 440 - SCRAPPED 1927
PD 474	CHARITY	65	38	15	81.3'	1903	SY 399 - SCRAPPED 1934
LT 1011	MAGNIFICIENT	64	44	15	79.5'	1904	KINLOCH FR 3 - SUNK FIRTH OF FORTH 1921
YH 879	THE QUEEN	77	28	28	81'	1904	SCRAPPED 1932
LT 300	FORWARD	74	42	25	82.3'	1905	BF 603, SH 281 - CEASED FISHING 1923
LT 360	RECORD	67	41	25	80'	1905	H 777 - SOLD TO FRANCE 1930
LT 338	CONDOR	63	29	25	79.3'	1905	WY 233 - SCRAPPED 1922
LT 564	GOOD HOPE	63	35	20	81'	1905	YH 756, BF 516 - HERRING CARRIER CLYDE ESTUARY - SCRAPPED 1925

ONWARD LT 907 - Built of wood by Henry Reynolds, Oulten Broad, Lowestoft during 1902. Seen here as PD 40 at East Anglia ca 1920s. Became INS 351. Sank Moray Firth 1930. Courtesy of Scottish Fisheries Museum.

WELCOME HOME LT 402 - Built of wood by Henry Reynolds, Oulten Broad, Lowestoft 1906. Sold to Spain 1925. Courtesy of Port of Lowestoft Research Society.

ANNEX IV   HENRY REYNOLDS - OULTON BROAD, LOWESTOFT (CONTINUED)   WOODEN

REG NO	NAME	G.R.T.	N.T.	H.P.	LENGTH	YR BUILT	HISTORY
LT 643	WELLAND	87	38	20	82'	1906	INS 1 - SCRAPPED 1929
LT 400	WITHAM	76	40	20	81.6'	1906	SH 123, BF 197 - SCRAPPED 1927
LT 402	WELCOME HOME	77	40	28	82.7'	1906	SOLD TO SPAIN 1925
LT 487	GLADYS	69	38	30	82.7'	1906	STAR OF MORAY, INS 368 - LOST 1931
LT 232	PROSIT	77	40	24	82.7'	1906	SOLD TO FRANCE 1929
LT 408	ENTERPRISE	84	44	25	83.4'	1906	MINED OFF BRINDISI 8.3.16
LT 421	HALCYON	72	35	24	82.1'	1906	LOST OFF OWERS LT. 1909
BF 392	TITANIA	92	39	25	86'	1906	BCK 195, GW2 (HERRING CARRIER) - SCRAPPED 1947
BF 366	ENTERPRISE	78	32	25	82.7'	1906	LOST 1922
BF 387	AURORA	74	33	23	84.6'	1906	BCK 379, SY 43 - LOST 1931
LT 510	PROSPERITY	72	33	20	81.3'	1906	BK 15, SH 194 - REG. CANC. 1920
LT 496	AULD LANG SYNE	75	38	24	82.7'	1906	WY 230 - SCRAPPED 1924
LT 461	PEARL	72	37	20	82'	1906	KITTIWAKE
BF 871	DOVE	81	34	23	83.8'	1907	SCRAPPED 1934
LT 1063	WELCOME STAR	81	34	28	83.5'	1907	FR 522, BF 326 - SCRAPPED 1934
FR 195	BENEFICIENT	80	34	23	83.5'	1907	SUNK BY GUNFIRE IN ADRIATIC 1.6.16
LT 1039	WEAR	82	34	20	83.6'	1907	SPERAVI
LT 1041	ROULETTE	81	34	24	85'	1907	SOLD TO SPAIN 1925
INS 422	ANNIE SMITH	84	35	24	84'	1907	SANK OFF LUNDY ISLAND 9.4.18
INS 433	EMBLEM	85	35	25	85'	1907	CITY OF PERTH, LT 755 - SANK TYNE 1944
LT 1037	EVERARD	82	34	20	83.6'	1907	INS 30 - SUNK OFF TUSKAR ROCKS 15.1.16
INS 461	COUNTY OF NAIRN	81	34	27	83.8'	1907	ACTIVELY BF 164 - SCRAPPED 1935
LT 1044	BLUEBELL	88	37	26	84.4'	1907	TO SPAIN 1925
LT 1071	IVY	83	35	23	84'	1907	SURE FIND
LT 1061	HEARTY	83	35	24	84.6'	1907	
LT 1034	SILVER KING	81	34	28	84'	1907	SCRAPPED 1939
LT 1042	RODNEY	81	34	24	84.3'	1907	BK 33 - LOST 1923

REG NO	NAME	G.R.T.	N.T.	H.P.	LENGTH	YR BUILT	HISTORY
LT 1051	LABURNUM	82	34	23	83.6'	1907	SOLD TO SPAIN 1925
LT 1081	FEARLESS	81	34	23	84'	1907	SCRAPPED 1936
LT 1076	OSPREY	82	34	24	83.4'	1907	SCRAPPED 1939
LT 1035	THANKFUL	55	28	15	73'	1907	WY 241 - SCRAPPED 1925
BCK 5	SPEY BAY	86	36	25	87'	1907	BF 601 - SCRAPPED 1928
BCK 2	EASTER MORN	81	34	23	83.8'	1907	SCRAPPED 1937
BF 859	JEANNIE SIMPSON	90	38	25	86.7'	1907	SCRAPPED 1935
BF 669	VICTORY	82	34	32	84.7'	1907	LOST 1923
BF 595	WATER LILY	82	35	25	85	1907	SUNK OFF ST. ALBANS HEAD 23.7.15.
LT 101	BRESSAY	81	36	30	84.6'	1908	LK 257
LT 11	WELCOME BOYS	92	41	32	88.4'	1908	LOST OFF TYNE 1937
BCK 281	CLUNY	83	36	20	84.1'	1908	BF 71, M 86 - WRECKED OFF IRELAND 1927
BCK 29	FREUCHNY	84	37	20	84.1'	1908	MINED OFF BRINDISI 8.1.16
BCK 23	IVY GREEN	76	32	25	84.5'	1908	SCRAPPED 1929
BCK 34	LILY OAK	84	35	25	85.1'	1908	LOST 1944
BCK 14	ROSIES	84	35	25	85.2'	1908	BOMBED IN ADRIATIC 26.8.16
LT 34	HOLMSGARTH	85	38	20	84.7'	1908	SCRAPPED 1938
YH 349	EMULATE	77	35	19	82'	1908	SCRAPPED 1939
LT 46	ESLEA	83	36	31	86.5'	1908	M 100 - SCRAPPED 1933
LT 127	ANCHOR STAR	82	35	30	85'	1908	SCRAPPED 1931
LT 29	BOY CHY	78	33	20	84.6'	1908	LOST NORTH SEA 1931
INS 610	CAWDOR CASTLE II	84	35	31	84.2'	1908	SCRAPPED 1937
INS 603	TREASURE TROVE	83	35	31	83.5'	1908	SCRAPPED 1937
LT 413	BOY EDWARD	80	34	30	85.5'	1909	LOST OFF SMITH'S KNOLL 1930
LT 313	EXPLORATOR	79	33	25	84.6'	1909	ML 12, LT 515, R 15 - SCRAPPED 1940
LT 328	EAST ANGLIA	83	35	32	84.6'	1909	SUNK BY SUBMARINE OFF SULISKER 24.7.15
YH 292	LLOYD GEORGE	79	34	32	84.8'	1910	PD 94, FR 65, PROTECT US - SCRAPPED 1936

REG NO	NAME	G.R.T.	N.T.	H.P.	LENGTH	YR BUILT	HISTORY
YH 272	ELLEN & IRENE	88	43	20	84.5'	1914	SY 29, BF 162 - SCRAPPED 1950
LT 334	FISHER BOY	91	44	20	86'	1914	SCRAPPED 1946
LT 375	WELCOME FRIEND	94	48	20	87.6'	1914	SCRAPPED 1939
LT 185	HAPPY DAYS	101	49	20	88.7'	1914	DORIENTA - SCRAPPED 1948
YH 174	W. P. G.	94	44	20	85.7'	1915	SWEET BUD - SCRAPPED 1939
LT 492	OUR ALLIES	91	44	25	86.5'	1915	BOY PAT GK 166 - WRECKED 1948

REG NO	NAME	G.R.T.	N.T.	H.P.	LENGTH	YR BUILT	HISTORY
LT 270	TEST	55	29	12	74'	1899	GY 204 - SOLD TO NORWAY 1924
LT 80	ADVENTURE	55	22	15	69'	1899	SUNK OFF WOLF ROCK 1917
A 200	GLENLYON	62	42	12	75'	1900	TO A COASTER., A 711 - SOLD TO DUBLIN 1930
A 195	GLENMORE	62	42	18	75'	1900	TO A COASTER 1920 - WRECKED 1922
A 190	GLENMUICK	62	42	12	75'	1900	PD 434 - SCRAPPED 1923

REG NO	NAME	G.R.T.	N.T.	H.P.	LENGTH	YR BUILT	HISTORY
A 205	GLENLOSSIE	62	42	12	75'	1900	SUNK OFF DOWNINGS BAY 15.5.1906
LT 161	SUCCESS	59	36	18	68.7'	1900	SN 71, D 10, LT 132
LT 207	PURSUIT	56	26	18	75.2'	1901	M 95
LT 274	DIADEM	55	34	18	76.1'	1901	
LT 269	DAILY BREAD	56	29	18	77.5'	1901	SOLD AS HOUSEBOAT 1920
LT 225	RESOLVE	56	35	18	76.1'	1901	PD 24 - SCRAPPED 1926
LT 261	LORD KITCHENER	56	34	16	77.5'	1901	SH 175, YH 490, BCK 269 - SCRAPPED 1927
LT 264	GENERAL FRENCH	57	33	18	77.5'	1901	PD 23 - SCRAPPED 1925
LT 306	LORD DUNDONALD	57	35	25	77.5'	1901	HAMNAVOE LK 400, SUNK BY U.BOAT OFF SUMBURGH HEAD 2.7.17
YH 664	BOADICEA	59	36	18	79'	1902	LOST 1917
LT 357	RESEARCH	60	36	18	79'	1902	SN 215, YH 421, PD 98 - SUNK BY GERMAN SUBMARINE OFF OUTER SKERRIES 23.6.15
LT 531	GIRL IVY	58	30	18	79'	1902	PD 577, SY 195 - SCRAPPED 1936
LT 929	AGNES WESTON	58	24	18	79'	1902	PD 105 - SCRAPPED 1926
LT 143	PROTECTOR	58	36	18	79'	1902	SY 388 - LOST 1920
LT 377	ASPIRE	66	39	20	79'	1903	WY 1
LT 961	GRATEFUL	62	39	20	79'	1903	PD 88 - SCRAPPED 1932
LT 587	RESCUE	63	36	25	79.5'	1903	INS 157, LT 297 - SCRAPPED 1926
LT 990	COMRADES	63	35	25	79.4'	1903	MINED OFF CAP D'ANTIFER 18.10.17
LT 746	HILDA	63	31	30	79.4'	1903	PD 106, BF 639, SY 14 - SANK NORTH MINCH 1922
LT 367	LILY MAUD	61	37	25	80'	1904	PD 86, BCK 366 - SCRAPPED 1934
LT 627	EMULATOR	66	40	25	80'	1904	SH 164 - MINED NORTH SEA 4.1919
LT 495	THISTLE	70	45	25	83.5'	1904	MINED OFF LOWESTOFT 8.5.41
LT 527	BOY WILLIE	66	40	20	80'	1904	PD 87 - SCRAPPED 1933
LT 617	DAWN OF DAY	65	39	25	81'	1904	
LT 500	GOLDEN RULE	65	39	25	81'	1905	WY 39
LT 505	AU REVOIR	66	37	20	81.7'	1906	BF 217 - SOLD TO ITALY 1931
LT 520	ACTIVE	65	39	35	81'	1906	
LT 441	BOY GEORGE	83	47	25	83.1'	1906	SCRAPPED 1931
LT 463	REWARD	78	42	25	83'	1906	LOST OFF GT. YARMOUTH 1929
LT 550	AU RETOUR	73	37	20	79.8'	1906	SH 120
LT 596	CONSOLATION	70	40	35	81.7'	1906	BK 316 - LOST 1924
LT 1017	BRITON	79	33	30	81.8'	1906	BUILT IN 40 WORKING DAYS - SCRAPPED 1936
LT 1030	ALERT	83	31	35	83.7'	1907	PD 131
LT 1032	PEACE	83	33	35	83'	1907	PD 130 - SCRAPPED 1934
LT 1043	EFFORT	82	34	35	83.4'	1907	SCRAPPED 1936
LT 1049	SHIELD	96	41	25	86'	1907	BK 317 - SCRAPPED 1927
LT 1053	ALFRED	96	41	25	85.5'	1907	SCRAPPED 1938
LT 1060	PILOT STAR	92	39	28	83'	1907	TO PORTUGAL 1920
LT 1052	HOLLY	93	39	23	84.2'	1907	FR 528 - SUNK OFF LAND'S END 11.5.18
LT 1065	BREADWINNER	93	39	25	84.2'	1907	BF 9 - SANK OFF BUCKIE 1927
LT 1072	ENDURANCE	94	40	25	86'	1907	FR 69 - SCRAPPED 1936
LT 1079	PLAYMATES	93	31	31	83.8'	1907	TO PORTUGAL 1920
LT 1083	GLADYS MAY	88	37	25	84.4'	1907	WY 277, WHITELINK BAY, FR 249 - SCRAPPED 1936
LT 1088	Q. E. F.	89	39	31	84.5'	1908	FR 532 - TO FRANCE 1920

ANNEX IV   S. RICHARDS & COMPANY THEN RICHARDS IRON WORKS - LOWESTOFT (CONTINUED) WOODEN

REG NO	NAME	G.R.T.	N.T.	H.P.	LENGTH	YR BUILT	HISTORY
LT 42	PERSISTIVE	82	37	30	84.1'	1908	MINED OFF DOVER 9.2.16
LT 71	COLONIAL	84	37	30	85'	1908	EASTERN DAWN - SCRAPPED 1951
LT 72	CAPE COLONY	82	38	30	84.7'	1908	FR 525 - MINED OFF HARWICH 8.1.17
LT 21	COURONNE	83	38	30	84.5'	1908	WRECKED 1925
LT 76	CAPE TOWN	83	39	30	85'	1908	SUNK ON ADMIRALTY SERVICE 1922
LT 125	HOMELAND	83	39	30	84.3'	1908	SCRAPPED 1928
LT 140	JOHN LINCOLN	83	36	30	84.2'	1908	MAY TAIT FR 108 - SCRAPPED 1936
LT 196	INDOMITABLE	83	37	31	84.2'	1908	SCRAPPED 1936
LT 210	KESSINGLAND	78	37	20	81.3'	1908	SH 212, REFLECT, LT 294
LT 318	BARNARDO	77	33	25	80.5'	1909	SMILECINA
LT 307	RENOVATE	81	36	30	84.2'	1909	
LT 339	TERRITORIAL	80	36	28	82.2'	1909	SCRAPPED 1936
LT 340	AJAX	81	37	28	82.2'	1909	SUNK BY GERMAN DESTROYERS DOVER STRAITS 27.10.16
LT 353	PILOT ME	83	39	30	84.4'	1909	SH 245
LT 358	CHILDREN'S HOPE	83	39	30	84.3'	1909	
LT 364	AU FAIT	83	39	30	84.3'	1909	SUNK BY GERMAN DESTROYERS OFF ZEEBRUGE 25.4.16
LT 448	PLEASANCE	80	36	25	83.4'	1909	SH 168
LT 465	QUICK SET	78	34	30	81.3'	1909	YH 44, LT 285
LT 473	MYRTLE SPRIG	77	38	20	79.7'	1910	GY 259 - SCRAPPED 1925
LT 553	PLACEO	83	36	30	83.5'	1910	FISHERMAN GY 169
LT 503	DATUM	90	44	30	85.7'	1910	SUNK BY GERMAN DESTROYERS DOVER STRAITS 27.10.16
LT 585	MIDAS	89	38	35	84.5'	1910	SUNK OFF DUNGENESS 3.2.41
LT 519	AMBITIOUS	90	45	30	85.7'	1910	SCRAPPED 1937
LT 685	VERACITY	96	42	35	89'	1910	SUNK BY GERMAN DESTROYERS DOVER STRAITS 15.2.18
LT 608	NINE SISTERS	92	45	30	85.5'	1910	SCRAPPED 1947
LT 706	GOLDEN GIFT	90	42	30	84.5'	1910	LOST AT OBAN 6.4.43
LT 719	WILL & MAGGIE	90	42	30	84.5'	1910	MINED OFF LOWESTOFT 3.11.14
LT 751	ALL'S WELL	87	42	28	85.7'	1910	SCRAPPED 1940
LT 768	PEACEMAKER	89	43	31	84.3'	1911	SCRAPPED 1947
LT 859	ORIENT III	93	44	30	86'	1911	
LT 1114	PAXTON	92	43	30	86'	1911	LOST AT DUNKIRK 26.5.40
LT 1123	CONTRIVE	95	45	30	88.6'	1911	SCRAPPED 1946
LT 1144	FAMILIAR FRIEND	92	43	30	87.3'	1911	SCRAPPED 1939
LT 1113	MANZANITA	93	45	30	87.3'	1911	WRECKED IN ADRIATIC 6.9.16
LT 1149	PAISABLE	90	42	30	86.2'	1911	SHOREBREEZE LT 1149 - LOST OFF CORNWALL 1938
LT 1151	BOUNTIFUL	91	43	30	85.8'	1911	LOST 1941
LT 1160	FORERUNNER	92	42	30	88.7'	1911	SUNK THAMES ESTUARY 14.10.41
LT 1170	GLEANER OF THE SEA	91	41	30	88.8'	1912	SUNK BY GERMAN DESTROYERS DOVER STRAITS 27.10.16
LT 1174	YOUNG LINNET	93	43	30	87.3'	1912	SUNK BY AUSTRIAN CRUISERS OFF FANO ISLANDS 15.5.17
YH 757	VIOLET AND ROSE	92	43	30	87.3'	1912	SCRAPPED 1954

ANNEX IV   S. RICHARDS & COMPANY THEN RICHARDS IRON WORKS - LOWESTOFT (CONTINUED) WOODEN

REG NO	NAME	G.R.T.	N.T.	H.P.	LENGTH	YR BUILT	HISTORY
LT 1185	MABEL VERA	98	47	30	89'	1912	LEEBREEZE LT 1185, PD 329
YH 264	OCEAN SPRAY	82	38	25	84.3'	1912	SCRAPPED 1957
LT 1184	ACCUMULATOR	85	38	30	86.4'	1912	LT 655, BF 27 - SCRAPPED 1949
LT 78	RECEPTIVE	93	39	25	85'	1913	YH 75 - MINED THAMES ESTUARY 3.7.41
LT 2	BOB READ	95	42	30	87.1'	1913	
LT 9	EXPECTANT	93	45	30	88.3'	1913	SCRAPPED 1939
LT 172	TRUE REWARD	93	40	30	85.8'	1913	SOLD TO NORWAY 1946
LT 135	SILVERY HARVEST	86	38	25	84.3'	1913	SUNK OF BERRY HEAD 16.5.18
YH 252	JACK GEORGE	98	47	25	89.5'	1913	SCRAPPED 1948
LT 87	ACHIEVABLE	89	42	25	85.5'	1913	
LT 221	JOHN MITCHELL	89	42	32	85.5'	1913	SUNK OFF ST. ALBAN'S HEAD 14.11.17
LT 226	SAM RICHARDS	88	40	25	86'	1913	MUTUAL ALLIANCE - SOLD TO NORWAY 1939
YH 766	KIAMI	93	44	30	87.5'	1914	LT 204, GIRL ELLEN YH 359 - REGISTRY CANCELLED 1947
LT 1011	GOLDEN HARVEST	87	41	25	86.1'	1914	SCRAPPED 1947
LT 757	REGAIN	87	41	25	86.5'	1914	LOST 1939
LT 89	PRESENT FRIENDS	89	41	30	86.5'	1914	SCRAPPED 1949
LT 19	JESSMAR	86	40	25	85.4'	1914	
LT 28	SAILOR KING	89	41	25	85'	1914	SCRAPPED 1951
LT 476	THE BOYS	92	43	30	86.3'	1914	SANK IN THE DOWNS 14.1.41
LT 457	YOUNG CROW	88	40	30	85.8'	1915	BURNT AT GARELOCH 1942
LT 447	EAST BRITON	88	42	30	86.5'	1915	SCRAPPED 1954
YH 627	G.A.W.	89	48	42	88.3'	1915	GEORGE ALBERT - SCRAPPED 1947
YH 762	PISCATORIAL II	93	43	30	86.7'	1916	DISAPPEARED OFF NEWHAVEN 29.12.17
LT 681	SINCERE	92	43	30	86.7'	1916	BF152, LT 143 - SCRAPPED 1952
YH 875	ROSE AND GLADYS	93	46	30	88.4'	1917	SCRAPPED 1939
YH 711	HARRY AND LEONARD	92	44	30	86	1917	SCRAPPED 1939
YH 657	HEATHER	94	44	30	87'	1917	LT 767 - SCRAPPED 1951
YH 530	QUEEN OF THE FLEET	96	45	40	88.3'	1917	SCRAPPED 1947

EAST BRITON LT 447 - Built of wood by S. Richard & Co. Lowestoft 1915. Scrapped 1954. Shown in Wartime Rig, ca 1917. Note small gun on foredeck. Courtesy of Scottish Fisheries Museum.

GIRL IVY LT 531 - Built of wood in 1902 by S. Richard & Co. Lowestoft. Seen at Lowestoft ca 1902.
Later became PD 577 then SY 195. Scrapped 1936. Courtesy of Port of Lowestoft Society.

ANNEX IV   W. & G. GARDINER OF CULLEN   WOODEN

REG NO	NAME	G.R.T.	N.T.	H.P.	LENGTH	YR BUILT	HISTORY
BF 448	VERDANT	87	29	27	86'	1906	SOLD TO SPAIN 1933
BF 680	SEAFIELD	86	28	27	86'	1907	SANK MORAY FIRTH 1920
BF 908	HERALD	86	28	27	86.2'	1907	BCK 329 - SCRAPPED 1937
BF 167	SUNNYSIDE	80	33	28	86.2'	1910	SCRAPPED 1936
BF 376	FLOWER O' MAY	80	33	28	85.7'	1911	SCRAPPED 1936
BF 80	HAWTHORN BUD	81	34	38	87.1'	1914	SCRAPPED 1935
BK 335	HARVESTER	95	40	31	89'	1914	SCRAPPED 1936

ANNEX IV   CHAMBERS & COLBY - LOWESTOFT   WOODEN

REG NO	NAME	G.R.T.	N.T.	H.P.	LENGTH	YR BUILT	HISTORY
LT 490	CHAMPION	37	24	5	59.4'	1892	SMACK CONVERTED TO STEAM
LT 718	CONSOLATION	55	39	15	72'	1897	1ST STEAM DRIFTER TO BE BUILT AT LOWESTOFT SOLD TO LERWICK - BURNT 1908
YH 292	CONTENT	47	32	40	71'	1897	WK 54, 1ST STEAM DRIFTER AT WICK, YH 780, LK 439 - CONVERTED TO MOTOR
YH 326	CONSTANCE	52	35	40	68.7'	1898	BK 310, YH 682 - SCRAPPED 1927
WK 771	PEEP O' DAY	54	28	14	76.4'	1898	YH 37, LT 187 - LOST OFF TYNE BY SUBMARINE 5.7.16
YH 77	ROCKET	53	23	15	76.4'	1899	SCRAPPED 1926
YH 434	LOTTIE	54	32	15	73.4'	1899	SCRAPPED 1927
YH 376	FANCY	53	27	15	76.4'	1899	BK 304, YH 376, LT 1228 - WRECKED WEST COAST 1926
INS 45	SUCCESS	61	25	15	68.7'	1899	BF 120 - SCRAPPED 1924
H 486	YARMOUTH	57	36	15	76.4'	1899	BF 613, SH 233, LT 104 - SCRAPPED 1923
H 610	NEWLYN	60	42	15	77.6'	1900	WK 102, PD 257 - TO BARROW AS PILOT CUTTER
YH 547	GRACE DARLING		37	15		1900	LOST IN COLLISION 1911
YH 573	HOMOCEA	58	39	15	76.1'	1900	LT 112
H 492	LOWESTOFT	54	30	15	76.6'	1900	YH 416 - SCRAPPED 1923
H 502	SCARBOROUGH	54	31	15	76.4'	1900	FR 276, LT 240 - SANK OFF EAST ANGLIA 1918

CHAMBERS & COLBY - LOWESTOFT (CONTINUED)

REG NO	NAME	G.R.T.	N.T.	H.P.	LENGTH	YR BUILT	HISTORY
SN 126	DAISY	57	37	15	71.5'	1900	YH 414 - SCRAPPED 1931
LT 164	BOUNTEOUS SEA	58	38	15	75'	1900	SCRAPPED 1927
WK 157	VIOLET	55		15	76.7	1900	WRECKED AT KEISS 1903
LT 387	OCEAN'S GIFT	58	38	15	75'	1900	INS 294 - SCRAPPED 1933
LT 289	JOHN AND SARAH	60	36	20	79.5'	1901	LOST OFF GORLESTON 1911
LT 241	FRIENDSHIP	56	38	15	75'	1901	WRECKED FRENCH COAST 1913
LT 139	NARCISSUS	58	39	15	76.1'	1901	SUNK BY SUBMARINE OFF TYNE 6.8.17
LT 250	WENSUM	56	38	15	73'	1901	SCRAPPED 1926
LT 629	REQUEST	56	34	15	75'	1901	SCRAPPED 1936
LT 222	WAVENEY	56	38	15	75'	1901	SUNK BY GERMAN DESTROYERS, DOVER STRAITS 27.10.16
LT 286	CHANTICLEER	56	34	15	79.5'	1901	M 206
YH 619	BERRY HEAD	58	39	15	76.1'	1901	LT 966, LT 659, YH 285 - SCRAPPED 1925
LT 372	EARLY MORN	58	39	15	76.1'	1901	BK 52 - SCRAPPED 1932
LT 396	UNITED	70	41	20	79.3'	1901	SH 148 - SCRAPPED 1923
LT 251	GAMESTER	54	39	15	76.1'	1901	YH 251 - LOST 1918
YH 314	LAVEROCK	54	39	15	76.1'	1901	LT 1182 - SCRAPPED 1934
LT 202	BOY ARCHIE	58	39	15	76.1'	1901	WK 10 - SCRAPPED 1926
YH 654	SUPERB	61		18		1901	SCRAPPED 1927
INS 493	VENTURE	58	39	15	76.1'	1902	WRECKED LOSSIEMOUTH HARBOUR 1909
H 548	MONTROSE	63	38	20	79.3'	1902	LOST OFF GT. YARMOUTH 1911
LT 179	SURPRISE	58	39	25	79.3'	1902	FR 383, SY 397, WK 326 - SCRAPPED 1934
LT 50	CARNATION	58	39	15	76.1'	1902	SY 399, LT 155, HERRING CARRIER CLYDE, GW 16
LT 60	STAR OF HOPE	56	38	15	74.4'	1902	WK 76 - SCRAPPED 1931
LT 509	RECOMPENCE	58	39	15	76.1'	1902	SCRAPPED 1926
LT 422	RELIANCE	60	41	15	75.5'	1902	D 328 - DISAPPEARED NORTH SEA - 10.17
SN 342	SARA	60	39	20	79.3'	1902	PD 100 - SCRAPPED 1932
LT 54	PROSPECT	58	39	15	76.1'	1902	SOLD TO CORK 1933
YH 252	BOY JACK	58	39	15	76'	1902	BK 302, LT 189, INS 299 - SUNK DECEMBER 1929
LT 231	ENERGY	66	39	28	79.3'	1902	WY 3, YH 636 - SCRAPPED 1925
YH 707	FORTUNATUS	58	39	15	76.1'	1902	SCRAPPED 1924
LT 508	LADY AUDREY	69	39	20	79.3'	1902	SOLD TO NORWAY 1925
YH 793	FOXGLOVE	58	39	15	74'	1903	ROVA HEAD, LK 385
LT 175	NIL DESPERANDUM	91	62	25	88.6'	1903	SCRAPPED 1936
LT 964	KATHLEEN	63	31	25	82.2'	1903	SUNK IN COLLISION 1907
LT 986	GUIDING STAR	60	41	17	80.5'	1903	LT 44, GY 685 - SCRAPPED 1923
YH 796	IVY	64	30	25	80.5'	1903	SCRAPPED 1924
YH 177	CICERO	56	39	15	74'	1903	SOLD TO FRANCE 1920
YH 799	HEATHER	58	39	15	74'	1903	SUNK BY SUBMARINE OFF BISHOP'S ROCK 24.4.17
YH 576	PETUNIA	58	39	15	74'	1903	SUNK BY SUBMARINE OFF TYNE - 6.7.16
BF 1142	ALEXANDRA MAUD	58	21	15	74'	1903	FR 435 SOLD TO SOUTHAMPTON 1923
YH 253	GERTRUDE	58	39	15	74'	1903	LOST OF HAISBOROUGH 1910
YH 789	SWEET BRIAR	58	39	15	74'	1903	BF 810, BCK 52 CEASED FISHING 1922
YH 820	TRIXIE	54	39	15	74.2'	1903	LT 220, YH 233
LT 693	EMILY	63	31	25	82'	1903	
THIS PARTNERSHIP ENDED 1903							

GUIDING STAR LT 986 - Built of wood by Chambers & Colby 1903. Became LT 44 then GY 685. Scrapped 1923. Courtesy of Scottish Fisheries Museum.

REG NO	NAME	G.R.T.	N.T.	H.P.	LENGTH	YR BUILT	HISTORY
ANNEX IV	**J. CHAMBERS & COMPANY LIMITED - LOWESTOFT**						**WOODEN**
YH 848	IMPERIAL	74	40	25	83.5'	1904	LOST NORTH SEA 1907
YH 377	DIADEM	75	44	25	83.5'	1904	SCRAPPED 1929
LT 693	EXCELSIOR	72	42	15	74'	1904	SOLD AS HOUSEBOAT 1920
YH 279	SUNBEAM	75	38	20	83.5'	1904	WK 104 - SUNK OFF INCHKEITH 16.4.18
LT 471	PRIDE	62	42	15	74.4'	1904	LOST 1924
BF 1492	STAR OF HOPE	60	36	15	75'	1904	PD 251 - SCRAPPED 1925
LT 741	ROSE	64	42	15	74'	1904	LOST 1929
YH 207	SUNSHINE	60	41	15	75'	1905	WK 755, SH 234, R 172
LT 672	SNOWDROP	62	42	15	74'	1905	SCRAPPED 1925
LT 570	ADVANCE	62	42	15	74'	1905	SCRAPPED 1936
LT 311	NEVER CAN TELL	62	42	15	74'	1905	GY 571, LT 871 - LOST OFF HUMBER 1921
LT 389	BEATRICE	62	42	15	74'	1905	INS 153 - SCRAPPED 1931
LT 545	LIVONIA	62	42	15	74'	1905	
LY 630	GUIDE ME	62	41	15	77'	1905	LK 106 SCRAPPED 1936
LT 435	GIRL BESSIE	62	42	15	74'	1905	SUNK BY SUBMARINE OFF TYNE - 6.7.16
INS 120	CAROL AND DOROTHY	89	37	25	86.4'	1905	1919 - SALVAGE VESSEL "RECOVERER"
YH 272	BOY JACOB	62	30	20	75'	1906	BK 236 LOST 1923
LT 668	TRYHAENA	69	38	20	78.3'	1906	SH 226 LOST 1929
YH 270	SPRAY	61	39	20	78.4'	1906	SY 517 LOST 1931
LT 212	BOY BEN	84	44	20	83.4'	1906	GIRL PHYLIS, LT 212 - LOST 1926
LT 366	FANCY	84	44	25	83.4'	1906	SOLD AS PILOT CUTTER 1920
INS 174	CALEDONIA	87	37	25	82.1'	1906	SCRAPPED 1919
LT 482	SUPERB	81	40	20	82.2'	1906	SUMBURGH HEAD, LK 367 - SCRAPPED 1937

REG NO	NAME	G.R.T.	N.T.	H.P.	LENGTH	YR BUILT	HISTORY
LT 1016	PRIMROSE	88	37	20	82.3'	1906	SUNK BY SUBMARINE OFF OUTER SKERRIES 23.5.15
BF 170	HONEYSUCKLE	64	42	15	74'	1906	PD 275 - SCRAPPED 1924
BF 382	RACER	84	35	25	82.7'	1906	SUNK IN MINCH 1923
BF 466	HELENA	87	37	25	83.8'	1906	SOLD TO SPAIN 1925
LT 1021	SAREPTA	89	37	25	82.5'	1906	YH 222 - SCRAPPED 1934
LT 418	PROLIFIC	63	39	15	73.3'	1906	
BF 623	JEANNIE MURRAY	90	38	25	84.5'	1907	SUNK BY GERMAN DESTROYERS DOVER STRAITS 15.2.18
BF 624	FORWARD	89	38	25	84.7'	1907	MINED OFF SHIPWASH 31.1.17
BF 619	FREEDOM	90	38	25	85'	1907	LOST OFF GT. YARMOUTH 1930
LT 1025	VIGILANT	87	37	25	84.2'	1907	INS 4 - SCRAPPED 1923
YH 265	OCEAN SPRAY	62	32	20	75.4'	1907	FITFUL HEAD, LK 174
LT 1038	MASCOT	60	26	20	74.4'	1907	
LT 1059	SPEARMINT	88	37	20	84'	1907	SUFFOLK COUNTY , KY 6, FR 30 - SCRAPPED 1936
LT 1077	SILVERDALE	62	32	20	74.3'	1907	SCRAPPED 1937
LT 1104	ZEALOT	66	34	20	75.6'	1907	
LT 1084	ARIMATHEA	87	37	25	84.1'	1907	LOST OFF GT. YARMOUTH 1937
YH 175	SILVER SPRAY	61	30	20	74.3'	1907	SCRAPPED 1937
YH 170	CHARM	62	31	20	74.4'	1907	SCRAPPED 1937
YH 570	PRIMROSE	62	32	20	74.4'	1907	SUNK BY SUBMARINE OFF BISHOP'S ROCK 18.5.17
INS 430	SCOTSMAN	88	30	25	84.6'	1907	SCRAPPED 1925
LT 1067	BOY CHARLEY	83	35	25	86.4'	1907	SCRAPPED 1928
LT 1040	GIRL HILDA	88	37	20	84.1'	1907	SCRAPPED 1930
YH 477	RENOWN	62	30	20	74.3'	1907	SUNK BY SUBMARINE OFF TYNE 28.7.16

SCOTSMAN INS 430 - Built of wood by J. Chambers & Co. Ltd. Lowestoft 1907. Seen here in Waveney Dock, Lowestoft October 1911. Scrapped 1925. Courtesy of A. Durrant, Kessingland.

REG NO	NAME	G.R.T.	N.T.	H.P.	LENGTH	YR BUILT	HISTORY
LT 1062	G. M. V.	94	42	25	87.3'	1907	SUNK OFF LARNE 13.3.15
LT 88	SPOTLESS PRINCE	85	36	25	84.3'	1908	SUNK BY GERMAN DESTROYERS DOVER STRAITS 27.10.16
LT 171	GIRL'S FRIEND	62	32	20	75.4'	1908	SUNK BY SUBMARINE OFF HARTLEPOOL 14.7.16
LT 290	SEARCHER	66	34	20	75.4'	1908	SCRAPPED 1937
LT 109	BON ESPOIR	86	38	25	84.1'	1908	FR 111 - SCRAPPED 1934
LT 234	GOLDEN SPUR	57	33	20	74.3'	1908	
LT 45	HERRING FISHER	76	33	23	84'	1908	SY 251 - SCRAPPED 1936
LT 219	YOUNG ROLAND	57	33	20	74.2'	1908	
LT 69	ANGELINA	86	38	25	84'	1908	LK 104 - SCRAPPED 1936
LT 112	GOOD FRIEND	86	37	26	85.3'	1908	AH 39, PD 115 - SCRAPPED 1935
YH 291	YOUNG ARCHIE	60	34	20	74.5'	1908	BK 24 - LOST 1935
INS 504	SPYNIE CASTLE	83	27	25	84.7'	1908	BURNT AT LOSSIEMOUTH 1915
INS 580	GLEN CORRAN	86	38	25	84.3'	1908	BF 434 - LOST WEST COAST OF SCOTLAND 12.23
PD 522	UGIE	83	37	25	84.3'	1908	SCRAPPED 1935
BF 1067	IVA	85	37	25	84'	1908	SUNK OFF SHIPWASH LIGHT VESSEL 1922
LT 23	PHYLLIS ANNE	88	40	25	87.4'	1908	

YOUNG ARCHIE YH 291 - Built of wood by Chambers of Lowestoft 1908. Shown here as YOUNG ARCHIE BK 24. Note unusual position of wheelhouse. Scrapped 1926. Courtesy of Scottish Fisheries Museum.

LT 344	LAUNCH OUT	67	33	20	75.4'	1908	SUNK BY GERMAN DESTROYERS DOVER STRAITS 27.10.16
LT 329	LONDON COUNTY	83	33	20	84.8'	1909	LOST OFF BEADNELL OCTOBER 1919
LT 355	TUBEROSE	67	34	20	75.4'	1909	MINED OFF LOWESTOFT 31.8.16
LT 423	TRUE FRIEND	83	37	25	84.8'	1909	YH 11, H 489, BF 109 - SCRAPPED 1948
LT 303	QUI SAIT	83	35	25	84.3'	1909	SOLD TO GIBRALTAR 1919
LT 324	HAWTHORNDALE	60	35	20	75'	1909	LT 748

REG NO	NAME	G.R.T.	N.T.	H.P.	LENGTH	YR BUILT	HISTORY
LT 470	JOHN ALFRED	81	34	20	84.1'	1909	
PD 543	GUIDING LIGHT	67	34	20	75'	1909	FR 323, BCK 332 - LOST 1923
LT 446	G. E. S.	60	34	20	75.6'	1909	SH 201
LT 309	E. B. C.	60	30	20	75.2'	1909	YH 240 - LOST 1930
LT 370	FRIENDLY STAR	58	33	20	75.4'	1909	WRECKED OFF CORNWALL W.W.II 1941
YH 97	GOLDEN SPRAY	59	34	20	75.8'	1909	BN 46 - SCRAPPED 1946
YH 557	RAMBLING ROSE	59	32	20	75.7'	1909	SCRAPPED 1946
YH 423	W. ELLIOT	60	35	20	74.3'	1909	SUNK BY GERMAN DESTROYERS DOVER STRAITS 15.2.18
YH 157	BOY EDDIE	59	34	20	74.3'	1909	SOLD TO ROYAL NAVY 1920
YH 485	H. F. E.	58	33	20	75.4'	1909	BK 50 - SCRAPPED 1937
LT 544	REMEMBRANCE	82	35	25	84.3'	1910	SY 51 - LOST 1921
LT 540	MAUD EVELYN	73	35	20	81.5'	1910	SH 335, LK 80
LT 480	WENLOCK	74	35	20	82.1'	1910	AUTUMN
LT 594	SMILAX	81	35	31	84.4'	1910	SCRAPPED 1936
LT 631	BIENVENU	77	35	25	84.5'	1910	LOST OFF BACTON 1920
LT 658	CONIFER	69	33	20	81.5'	1910	OCEAN SUNBEAM - SCRAPPED 1939
LT 714	BEN AND LUCY	83	38	25	84.2'	1910	SOLD TO NORWAY 1946 - SCRAPPED 1956
LT 638	PECHEUR	67	31	20	80.1'	1910	SUNK OFF SMALL'S LT. 3.4.16
LT 650	MARY ADELINE	73	24	20	81.7'	1910	LOST OFF TYNE 1930
LT 701	KING GEORGE V	68	32	20	80.1'	1910	MINED OFF DOVER 3.6.17
LT 692	DOROTHY ROSE	74	36	20	80.1'	1910	PEACE AND PLENTY - SCRAPPED 1936
LT 641	BON AVENIR	68	32	20	80.2'	1910	SH 114, WK 254 - SCRAPPED 1937
LT 528	WEST ANGLIA	75	33	29	84'	1910	SCRAPPED 1936
LT 717	YOUNG FRED	83	37	25	85.1'	1910	SCRAPPED 1937
PD 566	JOHN S. SUMMERS	62	36	20	77.4'	1910	SOLD TO CORK 1922
YH 176	JACOB GEORGE	67	31	20	80'	1910	SCRAPPED 1949
YH 167	GIRL NANCY	67	31	20	80.5'	1910	SCRAPPED 1946

JACOB GEORGE YH 176 - Built of wood by J. Chamber & Co. Ltd. Lowestoft 1910. Seen here ashore on Eyemouth Beach with crew being rescued by Breeches Buoy ca 1930s. Scrapped 1949. Courtesy of Scottish Fisheries Museum.

REG NO	NAME	G.R.T.	N.T.	H.P.	LENGTH	YR BUILT	HISTORY
YH 297	PISCATORIAL	84	35	25	84.5'	1910	SUNK BY SUBMARINE OFF OUTER SKERRIES 23.5.15
YH 719	OAKLAND	67	31	20	80.1'	1910	TO SALVAGE WORK SCRAPPED 1963
LT 577	SELECT	74	38	20	80.3'	1910	YH 577 - SUNK OFF ST. GOVANS LIGHT BUOY 16.4.18
YH 137	E. A. B.	67	32	20	80.7'	1910	
YH 697	YOUNG KENNETH	67	32	20	80.3'	1910	SCRAPPED 1943
YH 700	GIRL ANNIE	67	31	20	80.1'	1910	SH 47
LT 1126	REALITY	87	37	25	84.1'	1911	SCRAPPED 1943
LT 1152	LORD DUNWICH	75	36	20	81.8'	1911	LK 207 - SCRAPPED 1946
LT 1112	NESMAR	87	37	20	84.2'	1911	SCRAPPED 1936
LT 765	XMAS DAISY	88	39	25	84.2'	1911	SCRAPPED 1936
LT 1145	SILVER HERRING	86	36	32	84'	1911	SCRAPPED 1950
LT 1110	SPECULATION	83	35	33	84'	1911	SCRAPPED 1938
LT 1167	BOY ROY	95	42	25	86.2'	1911	LOST AT DUNKIRK 28.5.40 ALL WOODEN STANDARD DRIFTERS WERE DESIGNED FROM THIS VESSEL
LT 1119	SARAH MARIAN	89	39	20	86'	1911	LOST OFF LOWESTOFT 1930
LT 764	DOLLAR PRINCESS	74	34	20	82'	1911	SCRAPPED 1936
LT 1115	LILY JANE	74	35	20	82.1'	1911	BF 23, LONICERA - WRECKED OFF SCARBOROUGH 1933
LT 1135	GOLDEN GAIN	84	35	25	84.5'	1911	WY 260, YH 91 - SCRAPPED 1939
LT 1154	HERRING SEEKER	75	36	20	80.6'	1911	SCRAPPED 1936
LT 763	FORESIGHT	87	38	25	84.3'	1911	SOLD TO NORWAY 1946
LT 1117	EVENING PRIMROSE	88	38	25	84.6'	1911	SCRAPPED 1947
LT 1122	HEATHER BLOOM	88	38	25	84.4'	1911	FISHER KING - SCRAPPED 1939
LT 1147	YOUNG MUN	87	37	32	84.4'	1911	SCRAPPED 1956
LT 1157	TWO BOYS	91	41	25	87.3'	1911	SCRAPPED 1936
LT 1148	NEVERTHELESS	88	37	25	84.5'	1911	GENEROUS - LOST 1934
LT 1127	BOY HAROLD	74	36	20	82.3'	1911	MINED OFF BRINDISI - 3.3.16
LT 1139	DUSTY MILLER	73	38	20	82.2'	1911	YH 8 - LOST 1938
BF 370	GLEAM OF HOPE	72	32	20	82.3'	1911	LOST 1928
PD 20	DAVID. B. SUMMERS	61	31	20	77'	1911	SOLD TO GALWAY 1925
YH 876	OCEAN CREST	88	38	25	84.5'	1911	SCRAPPED 1951
YH 769	TESSIE	87	36	25	84.2'	1911	TRV AT ANSTRUTHER WW II SCRAPPED 1947
YH 713	DASHING SPRAY	69	32	20	80.4'	1911	BCK 56 - SCRAPPED 1951
YH 729	HALF MOON	95	43	25	87.4'	1911	LT 214
LT 1137	GIRL NORAH	75	36	20	82.2'	1911	LOST WITH ALL HANDS OFF FRENCH COAST
LT 1172	CONSTANT FRIEND	86	39	20	84.3'	1912	SCRAPPED 1947
LT 1178	ROSEMMA	92	40	25	84'	1912	SOLD TO GREECE 1947
LT 1190	VICTOR AND MARY	81	36	35	84.1'	1912	SCRAPPED 1939
LT 1168	EAST HOLME	75	35	20	82'	1912	YH 22, YH 291 - LOST 1934
LT 1181	HELPMATE	76	35	20	80.8'	1912	YH 129 - LOST OFF NEWLYN 31.3.41
LT 1188	HASTINGS CASTLE	73	35	20	81.5'	1912	SUNK AFTER COLLISION 1925
LT 1183	SCADAWN	101	46	35	92.6'	1912	LOST 1933
LT 1171	REDWALD	79	36	30	83.8'	1912	SCRAPPED 1953
LT 1200	RESTART	79	36	30	83.8'	1912	SCRAPPED 1947
YH 307	OCEAN RETRIEVER	94	44	25	87.4'	1912	MINED THAMES ESTUARY 22.9.43
YH 135	NEW SPRAY	70	33	20	80.5'	1912	LOST OFF SHEERNESS 3.1.41

J. CHAMBERS & COMPANY LIMITED - LOWESTOFT (CONTINUED)

REG NO	NAME	G.R.T.	N.T.	H.P.	LENGTH	YR BUILT	HISTORY
YH 704	MARY EVELYN	90	40	25	84.3'	1912	R 333
YH 924	SWEET PEA	73	35	20	80.3'	1912	WK 12, BCK 68 - SCRAPPED 1952
LT 271	NETSUKIS	85	39	30	83.3'	1913	SCRAPPED 1947
LT 1198	ROSEVINE	100	43	25	88'	1913	SUNK OFF GREAT YARMOUTH 24.5.17
LT 10	OCEAN SCOUT	86	39	20	84.1'	1913	
LT 33	FAITHFUL FRIEND	110	38	25	91.1'	1913	
YH 537	GEORGE BAKER	91	39	25	85'	1913	SUNK BY SUBMARINE OFF BISHOP'S ROCK 17.8.15
YH 927	MA FREEN	92	39	25	84.3'	1913	SCRAPPED 1939
LT 145	SILVER PRINCE	108	37	25	89.5'	1913	SOLD TO MILFORD HAVEN 1947
LT 64	LOYAL FRIEND	85	36	20	83.6'	1913	
LT 32	CONSTANT HOPE	92	41	20	84.5'	1913	SCRAPPED 1945
LT 61	DICK WHITTINGTON	80	40	20	82.2'	1913	SCRAPPED 1950
LT 1194	GOLDEN SUNSET	85	39	20	84.5'	1913	SUNK OFF SHAMBLES LIGHT VESSEL 4.1.18
LT 199	PEVENSEY CASTLE	101	47	25	86.2'	1913	
LT 72	OUR FRIEND	86	40	20	83.8'	1913	SCRAPPED 1937
LT 55	STAR OF THULE	91	40	20	84'	1913	UNITED FRIENDS - SCRAPPED 1939
YH 574	OCEAN TREASURE	92	39	25	84.3'	1913	SOLD TO NORWAY 1946
YH 718	BROADLAND	76	36	20	80.7'	1913	LOST IN NORTH ATLANTIC 6.6.45
LT 213	LA PARISIENNE	85	39	25	84'	1913	
YH 346	GIRL EVA	76	36	20	83'	1913	MINED OFF ELBOW LIGHT BUOY 2.10.16
LT 17	BOY SCOUT	80	39	20	82.1'	1913	SOLD TO GREECE 1947 - LOST 1947
LT 277	DULCIE DORIS	85	39	20	84.5'	1913	SOLD TO GREECE 1920
LT 350	EX FORTIS	90	42	20	85.3'	1914	SCRAPPED 1954
YH 702	DORIS MAUD	79	40	20	84.5'	1914	SOLD TO GREECE 1921
SN 37	LERITA	79	39	20	82.5'	1914	FR 197, BCK 188 - SCRAPPED 1949
SN 44	NOREEN	79	39	20	82.3'	1914	
LT 376	WELWYN	78	37	20	82'	1914	TRV AT ANSTRUTHER W.W.II SCRAPPED 1947
WY 14	WYE BURN	94	41	26	85.2'	1914	
YH 24	OCEAN GUIDE	75	35	20	80.3'	1914	SCRAPPED 1955
YH 33	OCEAN RETRIEVER II	94	44	25	87.5'	1914	WRECKED OFF MALLAIG 1934
LT 342	EILEEN EMMA	102	46	25	86.6'	1914	TO NORWAY 1946
LT 322	LINDSELL	88	39	25	84'	1914	MINED OFF OUTER DOWSING 3.9.14
YH 160	OCEAN TRUST	77	37	20	80.7'	1914	SCRAPPED 1954
YH 271	J. H. F.	78	37	20	81.8'	1914	LOST 1942
LT 215	RESTORE	93	39	32	85'	1914	SUNK BY SUBMARINE IN ADRIATIC 12.10.15
LT 371	GOLDEN CHANCE	85	36	32	84'	1914	WY 231, LT 1227 - TO FALKLANDS 1946
LT 141	YOUNG FISHERMAN	95	43	25	86'	1914	YH 297 - WRECKED AT OBAN 29.11.40
LT 283	GIRL ETHEL	88	39	32	83.8'	1914	SH 260, LT 60, SH 216, BCK 2 - SCRAPPED 1950
LT 77	FISHER GIRL	85	36	32	83.6'	1914	SUNK AT FALMOUTH - BOMBED 25.11.41
LT 365	REALIZE	108	50	25	86.2'	1914	
YH 87	F. & G. G.	85	38	20	83.5'	1914	SCRAPPED 1953
LT 331	BOY ALAN	109	51	25	89.4'	1914	SUNK AT THAMES ESTUARY 10.2.41
YH 184	OCEAN GAIN	77	38	20	80.6'	1915	SCRAPPED 1954
LT 323	PRESENTER	96	45	39	89.4'	1915	AH 95, CRAIGEARN FR 477 - SCRAPPED 1948
LT 45	DRIFT FISHER	96	41	32	84.5'	1916	WK 93, BF 176 - SCRAPPED 1949
LT 695	BRACKENDALE	88	41	30	83.6'	1916	H 859, FR 147 - SCRAPPED OCTOBER 1952

LERITA SN 37 - Built of wood by J. Chambers & Co. Ltd. of Lowestoft 1914. Shown as FR 197 became BCK 188. Scrapped 1949. Courtesy of Scottish Fisheries Museum.

ANNEX IV J. CHAMBERS & COMPANY LIMITED - LOWESTOFT (CONTINUED) WOODEN

REG NO	NAME	G.R.T.	N.T.	H.P.	LENGTH	YR BUILT	HISTORY
LT 679	FISHER QUEEN	88	40	32	83.6'	1916	SCRAPPED 1955
LT 703	EMPIRE'S HEROES	89	38	20	83.7'	1916	SCRAPPED 1937
LT 730	IMPLACABLE	88	40	32	83.6'	1916	SCRAPPED 1955
YH 622	ANIMATE	88	43	24	83.5'	1917	SCRAPPED 1957
LT 100	FORMIDABLE	87	40	33	85.5'	1917	SOLD TO NORWAY 1946
YH 497	OCEAN ROAMER	90	44	26	85.1'	1917	C. & A., BK 180 - SCRAPPED 1946
WY 172	LAVINIA L	73	31	24	80.6'	1917	LT 1299, YH 448 - BOMBED - SUNK OFF SHEERNESS 5.6.41
WY 225	WYDALE	102	48	37	89'	1917	YH 105 - SCRAPPED 1961
YH 571	CHOICE LASS	75	35	20	80.5'	1917	LORD HOWE, LT 1257 - SCRAPPED 1947
YH 580	LYDIA LONG	76	36	20	80.6'	1918	INS 38 - SCRAPPED 1946
LT 25	TRIPLE ALLIANCE	87	40	30	84.3'	1924	FR 89 - SCRAPPED 1950
LT 27	FORETHOUGHT	96	37	20	86.5'	1924	FR 87 - SCRAPPED 1952
LT 90	PEACEFUL STAR	97	43	30	87'	1924	SUNK - BOMBED OFF ROCKABILL LIGHT HOUSE 14.3.41
YH 63	ROMANY ROSE	95	40	30	86.5'	1924	SCRAPPED 1956
YH 55	YOUNG ERNIE	96	41	30	86.5'	1924	SUNK OFF TYNE 18.4.41
LT 230	RAY OF HOPE	99	46	33	88.3'	1924	MINED THAMES ESTUARY 10.12.39
LT 223	FORECAST	98	44	30	88.3'	1925	SUNK OFF GREENOCK 14.4.44
LT 264	CHARTER	98	44	36	88.5'	1925	WRECKED OFF DEVON 1934
LT 256	WELCOME HOME	104	44	32	88.1'	1925	SCRAPPED 1957
LT 194	SILVER DAWN	98	43	34	88.1'	1925	YH 112 - SCRAPPED 1956
YH 138	ANIMATION	99	45	37	88.2'	1925	TRV AT ANSTRUTHER W.W.II - SCRAPPED 1957
YH 126	PLANKTON	99	45	34	88.1'	1925	YOUNG CLIFF, YH 126 - SCRAPPED 1959
LT 231	MERIT	97	42	27	87.7'	1925	SOLD TO DENMARK 1939
YH 169	UT PROSIN	97	42	23	87.7'	1925	SUNK OFF DOVER 2.3.43
LT 296	RENOUELLE	97	42	27	88'	1926	JACKETA , LT 296 - SOLD TO DENMARK April 1947
LT 341	ACHIEVABLE	98	43	34	88.1'	1927	YH 92 - SCRAPPED 1958

ANNEX IV · GARMOUTH · WOODEN

REG NO	NAME	G.R.T.	N.T.	H.P.	LENGTH	YR BUILT	HISTORY
BCK 1	HANDSOME (A)	84	24	20	85'	1907	FR 102, SY 706 - SCRAPPED 1951
BCK 6	ROSEDALE (B)	93	39	23	83.4'	1907	CONVERTED TO COASTER 1936
BF 882	PISCES (B)	94	33	31	83.3'	1907	SY 223 - CEASED FISHING 1925
BF 912	WINSOME (A)	80	28	30	84.1'	1908	SCRAPPED 1936
BCK 16	BLITHSOME (A)	81	34	30	86.1'	1908	SOLD TO FAEROES 1934
BUILDERS WERE JOHN HAY (A)							
THOMAS DUNCAN & SON (B)							

HANDSOME BCK 1 - Built of wood by J. Hay of Garmouth during 1907. Became FR 102 and SY 706. Scrapped 1951.
Courtesy of Scottish Fisheries Museum.

ANNEX IV · SANDERS AND GIBBS & Co., BOTH OFF GALMPTON, DEVON · WOODEN

REG NO	NAME	G.R.T.	N.T.	H.P.	LENGTH	YR BUILT	HISTORY
SN 267	LOTTIE	60	29	20	77'	1900	YH 430
LT 507	MAGGIE (B)	55	29	15	76.2'	1900	YH 330, PD 243 - SCRAPPED 1925
LT 440	SUNNY DEVON (B)	61	34	25	77.8'	1901	WK 91 - SCRAPPED 1924
YH 616	BERRY CASTLE	59	40	15	71.7'	1901	
SN 294	CISSY (B)	59	23	20	78'	1901	BCK 331 - SCRAPPED 1927
YH 571	MARGERY (B)	64	31	20	76.1'	1901	LH 158, INS 33, BCK 315 - HERRING CARRIER CLYDE - SCRAPPED 1931
LT 262	GENERAL MACDONALD (B)	59	35	16	77.6'	1901	FR 396 - SCRAPPED 1922
SN 302	DOROTHY (B)	70	28	29	78.8'	1901	PD 109 - SCRAPPED 1923
LT 239	MARJORIE	62	30	14	78.3'	1901	BCK 54 - SCRAPPED 1924
LT 507	BOY JIM	63	26	24	77.3'	1901	LK 490, BF 277, YH 257 - SCRAPPED 1927
LT 897	LORD METHVEN	62	37	20	76.5'	1902	SY 325
LT 506	MARYLAND	61	35	25	78.6'	1902	

SANDERS AND GIBBS & Co., BOTH OFF GALMPTON, DEVON **WOODEN**

REG NO	NAME	G.R.T.	N.T.	H.P.	LENGTH	YR BUILT	HISTORY
LT 497	FEAR NOT	60	33	25	78'	1902	SH 105
YH 976	UNITY	56	30	25	76'	1902	GY 62
LT 147	CRESCENT	63	27	28	78.4'	1902	
LT 889	BRITISH MONARCH	57	25	25	75.1'	1902	
LT 177	GRATITUDE	60	33	25	78.4'	1902	WY 25
LT 488	GEN, BRUCE HAMILTON (B)	61	38	18	78'	1902	FR 404 - SCRAPPED 1922
YH 711	RHODA (B)	66	37	25	75.6'	1902	PD 90, SY 361 - SCRAPPED 1924
LT 994	I'LL TRY (B)	59	33	25	77.5'	1902	PD 576, BF 64 - SCRAPPED 1929
YH 751	GUIDE ME	62	36	18	79.2'	1902	
INS 538	MAGNIFICIENT (B)	68	29	26	79'	1903	BCK 403 - SCRAPPED 1929
YH 821	TORBAY (B)	66	28	20	79'	1903	LT 521, FR 391 - REGISTRY CANC. 1924
YH 827	BRACKEN (B)	66	28	20	78.7'	1903	PD 200 - LOST 1929
YH 791	HONEYSUCKLE (B)	62	36	20	78.8'	1903	PD 11 - SOLD TO METHIL AS A CARGO BOAT
LT 975	EAGLE	61	35	25	78.4'	1903	
LT 255	MORNING STAR (B)	68	29	25	81.6'	1904	YH 479, PD 135 - SCRAPPED 1927
YH 762	VIOLET MAY (A)	74	35	31	82.1'	1906	FR 476 - SCRAPPED 1934
YH 711	BOY WILLIE (A)	81	34	31	83.7'	1907	FR 486 - SCRAPPED 1933
SN 61	DORIS	82	34	20	83'	1907	BCK 325 - CEASED FISHING 1920
YH 105	PISCATOR	83	34	31	85.1'	1907	BK 26 - SCRAPPED 1936
SN 73	FELICIA	75	32	25	80.8'	1908	YH 633
WY 137	ROBURN	83	36	21	85.2'	1913	SUNK BY GERMAN DESTROYERS DOVER STRAITS 27.10.16
BUILDERS WERE SANDERS = (A), AND GIBB & CO = (B), NO BRACKETS = UNKNOWN							

MARJORIE LT 239 - Built of wood by Saunders of Galmpton, Devon 1901. Later became BCK 54. Scrapped 1924.
Seen here ashore on Yorkshire coast, note wheel house aft of funnel. Courtesy of Scottish Fisheries Museum.

*BRITISH MONARCH LT 889 - Built of wood by Saunders of Galmpton, Devon 1902.
Note furled sail on foremast yard. Courtesy of Port of Lowestoft Research Society.*

*I'LL TRY PD 576 - Built of wood by Gibb's & Co. of Galmpton, Devon during 1902 as I'LL TRY LT 994.
Became PD 576 then BF 64. Shown as PD 576 leaving Lowestoft ca 1912. Courtesy of A. Durrant, Kessingland.*

REG NO	NAME	G.R.T.	N.T.	H.P.	LENGTH	YR BUILT	HISTORY
LT 753	WILD FLOWER	33	17	15	55.7'	1896	BUILT AS SAIL, CONVERTED TO STEAM THEN BACK TO SAIL
LT 153	PRETORIA (B)	58	36	15	76.7'	1900	BF 515, SY 267 - SCRAPPED 15.12.26
A 201	GLENISLA (B)	60	41	12	75.1'	1900	FR 601 - SCRAPPED 1924
A 202	GLENTILT (A)	61	23	12	77.3'	1900	GN 45, FR 278 - SCRAPPED 1924
A 364	GLENBERVIE	65	27	17	78.4'	1901	SANK OFF CORTON LIGHT VESSEL 15.10.1909
A 380	GLENTANA (B)	67	30	17	76.4'	1901	FR 480 - SCRAPPED 1924
A 385	GLENURIE (A)	68	21	17	78.4'	1901	FR 479 - CONVERTED TO COASTER 1930
SD 57	ADA (B)	65	30	18	75.6'	1901	SN 57, WK 688, LT 123, WY 224
SN 58	BERTHA	65	29	18	75.8'	1901	WK 689, YH 458, LT 207
SN 59	CLARA (B)	65	30	18	76.7'	1901	WK 696, YH 478, LT 1237
SD 60	DORA	67	30	18	76.7'	1902	WK 700, YH 481, D 386
LT 529	ROSE OF SHARON	59	40	15	74'	1902	
LT 988	LILY OF THE VALLEY	60	41	15	74.5'	1903	
LT 216	BROTHERS	65	30	28	79.1'	1903	
LT 644	BUSY BEE	58	24	25	76.5'	1903	PD 9 - SCRAPPED 1924
BF 281	WHITE HEATHER (A)	58	39	15	74'	1906	WRECKED COMING HOME FROM GREAT YARMOUTH 1913
LT 1054	ENERGETIC	83	29	23	83.6'	1907	
INS 286	VIOLET (A)	82	34	30	83.7'	1907	BCK 234 - SCRAPPED 1933
INS 310	CLUPEA	83	35	30	85'	1907	WRECKED OFF NORFOLK NOVEMBER 1920
YH 598	GIRL MAY	81	34	20	82.8'	1907	FR 473, GK 89 - TO COASTER, CLYDE AREA 1932
BF 896	BUSY BEE (A)	84	35	31	84.1'	1907	BCK 205 - SCRAPPED 1937
BF 941	ASPIRE (A)	87	36	30	84'	1907	SCRAPPED 1934
LT 31	MARVELLOUS	82	35	30	86'	1908	FR 474, FR 163 - SCRAPPED 1933
BCK 32	BARTONIA (A)	82	41	20	86'	1908	LOST 1919
BCK 30	GENTIANA (A)	81	34	30	85.6'	1908	SANK NORTH SEA 1910
BCK 47	CRAIGMIN (A)	74	34	25	81'	1909	SANK OFF GT. YARMOUTH 1926
LT 562	EXPECTATIONS	77	34	25	85.4'	1910	PD 127 PREVALOIR - SCRAPPED 1936
YH 503	FRANK ARNOLD (A)	88	38	30	84.3'	1917	MORNING RAYS FR 311, BCK 161 - SCRAPPED 1951

BUILDERS WERE: R. KITTO & SONS (A)   J. BOWDEN (B)   WHERE NO BRACKETS BUILDER UNKNOWN

LILY OF THE VALLEY LT 988 - Built of wood by R. Kitto & Sons of Porthleven, Cornwall 1903. Note wheel house aft of funnel and sail on foremast yard. Courtesy of Port of Lowestoft Research Society.

ANNEX IV — GEORGE THOMSON - BUCKIE — WOODEN

REG NO	NAME	G.R.T.	N.T.	H.P.	LENGTH	YR BUILT	HISTORY
BF 18	IVY	71	24	25	72.3'	1905	INS 10 - SCRAPPED 1936
BF 344	EXCEL	77	27	24	81.2'	1906	BCK 362, SY 829 - SCRAPPED 2.51
BF 622	GOOD HOPE	85	30	30	83.4'	1907	BCK 322 - SCRAPPED 1937
BF 956	PROGRESS	84	27	31	85.1'	1907	BCK 347, APPLE TREE - SUNK AT OBAN 13.10.40
BF 597	SILVER THYME	84	29	30	86.4'	1907	RANNAS BCK 122, SH 263, BCK 441 - SCRAPPED 1936
BCK 3	GOWAN	84	28	31	86.4'	1907	PD 110 SCRAPPED 1950
BCK 33	LEA RIG	83	28	32	87.2'	1908	SY 820 - CEASED FISHING 10.52
BCK 12	MARY COWIE	83	35	28	86'	1908	LY 48, BCK 338 - TO SALVAGE 1933
BCK 182	EXCHEQUER	86	36	35	87.2'	1914	INS 287, BF 423, SY 787 - SCRAPPED 1952
BCK 212	RECRUIT	94	40	44	91.3'	1915	PD 72 - SOLD AS HERRING CARRIER CLYDE 1949 SANK IRISH SEA 1953

ANNEX IV — WICK — WOODEN

REG NO	NAME	G.R.T.	N.T.	H.P.	LENGTH	YR BUILT	HISTORY
WK 151	SUSIE ROSS	52	35	15	73.1'	1900	YH 383, WK 325 - LOST 1919
WK 210	ELSAY	67	23	23	77.5'	1901	SCRAPPED 1938
WK 544	FISHER	81		20	88.5	1901	LOST OFF GT. YARMOUTH 1904
WK 256	LORD ROBERTS	60	34	10	71'	1901	PD 271 - CONVERTED TO MOTOR AS CARGO VESSEL GADLE BRAES 1922
WK 424	CORDELIA	69	23	17	77'	1901	PD 261 - LOST EAST ANGLIA 1923
WK 582	PRIMROSE	73		21	80.25	1903	SY 269 - SCRAPPED 1929
WK 563	FIDELIA	74	25	21	79.4'	1903	SUNK 1920
WK 15	LOTTIE	71	23	25	80.5'	1904	SCRAPPED 1946
WK 127	LAURELIA	96	35	25	89.7'	1907	SCRAPPED 1937
WK 270	CHANCE	92	28	39	86'	1908	SANK OFF ORKNEY 26.1.16

BUILDERS WERE
J.D.HARPER
A.McEWEN AND SONS
A. DAVIDSON
D.HARPER
D.ALEXANDER
A.ALEXANDER

ANNEX IV — FRED. W. STANGER - STROMNESS, ORKNEY — WOODEN

REG NO	NAME	G.R.T.	N.T.	H.P.	LENGTH	YR BUILT	HISTORY
LT 786	PANSY	58	39	15	76.1'	1902	TAROOL WK 578 - SCRAPPED 1934
LK 663	THULE ROCK	98	41	38	90'	1917	LORD HOWARD, LT 212 - SANK AT DOVER 24.12.40

REG NO	NAME	G.R.T.	N.T.	H.P.	LENGTH	YR BUILT	HISTORY
BF 1466	PURSUIT	72	22	24	79'	1904	PD 394 - SCRAPPED 1937
BF 313	GEM	77	27	28	83.1'	1906	SUNK BY SUBMARINE OFF RATTRAY HEAD 29.6.17
BF 500	PARAGON	83	37	24	84.3'	1906	BCK 356 - LOST 1944
BF 581	MONARCH	82	29	30	85'	1907	BCK 381 - SCRAPPED 1945
BF 762	MORNING STAR	84	29	30	84.4'	1907	BCK 201 - SANK MORAY FIRTH 1922
BF 987	PRESTIGE	81	34	20	85.7'	1907	BCK 156 - SUNK OFF PETERHEAD 1929
BF 961	THRIFT	81	34	20	85.1'	1907	M 69 - WRECKED IRISH SEA 1922
BF 850	CHRYSANTHEMUM	82	34	25	85.5'	1907	SCRAPPED 1930
BF 645	FLEETWING	84	35	30	85.1'	1907	SOLD TO SPAIN 1925
BCK 4	FLOWER	83	35	20	86'	1907	SCRAPPED 1950
BF 1108	SERENITY	81	34	28	85.8'	1908	ARRADOUL, BCK 127 - LOST 1938
BF 1144	WHITE LILAC	83	35	39	86.4'	1908	SCRAPPED 1945
BCK 22	MARA SMITH	88	30	36	83.4'	1908	FR 164, TOIL ON, SILVER SEA, BF 200 - SCRAPPED 1937
BCK 86	MARY BOWIE	79	33	27	86'	1911	SCRAPPED 1938
INS 355	COUNTY OF INVERNESS	84	35	33	87'	1913	CORAL HAVEN, FR 195 - SCRAPPED 1938
BCK 177	NORLAN	90	38	42	90.1'	1914	SCRAPPED 1950
BCK 206	HELEN ANN	90	38	36	88.2'	1915	INS 56, BK 148, BF 119 - WRECKED AT LOWESTOFT 1946
BCK 237	GREEN PASTURES	99	42	42	87.2'	1917	GERVAIS RENTOUL, LT 740 - SCRAPPED 1952
BCK 289	HELEN SLATER	102	43	44	88'	1918	SCRAPPED 1949

GERVAIS RENTOUL LT 740 - Built of wood by G. Smith of Buckie 1917 as GREEN PASTURES BCK 237.
Scrapped 1952. Courtesy of Scottish Fisheries Museum.

ANNEX IV — MCKENZIE - THURSO — WOODEN

REG NO	NAME	G.R.T.	N.T.	H.P.	LENGTH	YR BUILT	HISTORY
WK 71	ALPHA	46	23	24	66.6'	1879	THE 1ST STEAM DRIFTER LISTED HERE, TO ARBROATH AS HARBOUR TUG 1881 - TO GREAT YARMOUTH CA. 1917 - YH 421

ANNEX IV — SANDWICK - SHETLAND — WOODEN

REG NO	NAME	G.R.T.	N.T.	H.P.	LENGTH	YR BUILT	HISTORY
LK 588	PRINCESS OF SANDWICK	50	21	14	71.1'	1907	SAILING SMACK CONVERTED TO STEAM

PRINCESS OF SANDWICK LK 588 - Originally sailboat BRITANNIA, lengthed by 20' to give a keel length of 75' and a steam boiler and steam engine installed during 1907. Became first steam drifter of Shetland.
Courtesy of A. Smith, Shetland.

ANNEX IV — MC INTOSH - PORTESSIE AND IANSTOWN, BUCKIE — WOODEN

REG NO	NAME	G.R.T.	N.T.	H.P.	LENGTH	YR BUILT	HISTORY
A 149	WHITE ROSE	94	41	30	87.1'	1900	KY 179, SILVERNIA, GY 41
BF 398	FRIGATE BIRD	80		37	86'	1900	WRECKED GT. YARMOUTH 1903
BF 1553	STATELY	72	28	28	80.4'	1904	SUNK 6.9.27
BF 188	MISTLETOE	80	30	33	83'	1906	LOST ENTERING GREAT YARMOUTH 5.10.10
BF 304	GUIDING STAR	81	30	26	83.5'	1906	WRECKED OFF LEWIS 1914
BF 162	CONCORD	81	30	33	83'	1906	WRECKED OFF KINCARDINE 1932
BF 274	BOY GEORGE	84	37	34	84'	1906	BCK 55 - SOLD TO SPAIN 1928
BF 573	HOPE	79	38	25	82.4'	1907	BCK 363 SCRAPPED 1935
BF 574	VINTAGE	80	33	25	83.5'	1907	BCK 380 - SANK OFF EAST ANGLIA 1922
BF 846	ZODIAC	80	26	31	83.6'	1907	SCRAPPED 1937
BF 933	BLOOM	87	36	27	85'	1907	SH 217, GY 329 - SCRAPPED 1935
BF 722	UNION	84	35	35	84.5'	1907	LOST 1921
BCK 9	FEAR NOT	101	43	27	88.4'	1908	SCRAPPED 1938
BCK 20	HAZAEL	85	36	31	84.5'	1908	SCRAPPED 1935

REG NO	NAME	G.R.T.	N.T.	H.P.	LENGTH	YR BUILT	HISTORY
BCK 13	BRAMBLE	91	38	25	84.2'	1908	BCK 137 - SCRAPPED 1936
BCK 45	CON - AMORE	88	37	25	86.1'	1909	BF 210, BCK 76 - SCRAPPED 1937
BF 343	SILVERSCALE	91	38	28	85.35'	1911	LH 12, KY 26 - LOST GREAT YARMOUTH 15.11.33
BF 453	PLANTIN	84	35	27	87'	1912	MINED OFF STANDFAST PT. 1917
INS 372	HOLME ROSE	89	37	35	86.6'	1913	SCRAPPED 1937
BCK 190	EN AVANT	90	38	30	87.5'	1914	SCRAPPED 1937
BCK 209	JEANNIE McINTOSH	88	37	40	91.5'	1915	SCRAPPED 1947

*WHITE ROSE A 149 - Built of wood by McIntosh of Portessie 1900. Became KY 179 and GY 41,
shown with crew "redding down" nets. Courtesy of Scottish Fisheries Museum.*

REG NO	NAME	G.R.T.	N.T.	H.P.	LENGTH	YR BUILT	HISTORY
BK 1104	CORMORANT	55	22	10	71.2'	1885	
SN 67	ANGLIA	58	7	20	74.1'	1889	
SN 85	CAMBRIA	105	42	45	96'	1890	

REG NO	NAME	G.R.T.	N.T.	H.P.	LENGTH	YR BUILT	HISTORY
LT 128	MAY QUEEN	59	24	19	69.4'	1900	BF 521 - BUILT AS A SAILING SMACK CONVERTED TO STEAM - SANK 1921
PD 424	ENERGY	78	43	23	79.4'	1901	LOST 1925
PD 475	QUIET WATERS	67	40	26	79'	1903	SUNK BY SUBMARINE OFF BALTA 23.6.15

REG NO	NAME	G.R.T.	N.T.	H.P.	LENGTH	YR BUILT	HISTORY
INS 522	LADY HILL	60	37	42	80'	1903	BUILT AS A ZULU - FITTED WITH STEAM SUNK LOSSIEMOUTH NOVEMBER 1915
INS 181	GOWAN BRAE	82	36	30	83.2'	1906	SCRAPPED 1937
INS 188	RISING SUN	81	35	30	82.3'	1906	SCRAPPED 1936
INS 262	FAITHFUL	80	30	30	84'	1907	WRECKED AT LOWESROFT NOVEMBER 1909
INS 319	BEGONIA	91	30	25	84.5'	1907	SCRAPPED 1937
INS 326	SUBLIME	78	31	35	84.3'	1907	SUNK OFF STRATHY POINT 1920
BF 971	WHITE ROSE	79	33	30	85'	1907	BCK 120 - SUNK OFF DOVER 26.7.16
INS 500	ARNDILLY CASTLE	78	32	32	86'	1908	SANK OFF BRIDLINGTON NOV 1924
INS 584	FLOWER O' MORAY	84	35	24	87.5'	1908	INS 102 - WRECKED AT LOSSIEMOUTH 1935
INS 551	COULARD HILL	86	36	22	87.1'	1908	SCRAPPED 1939
INS 432	GRATITUDE	85	35	32	87.7'	1908	LOST OFF LOWESTOFT 1910
INS 173	LOCH SPYNIE	80	33	25	83.2'	1910	SCRAPPED 1937
INS 112	LOCHNABO	76	31	30	82.7'	1910	SCRAPPED 1937
INS 212	DAISY ROCK	76	32	30	82.2'	1911	SCRAPPED 1936
INS 267	GRANT HAY	77	32	30	86.4'	1911	SCRAPPED 1933
INS 206	MORAY GEM	73	30	20	82.4'	1911	BCK 455 - SCRAPPED 1937
INS 99	ADMIRATION	77	32	30	85.1'	1914	SCRAPPED 1937
INS 86	ST. AETHAN'S	76	31	30	84'	1914	HELENS, FR 314 - SCRAPPED 1936
INS 65	CALEDONIA	81	35	25	86.5'	1919	SCRAPPED 1934
INS 84	GIRL ISOBEL	96	40	25	88'	1925	JEANNIE JACK FR 244, KILMANY, BF 448, LT 90 - SCRAPPED 1952

GOWANBRAE INS 181 - Built of wood by Wm. Wood of Lossiemouth 1906. Seen here leaving
Lowestoft ca 1911. Scrapped 1937. Courtesy of A. Durrant of Kessingland.

LADY HILL INS 522 - Built as a Zulu, fitted with boiler and steam engine by Wm. Wood of Lossiemouth 1903. Sank at Lossiemouth November 1915, seen here at Aberdeen. Courtesy of Scottish Fisheries Museum.

ANNEX IV   DANIEL MAIN - HOPEMAN   WOODEN

REG NO	NAME	G.R.T.	N.T.	H.P.	LENGTH	YR BUILT	HISTORY
INS 31	LAICH O' MORAY	79	32	27	84.1'	1909	FR 37, RUSHING WATER, LAUNCH OUT - SCRAPPED 1936

ANNEX IV   G. WALKER - NAIRN   WOODEN

REG NO	NAME	G.R.T.	N.T.	H.P.	LENGTH	YR BUILT	HISTORY
BCK 223	GOLDEN SHEAF	88	40	37	89.1'	1916	FR 20 - SCRAPPED OCTOBER 1951

ANNEX IV   ALEXANDER SLATER - LOSSIEMOUTH   WOODEN

REG NO	NAME	G.R.T.	N.T.	H.P.	LENGTH	YR BUILT	HISTORY
INS 163	THISTLE	71	26	20	80.6'	1906	SUNK OFF GREAT ORME'S HEAD 30.6.15
INS 403	BELLONA	92	33	25	84.5'	1907	SCRAPPED 1934
INS 470	UTOPIA	75	31	25	85.7'	1907	CHARLES HAY, INS 470 - LOST OFF EAST ANGLIA NOVEMBER 1920
INS 353	BERYL	81	30	30	84.1'	1907	EMERGENCY - SCRAPPED 1932
INS 259	MARINER	88	33	34	88'	1907	BURNT 1930
INS 553	GLEN URQUHART	76	31	27	87.3'	1908	SUNK JULY 1932
INS 171	FERNDALE	75	31	25	83.4'	1910	WRECKED AT ST. ANN'S HEAD 27.12.15
INS 167	INCHBROOM	78	32	27	85.5'	1910	CAUPONA, FR 9 - SCRAPPED 1937
INS 113	THYRSUS	75	31	31	85.6'	1910	WRECKED LOSSIEMOUTH MARCH 1919
INS 207	BRANDERBURGH	79	33	27	88.5'	1911	WRECKED LOSSIEMOUTH FEBRUARY 1933
INS 243	MARY SLATER	79	33	26	83.6'	1911	HILLOCKS SCRAPPED 1937
INS 57	CRAIGMOUNT	80	33	30	87.7'	1914	SCRAPPED 1933
INS 97	GOWAN CRAIG	82	34	36	83.2'	1915	CEASED FISHING 1939
INS 451	GUIDE ON	88	37	36	87'	1917	BCK 112 - SCRAPPED 1946

GOWANCRAIG INS 97 - Built of wood by A. Slater of Lossiemouth 1915. Seen here entering Scarborough possibly en route to East Anglia ca 1920s. Ceased fishing 1939, scrapped 1946. Courtesy of Scottish Fisheries Museum.

ANNEX IV — WILLIAM ALEXANDER & Co. - GOVAN — WOODEN

REG NO	NAME	G.R.T.	N.T.	H.P.	LENGTH	YR BUILT	HISTORY
A 854	PERI	34	19	6	59.2'	1884	BUILT AS PLEASURE SAILING SMACK LATER CONVERTED TO STEAM - SY 458 - LOST 1920

ANNEX IV — YARE DRY DOCK COMPANY LIMITED - GREAT YARMOUTH — WOODEN

REG NO	NAME	G.R.T.	N.T.	H.P.	LENGTH	YR BUILT	HISTORY
YH 278	HARRY EASTICK	107	45	33	86'	1926	LAUNCHED AS OCEAN RIDER - NAME CHANGED BEFORE COMPLETION - RE- ENGINED 1946 SCRAPPED 1961

ANNEX IV — J. TYRRELL & SONS - ARKLOW — WOODEN

REG NO	NAME	G.R.T.	N.T.	H.P.	LENGTH	YR BUILT	HISTORY
D 146	DAN O' CONNELL	52	15	10		1911	PD 260 SOLD TO DUBLIN 1919

ANNEX IV — HAWTHORN & Co. - GRANTON — WOODEN

REG NO	NAME	G.R.T.	N.T.	H.P.	LENGTH	YR BUILT	HISTORY
GN 4	KINGFISHER	76	35	25	86.4'	1882	A 613 - SANK OBAN BAY 1.4.24
LH 1133	GRACE	43	15	16	63.1'	1884	YH 67
YH 515	BELOS	68	28	26	75.5'	1900	K 157 - SCRAPPED 1934

SMITH DOCK COMPANY LIMITED - NORTH SHIELDS, MIDDLESBOROUGH

REG NO	NAME	G.R.T.	N.T.	H.P.	LENGTH	YR BUILT	HISTORY
YH 463	ONE	84	29	24	80'	1900	FAIRY HILL WK 757, INS 19 - SCRAPPED 1935
YH 473	TWO	89	37	44	80'	1900	LEONARD BF 632 - LOST AT SEA JANUARY 1920
YH 478	THREE	84	42	23	80'	1900	LEAL BCK 38, TWO YH 415, PELAGIA, CE 227 - MINED OFF NAB LIGHT VESSEL 28.11.16
YH 480	FOUR	84	42	23	80'	1901	SA 10, PD 108 - SUNK BY SUBMARINE OFF OUTER SKERRIES 23.6.15
YH 530	FIVE	72	33	22	80'	1901	ROSEBINE PD 528 - SCRAPPED AUGUST 1936
YH 531	SIX	77	33	22	80'	1901	MAYBERRY WK 79 - SCRAPPED JUNE 1931
YH 542	SEVEN	77	33	22	80'	1901	LINUM PD 151 - SCRAPPED OCTOBER 1934
YH 500	EIGHT	77	33	22	80'	1901	NIGELLA II PD 152 - SCRAPPED DECEMBER 1928
YH 543	NINE	77	33	22	80'	1901	CONNAGE BCK 197 - SCRAPPED JULY 1935
YH 545	TEN	77	33	22	80'	1901	MON AMI INS 52, YH 178 - SUNK OFF BERWICK 1922
YH 558	ELEVEN	77	33	21	80'	1901	RHYNE BCK 416 - SCRAPPED APRIL 1933
YH 562	TWELVE	77	33	22	80'	1901	GARTLEY BF 658 - SCRAPPED APRIL 1930
YH 581	THIRTEEN	77	33	22	80'	1901	G. C. D. BCK 189 - SCRAPPED OCTOBER 1935
YH 584	FOURTEEN	77	38	22	80'	1901	DENFORD BCK 191 - SOLD TO ADMIRALITY 9.21
YH 595	FIFTEEN	78	33	22	80'	1901	JAMES REIACH BCK 193 - SOLD TO ITALY OCTOBER 1927
YH 596	SIXTEEN	78	33	22	80'	1901	A 75 - SOLD TO ITALY OCTOBER 1927
YH 607	SEVENTEEN	77	33	22	80'	1901	BRAE LOSSIE INS 36 - AS COAL HULK 1930
YH 611	EIGHTEEN	78	34	22	80'	1901	W. J. R. PD 150 - SCRAPPED APRIL 1925
YH 613	NINETEEN	77	33	22	80'	1901	ROCK DAISY PD 157 - SCRAPPED MAY 1938
YH 614	TWENTY	78	33	22	80'	1901	ELEVATE BCK 199-SCRAPPED OCTOBER 1927
GY 1221	FAVO	77	33	22	80'	1901	BF 477 - SCRAPPED 1933
GY 1228	CATO	77	33	22	80'	1901	MIZPAH BF 494, PD 552, BF 114 - SCRAPPED 1927
YH 668	TWENTY ONE	79	33	22	80'	1902	LOST OFF BERWICK JULY 1906
YH 670	TWENTY TWO	79	33	22	80'	1902	UGIE BRAE PD 63 - SUNK BY SUBMARINE OFF SKERRIES 23.6.15
YH 672	TWENTY THREE	80	34	22	80'	1902	LYRE BIRD BCK 174 - SCRAPPED OCTOBER 1925
YH 674	TWENTY FOUR	81	34	22	80'	1902	HILARY II - ADMIRALTY NAME - MINED OFF SPIT BUOY 25.3.16
YH 675	TWENTY FIVE	79	34	22	80'	1902	XERANTHEMUM BF 552 - SCRAPPED DECEMBER 1935
YH 678	TWENTY SIX	80	33	22	80'	1902	CARPE DIEM LT 1207 - BF 226 - SCRAPPED MAY 1935
YH 680	TWENTY SEVEN	80	33	22	80'	1902	PITNESS BF 98 - SCRAPPED MAY 1936
YH 681	TWENTY EIGHT	79	33	22	80'	1902	RESOURCE BF 343 - SCRAPPED JULY 1935
YH 691	TWENTY NINE	80	33	22	80'	1902	ELSIE BUDGE WK 224 - SCRAPPED AUGUST 1934
YH 695	THIRTY	80	33	22	80'	1902	MAGGIE GARDEN BCK 130 - SCRAPPED OCTOBER 1935
YH 701	THIRTY ONE	79	34	22	80'	1902	EXUBERANT BCK 148 - SCRAPPED FEBRUARY 1937
YH 709	THIRTY TWO	80	33	22	80'	1902	LEMNOS BF 110 - SOLD TO ITALY MARCH 1928
YH 712	THIRTY THREE	80	33	22	80'	1902	SOLD TO CANADA 1904
YH 721	THIRTY FOUR	84	34	22	80'	1902	BRIAR ROSE BF 300 - SCRAPPED APRIL 1924
YH 725	THIRTY FIVE	80	34	21	80'	1902	TRIDENT BF 1049 - SCRAPPED JANUARY 1936
YH 730	THIRTY SIX	76	34	22	80	1902	POPPY LT 965, BCK 175 - SCRAPPED OCTOBER 1932
YH 732	THIRTY SEVEN	80	34	22	80'	1902	DILIGENT BF 1138 - SCRAPPED DECEMBER 1931
YH 743	THIRTY EIGHT	79	34	22	80'	1902	BLUEBELL BF 1048, LT 527 - SCRAPPED DECEMBER 1930

SMITH DOCK COMPANY LIMITED - NORTH SHIELDS, MIDDLESBOROUGH (CONTINUED)

REG NO	NAME	G.R.T.	N.T.	H.P.	LENGTH	YR BUILT	HISTORY
INS 474	NELLIE	78	34	22	80'	1902	BF 760, FR 760, LT 1221 - SOLD TO HOLLAND 1923
BF 940	VIGILANT	77	28	21	80'	1902	SCRAPPED 1936
LT 890	DORIS	77	33	22	80'	1902	
PD 481	PURSUIT	78	32	23	80'	1903	KY 62 - SOLD ABROAD
BF 1410	GUIDE ME	77	29	25	80'	1903	BK 247 - TO SOUTH AFRICA 1923
BF 1399	SUCCEED	77	33	22	80'	1903	SANK NORTH MINCH 1933
LT 997	HYACINTH	79	28	22	80'	1903	M 173
WK 605	BESSIE	79	28	22	80'	1903	SCRAPPED
WK 638	SUNBEAM	79	28	22	80'	1903	LOST 1925
WK 643	LIVELY	79	30	30	80'	1903	BF 262 - SCRAPPED 1936
BF 1296	WELFARE	79	28	22	80'	1903	SCRAPPED 1935
WK 608	SCOT	79	28	22	80'	1903	KY 139 - SCRAPPED 1935
FR 985	FAITHLIE	79	28	23	80'	1903	KY 32 - SCRAPPED 1936 -
PD 492	A. M. LEASK	79	29	23	80'	1903	SPRING BUD BF 219 - SCRAPPED 1935
PD 483	JEANNIE	79	30	23	80'	1903	BF 356 - SCRAPPED 1935
PD 491	SPEEDWELL	79	30	23	80'	1903	SOLD TO SPAIN
PD 484	ANCHOR OF HOPE	79	30	23	80'	1903	SCRAPPED 1938
INS 573	VINE	77	28	22	80'	1904	KY 127, PD 156, FR 209 - SCRAPPED JANUARY 1952
YH 828	BLACKTHORN	79	28	22	80'	1904	BF 474 - SCRAPPED 1936
YH 831	HOLLY	79	28	22	80'	1904	
YH 833	MISTLETOE	79	27	22	80'	1904	WK 186 - SCRAPPED 1937
YH 829	THISTLE	79	28	22	80'	1904	MINED THAMES ESTUARY MAY 1941
BF 1461	THRIVE	81	30	24	80'	1904	SOLD TO FALMOUTH - SCRAPPED 1936
PD 497	NINA	83	31	28	82' 1"	1904	MINED OFF PRAWLIE POINT 2.8.17
PD 48	RESOLUTE	90	31	27	85'	1904	FR 556, INS 16, BF 57, FR 58 - SCRAPPED 1937
FR 26	CHRISOBEL	84	31	27	82.1'	1904	SCRAPPED 1937
KY 693	VANGUARD III	83	31	28	82'	1904	BCK 419 - SCRAPPED 1936
BF 1465	BURD	93	31	27	82.1'	1904	SCRAPPED 1937
PD 496	EMILY REAICH	84	31	28	82'	1904	BF 745, BCK 85, BK 208 - SANK NORTH SEA 1924
YH 211	TWO II	91	45	25	82.1'	1907	CORRIEDOUNE BCK 417, FR 481 - SCRAPPED JULY 1949
YH 874	THREE II	87	29	37	82.5'	1907	JOHN WATT BF 641, FR 240 - SCRAPPED JULY 1949
YH 212	FOUR II	91	45	25	82.2'	1907	THOMPSON'S BCK 420, GY 502 - SCRAPPED SEPTEMBER 1947
YH 971	ROSE	91	45	25	82. 2'	1907	LT 293 - SUNK 11.9.43
YH 972	BULLRUSH	90	44	25	82. 2'	1907	YOUNG SAM YH 972
YH 574	OCEAN GIFT	91	45	25	82.1'	1907	FR 563 - SCRAPPED 1947
INS 11	PITGAVENNY	88	29	25	82. 1'	1908	BF 151 - WRECKED GREAT YARMOUTH NOVEMBER 1936
BCK 39	RATHVEN	87	29	37	82. 5'	1908	SCRAPPED 1938
BCK 19	LIZZIE ANNE	87	29	37	82. 5'	1908	SCRAPPED 1938
BF 1117	DEXTERITY	87	29	37	82.5'	1908	SCRAPPED 1937
BF 1056	CELOSIA	87	29	37	82.5'	1908	SCRAPPED 1938
BCK 11	LILY REAICH	88	30	36	82.5'	1908	MINED OFF DURAZZO 26.2.16
BCK 10	M. THOMPSON	87	29	37	82.5'	1908	SCRAPPED 1951
BF 543	TROPIC BIRD	96	39	35	82.3'	1909	SCRAPPED 1936
INS 9	CLUNY	86	29	38	82.3'	1909	CITY OF ELGIN INS 9 - SCRAPPED 1938

SMITH DOCK COMPANY LIMITED - NORTH SHIELDS, MIDDLESBOROUGH (CONTINUED)

REG NO	NAME	G.R.T.	N.T.	H.P.	LENGTH	YR BUILT	HISTORY
KY 8	LILY & MAGGIE	87	31	38	82.1'	1909	ML 119, LENA & FRANCOIS KY 8 - SCRAPPED 1936
BCK 48	JANET GEDDES	88	31	38	82.3'	1909	SCRAPPED 1938
YH 510	FIVE II	84	28	38	82'	1910	REGINA STELLA BCK 422 - SCRAPPED SEPTEMBER 1947
YH 511	TEN II	84	28	38	82'	1910	BREME BF 638, FR 74 - SCRAPPED MAY 1951
INS 135	LASSIE MAIN	84	31	38	82'	1910	FR 382 - SCRAPPED 1945
KY 73	CROMORNA	85	31	37	82'	1910	LEMNOS BF 2, PD 141 - SCRAPPED 1950
SN 118	CHRIS	81	30	32	80'	1910	RAMBLER ROSE BF 263 - TO NORWAY 1945
INS 116	WATER BIRD III	79	29	29	80'	1910	ROSECRAIG BCK 217, PD 127 - SCRAPPED MAY 1950
INS 110	J. A. C.	79	28	29	80'	1910	MAGGIE SMITH BCK 11, LOVENNA - SCRAPPED 1938
INS 100	MARY THOMPSON	76	28	29	80'	1910	WK 45, PRIMROSE BAY, INS 120, PD 181 - SCRAPPED FEBRUARY 1952
INS 111	EMINENT	79	28	29	80'	1910	WK 174 - SCRAPPED 1936
INS 124	DAIRLIE	79	28	29	80'	1910	SCRAPPED 1937
BCK 66	GOOD DESIGN II	79	29	29	80'	1910	FR 85, GW 29 - HERRING CARRIER, SILVER DRIFT INS 62 - SCRAPPED 1937
BF 151	DELIVERER	79	28	29	80'	1910	SUNK BY SUBMARINE OFF DUBLIN BAY 3.11.17
BCK 63	UNISON	79	29	22	80'	1910	SCRAPPED 1946
BCK 62	ROCHOMIE	79	29	22	80'	1910	SCRAPPED 1945
INS 175	TRUST ON	79	28	29	80'	1911	INVERBOYNDIE BF 195 - SUNK OFF BELL ROCK JULY 1932
YH 172	OCEAN PRIDE	95	36	45	86'	1911	FR 104, R 243, INS 53 - LOST WEST OF SCOTLAND 1. 28

*VANGUARD III KY 693 - Built of steel by Smith Dock Co. Ltd. North Shields 1904. Became BCK 419, scrapped 1936.
Seen here in Anstruther Harbour 1904 having newly arrived from builders. Courtesy of Scottish Fisheries Museum.*

SCOT KY 139 - Built of steel by Smith Dock Co. Ltd. North Shields as SCOT WK608 during 1903. Seen leaving Gt. Yarmouth ca 1920s. Scrapped 1935. Courtesy of Scottish Fisheries Museum.

ANNEX V   MACKAY BROS - ALLOA   STEEL DRIFTERS

REG NO	NAME	G.R.T.	N.T.	H.P.	LENGTH	YR BUILT	HISTORY
LH 30	REDRIFT	97	33	32	86. 1'	1908	FR 419, BCK 430 - SCRAPPED 1938
LH 41	TERFRID	97	33	32	86. 1'	1908	DREEL CASTLE KY 71, BCK 74 - SCRAPPED 1951
BCK 83	CORNRIG	97	33	32	87'	1911	HAZELDALE BCK 83 - CONVERTED TO MOTOR 1950 - SCRAPPED 1974
BCK 92	RIG	96	33	40	87'	1911	R 139 - SCRAPPED 1953

HAWTHORN & COMPANY - LEITH   STEEL DRIFTERS

REG NO	NAME	G.R.T.	N.T.	H.P.	LENGTH	YR BUILT	HISTORY
KY 569	ISLE OF MAY	119	31	34	90. 1'	1896	HERRING CARRIER FROM 1901
KY 567	KELLIE CASTLE	119	31	34	90. 2'	1896	TO EAST LONDON SOUTH AFRICA 1902
KY 572	COUNTY OF FIFE	114	43	34	90. 1'	1896	YH 514
GN 47	CAVALIER	107	40	35	90. 4'	1907	PD 601 - SCRAPPED 1945
GN 66	CHIMERA	107	40	35	90. 4'	1907	LT 118 - GY 19 WRECKED SCURDY NESS 1926

COUNTY OF FIFE KY 572 - Built of steel by Hawthorn & Co. Leith 1896 as a Liner. Note no steam capstan. Became YH 514. Shown here in Anstruther Harbour having arrived from Builders 1896. Courtesy of Scottish Fisheries Museum.

ANNEX V   WM. CHALMERS & Co. - RUTHERGLEN   STEEL DRIFTERS

REG NO	NAME	G.R.T.	N.T.	H.P.	LENGTH	YR BUILT	HISTORY
BF 1417	FLOURISH	82	31	18	80'	1903	GY 301, SEVEN GY 424 - SCRAPPED 1932

STEEL DRIFTERS
ARDROSSAN DRY DOCK & SHIP BUILDING COMPANY LIMITED - ARDROSSAN

REG NO	NAME	G.R.T.	N.T.	H.P.	LENGTH	YR BUILT	HISTORY
WK 425	JANE	104	40	24	91. 7'	1901	SY 50 - AS HERRING CARRIER - GW 28
WK 619	VICTORY	91	33	22	80. 4'	1903	YH 601, BCK 147 - SCRAPPED 1930

STEEL DRIFTERS   MACKIE & THOMSON LIMITED - GOVAN

REG NO	NAME	G.R.T.	N.T.	H.P.	LENGTH	YR BUILT	HISTORY
PD 477	FAITHFUL	92	35	27	82. 3'	1903	SCRAPPED 1938
INS 558	CORYPHAENA	92	35	25	82. 3'	1903	FLOWERDALE BF 5 - SCRAPPED 1938
INS 559	ALPHA	92	35	25	82. 2'	1903	BF 58 - SCRAPPED 1937
PD 17	PRIMROSE	91	35	27	82. 4'	1904	SUNK BY SUBMARINE OFF OUTER SKERRIES 23.6.17
PD 22	HEATHERBELL	91	35	27	82. 4'	1904	BF 198 - SCRAPPED 1949
PD 501	SNOWDROP	94	35	30	86. 1'	1907	SCRAPPED MARCH 1952
PD 503	BRUCES	94	35	30	86. 1'	1907	LUCY MACKAY KY 172 - SCRAPPED 1938
PD 504	HOPEFUL	94	35	30	86. 1'	1907	SEA GLEANER FR 274 - SCRAPPED 1951
FR 238	JEAN	94	35	30	86. 1'	1907	MINED OFF CAPE SANTA MARIA DI LEUCA 17.10.17
INS 402	EMBRACE	94	35	30	86. 1'	1907	WRECKED KYLE OF LOCHALSH 2.8.40
INS 404	GOLDEN HARP	94	35	30	87. 1'	1907	ACQUIRE BF 313, PD 102 - SCRAPPED MARCH 1951
GW 19	ST. MUNGO	95	35	40	86. 1'	1907	SILVERY DAWN A 550, TANSY PD 598 - SCRAPPED 3.51
PD 359	COMELY	95	35	39	86. 1'	1907	FR 195 - SCRAPPED 1950
PD 347	RIVAL	95	35	39	86. 1'	1907	A 347 - SCRAPPED FEBRUARY 1952
PD 177	TRUSTFUL	95	35	39	86. 1'	1907	SCRAPPED 1952
PD 407	IDA	94	35	39	86. 1'	1907	STRATHBEG, FR 180 - SCRAPPED 1938
PD 417	TRUE VINE	95	35	39	86. 1'	1907	BF 198, FR 97, PD 349 - SCRAPPED NOVEMBER 1950
PD 193	JEANNIE LEASK	95	35	39	86. 1'	1907	SOLD TO AIR MINISTRY
PD 500	FAVOURITE	95	35	39	86. 1'	1907	LY 32, PD 184, INS 163 - SCRAPPED 1937
INS 391	SAPPHIRE	95	35	39	86. 1'	1907	BF 117 - SCRAPPED 1938
INS 291	OPTIMISTIC	95	35	39	86. 1'	1907	SCRAPPED 1939
LH 251	TRUSTFUL	95	35	39	86. 2'	1907	INS 142, CONFIDE PD 64 - SCRAPPED MARCH 1952
BF 860	EGLANTINE	95	35	39	86. 1'	1907	SCRAPPED 1937
BCK 31	ENZIE	93	35	30	86. 3'	1908	SY 524 - SUNK OFF LEWIS 1949
PD 516	BRANCH	93	36	39	86. 3'	1908	SCRAPPED DECEMBER 1951
PD 521	NELLIE MCGEE	93	36	39	86. 2'	1908	TO ROYAL NAVY THEN PD 604 - SCRAPPED DECEMBER 1952
PD 511	INVERUGIE	93	36	39	86. 2'	1908	SCRAPPED
INS 600	BEN AIGEN	93	36	38	86. 3'	1908	SUSTAIN BF 315, PD 289 - SCRAPPED 30.3.54
A 221	NEW DAWN	93	35	39	86. 3'	1908	MINED OFF NEEDLES 23.3.18
BCK 21	EUNICE AND NELLIE	93	36	39	86. 3'	1908	INTER NOS BCK 21, BF 137 - SCRAPPED 22.12.50
INS 530	FAVOUR	93	36	39	86. 2'	1908	PD 88 - SCRAPPED 1952
INS 518	ADMIRE	93	35	39	86. 2'	1908	PD 361 - SCRAPPED 1951
INS 534	WEAL	93	35	39	86. 5'	1908	SCRAPPED 1939
INS 549	CRAIGHEAD	93	36	39	84. 4'	1908	GOLDEN ROD PD 10 - SCRAPPED MARCH 1951

MACKIE & THOMSON LIMITED - GOVAN (CONTINUED) STEEL DRIFTERS

REG NO	NAME	G.R.T.	N.T.	H.P.	LENGTH	YR BUILT	HISTORY
INS 545	THE PROVOST	93	35	39	86. 4'	1908	OPHIRLAND BF 483 - TO NORWAY 1946
INS 599	PROMINENT	93	36	39	86. 3'	1908	WRECKED OFF DONEGAL 1913
INS 22	MORAY VIEW	93	36	39	86. 3'	1909	PD 235 - SCRAPPED 1952
INS 23	MAGNIFICIENT III	93	36	41	86. 5'	1909	PD 57 - SCRAPPED 1952
A 277	ELYSIAN DAWN	91	33	41	82. 2'	1909	BCK 424, INS 370, FR 411 - SCRAPPED 1946
A 278	EASTERN DAWN	91	33	41	82. 2'	1909	CAMPANIA BCK 98 - SCRAPPED 1944
YH 365	OAKAPPLE	98	36	40	86' 3'	1910	LT 277 - TRV AT ANSTRUTHER W.W.II
YH 738	REED	99	38	40	86. 4'	1911	LT 270 - MINED OFF THAMES ESTUARY 7.11.40
YH 723	FURZE	99	38	40	86. 4'	1911	BCK 42, LT 95 - SCRAPPED 1955
YH 734	MOSS	99	38	40	86. 3'	1911	GUIDING LIGHT PD 172 - SCRAPPED OCTOBER 1952
YH 724	GORSE	99	38	40	86. 5'	1911	PD 197 - TO SALVAGE WORK MARCH 1952
YH 728	LICHEN	99	38	40	86. 3'	1911	PD 195, LT 64, PD 338 - SCRAPPED JULY 1952
BCK 84	WALKERDALE	99	34	40	87. 5'	1911	BF 107, HAZELGROVE BCK 35 - CONVERTED TO MOTOR VESSEL - SCRAPPED 1974
BCK 99	DARDA	99	34	40	87. 4'	1911	OCEAN VETERAN YH 151 - SCRAPPED SEPTEMBER 1954
BCK 96	HONEYDEW	99	36	40	87. 4'	1911	BF 122 - SCRAPPED JANUARY 1951

GOLDEN ROD PD 10 - Built of steel by Mackie & Thomson Ltd. Govan, 1908 as CRAIGHEAD INS 549.
Shown here leaving Peterhead ca 1947. Courtesy of Aberdeen Libraries - Benzie Collection.

CHARLTON & DOUGHTY LTD. - GRIMSBY STEEL DRIFTERS

REG NO	NAME	G.R.T.	N.T.	H.P.	LENGTH	YR BUILT	HISTORY
GY 112	MARGARET	115	39	30	89'	1896	PD 435 - LOST 1921
FR 224	CAIRNBULG	104	36	32	87'	1907	A 187, SERO ET BF 650 - SOLD TO PORTUGAL 1926
FR 241	BROTHER'S GEM	96	36	31	86. 1'	1907	SCRAPPED 37
LT 1090	W.A.MASSEY	84	36	28	82. 1'	1907	MINED OFF HANDY ISLAND 11.3.18
A 204	BUCHAN NESS	95	35	40	86. 1'	1908	F. H. S., YH 809, THEALBY GY 28, BF 61 - SCRAPPED 1937
A 203	TARBERT NESS	95	35	40	86' 1'	1908	I. F. S., YH 188, ACCEDE PD 191
BCK 25	FLOREAT	93	32	30	86'	1908	GY 351, BF 101 - SCRAPPED 1933
H 72	VAL	93	32	28	86'	1909	M72, BF 19 - SCRAPPED 1938
LT 691	HUMOROUS	101	39	36	87. 4'	1916	
LT 664	SENTINEL STAR	105	37	30	87. 4'	1916	SOLD TO FRANCE
H 295	CATHERINE CHARLTON	91	39	30	87. 2'	1921	TRUE ACCORD, LT 424 - SUNK OFF GREAT YARMOUTH 26.12.40

G. BROWN & COMPANY - GREENOCK STEEL DRIFTERS

REG NO	NAME	G.R.T.	N.T.	H.P.	LENGTH	YR BUILT	HISTORY
INS 348	ROOSEVELT	97	37	35	86'	1907	WK 212 - SCRAPPED 1929
BF 866	CLYDE	97	36	35	86'	1907	TO CARGO 1921 - WRECKED NEAR FRASERBURGH 1924
BF 715	MARITANA	97	36	35	86'	1907	BCK 408 - WRECKED OFF EYEMOUTH 1927
BF 579	COMMONWEALTH	97	37	35	86'	1907	TYNET BCK 160 - SUNK NORTH MINCH 1928
LK 491	MAYFLOWER	97	37	35	86'	1907	INS 75 - SCRAPPED 1937

MONTROSE SHIPBUILDING COMPANY LIMITED - MONTROSE STEEL DRIFTERS

REG NO	NAME	G.R.T.	N.T.	H.P.	LENGTH	YR BUILT	HISTORY
BF 840	THRUSH	92	39	25	84. 5'	1907	BCK 186, PD 290 - SCRAPPED MARCH 1951
BF 753	BRUCE'S	92	39	25	84. 7'	1907	FR 62 - SCRAPPED 1952
BF 960	OCEAN STAR	92	39	25	84. 6'	1907	MINED OFF NAB LIGHT 26.9.17
BF 877	JEANNIE GILCHRIST	92	39	25	84. 7'	1907	CRANNOCH - SCRAPPED 1938
BF 1016	DAISY	92	39	25	84. 6'	1907	BCK 154 - SCRAPPED NOVEMBER 1950
LT 1056	VICTORIA	92	35	25	84. 4'	1907	PROFLUENT BCK 117 - SCRAPPED 1938
KY 300	CARMI III	88	36	39	86'	1908	J. T. HENDRY BCK 22, BF 42 - SCRAPPED APRIL 1951
KY 304	KILMANY	88	36	39	86'	1908	BF 1 - SCRAPPED 1938
BF 322	INVERBOYNDIE	89	37	35	86'	1910	ROSE IN BLOOM, SAPPHIRE - SCRAPPED APRIL 1951
BF 102	XMAS MORN	89	37	41	85. 6'	1914	FR 126 - SCRAPPED MARCH 1951
BCK 203	ADMIRABLE	90	37	41	85. 6'	1914	SUNK BY AUSTRIAN CRUISERS OFF FANO ISLANDS - ADRIATIC 15.5.17
BF 191	CLANS	89	37	41	85. 6'	1915	SCRAPPED JANUARY 1952
PD 238	PRIMROSE	89	37	41	85. 6'	1915	SCRAPPED DECEMBER 1952
R 355	LADY LUCK	95	39	34	87'	1920	SCRAPPED 1957
R 356	TWEENWAYS	95	39	34	87'	1920	

CARMI III KY 300 - Built of steel by Montrose Shipbuilding Co. Ltd. 1908. Became J. T. HENDRY BCK22 and BF42. Scrapped 1951, shown in Anstruther Harbour ca 1922. Courtesy of Scottish Fisheries Museum.

ANNEX V — LIVINGSTONE & COOPER LTD. - HESSLE, YORKSHIRE — STEEL DRIFTERS

REG NO	NAME	G.R.T.	N.T.	H.P.	LENGTH	YR BUILT	HISTORY
YH 25	THE MAJESTY	99	42	33	87. 7'	1914	FELLOWSHIP LT 65
YH 51	HERRING SEARCHER	99	42	33	87. 7'	1914	PD 79, BF 19, LT 276 - SCRAPPED 1954
YH 68	JACK SALMON	99	42	33	87. 7'	1914	YOUNG JACOB YH 68

J. CHAMBERS & COMPANY LIMITED - LOWESTOFT — STEEL DRIFTERS

REG NO	NAME	G.R.T.	N.T.	H.P.	LENGTH	YR BUILT	HISTORY
LT 343	OCEAN BREEZE	112	48	36	90. 6'	1927	CONVERTED TO MOTOR 1958 - TO GREECE 1975
LT 79	LORD ST. VINCENT	115	48	30	90'	1929	MINED THAMES ESTUARY 7.7.41
LT 44	LORD SUFFOLK	115	48	30	92'	1929	CONVERTED TO MOTOR 1959 - SCRAPPED 1976
LT 108	ASCONA	138	59	28	98'	1929	CONVERTED TO MOTOR 1958 - SCRAPPED 1970
LT 177	KINDRED STAR	115	49	29	92. 1'	1930	CONVERTED TO MOTOR 1954
LT 167	HOSANNA	132	62	28	96. 3'	1930	CONVERTED TO MOTOR 1960 - SCRAPPED 1976
LT 188	TRITONIA	115	52	50	92'	1930	CONVERTED TO MOTOR 1958 - SCRAPPED 1976
LT 168	ADVISABLE	115	52	50	92'	1930	SOLD TO CANADA 1954 - SCRAPPED 1975
LT 737	WILLING BOYS	138	59	28	98'	1930	CONVERTED TO MOTOR 1957 - SCRAPPED 1976

LORD SUFFOLK LT 44 - Rigged for trawling, built 1929 of steel by J. Chambers Ltd. of Lowestoft. Converted to motor 1959 and scrapped 1976. Courtesy of Scottish Fisheries Museum.

HOSANNA LT 167 - Rigged for trawling, built of steel by J. Chambers Ltd. of Lowestoft. converted to motor 1960 and scrapped 1976. Courtesy of Port of Lowestoft Research Society.

ANNEX V   COOK, WELTON & GEMMELL LIMITED - BEVERLEY STEEL DRIFTERS

REG NO	NAME	G.R.T.	N.T.	H.P.	LENGTH	YR BUILT	HISTORY
PD 498	WATCHFUL	88	38	33	82'	1903	GW 19 - AS HERRING CARRIER - SCRAPPED 1938
BF 1436	VALKYRIE	88	33	33	82'	1903	SCRAPPED 1935
YH 878	THE PRINCE	77	28	28	78'	1904	MAGNELPHYL BF 294 - SCRAPPED 1933
YH 879	THE PRINCESS	77	28	28	78'	1904	BF 40 - SCRAPPED 1937
H 548	W.J.COOK	94	34	20	82. 1'	1922	* SOLD TO SPAIN - SCRAPPED 1976
H 582	W.M.GEMMELL	94	35	20	82. 1'	1922	* SOLD TO SPAIN - SUNK 1976
H 600	C.K.WALTON	94	35	20	82. 1'	1922	* SOLD TO GREENLAND - SCRAPPED 1950
							* THESE THREE VESSELS WERE FITTED WITH ENGINES AND BOILERS TAKEN FROM SCRAPPED WOODEN STANDARD DRIFTERS

WATCHFUL GW 19 - Built of steel by Cook, Welton & Gemmell Ltd. Beverley 1903 as PD 498, scrapped 1938. Shown as WATCHFUL GW 19 as a herring carrier based on the Clyde. Courtesy of Scottish Fisheries Museum.

ANNEX V — DUTCH STEAM DRIFTERS — STEEL DRIFTERS

REG NO	NAME	G.R.T.	N.T.	H.P.	LENGTH	YR BUILT	WHERE BUILT	HISTORY
BF 1539	SWALLOW	85	35	30	81. 4'	1904	ZALT BOMMEL	BCK 351, FR 65, BF 226 - SCRAPPED 1952
PD 62	RENOWN	86	36	29	81. 4'	1904	ZALT BOMMEL	TO LONDON DERRY THEN BACK TO PETERHEAD, 1915 AS PD 225 - SCRAPPED 1937
PD 126	MAGGIE LEASK	94	39	35	86'	1904	AMBACHT	YH 199, GOLDEN SUNRAY KY 188, CHANCELOT - SCRAPPED 1937
LT 149	LEONARD	101	45	22	90. 6'	1913	LIEDERDORP	EX. HELGA, EGON AND MAJESTIC - SCRAPPED 1955
LT 151	BOY'S FRIEND	120	52	27	94'	1915	LIEDORDORP	EX. MARTINA, ANNIE - SCRAPPED 1955
LT 48	ALCMARIA	148	64	25	102. 1'	1916	LIEDORDORP	EX ZAANSTROOM IV, MASTROOM II, ARIA.
LT 178	PATRIA	148	66	25	102. 3'	1916	LIEDORDORP	EX. ATLANTIC, IRMA - SCRAPPED 1954
LT 152	THRIFTY	139	68	25	100. 4'	1916	LIEDORDORP	EX. FERNAND - CONVERTED TO MOTOR, FD 201, CATHERINE, SHAUN
LT 241	AMALIA	145	61	27	101. 7'	1917	LIEDERDORP	
LT 158	TRIER	136	61	25	100. 2'	1917	LIEDERDORP	EX.OCEANI, LISETTE, ZEELANDIA, ADOLPHINE - SCRAPPED 1955
LT 216	WEST HOLME	138	67	35	102. 4'	1918	ROTTERDAM	EX. WITTE ZEE
M 148	DILIMER	150	54	36	102. 2'	1918	LIEDORDORP	EX. MARIA ALDIA, MARIE LOUISE

BUILDERS WERE - J. MEIER - ZALT BOMMEL

UNKNOWN - AMBACHT

GEBRODERS BOOT - LEIDERDORP

M.S BURGERHOUTS NV - ROTTERDAM

SWALLOW BF 226 - Built of steel by J. Meier of Zalt Bommel, Holland 1904 as SWALLOW BF 1539.
Became BCK 351, FR 65, BF 226. Scrapped 1952. Courtesy of Scottish Fisheries Museum.

ANNEX V   A. HALL & COMPANY LIMITED - ABERDEEN   STEEL DRIFTERS

REG NO	NAME	G.R.T.	N.T.	H.P.	LENGTH	YR BUILT	HISTORY
INS 544	COMMODORE	88	33	30	83. 5'	1903	SCRAPPED 1938
PD 479	BUSY BEE	92	34	31	86. 1'	1903	BCK 444, PD 95 - SCRAPPED 1950
PD 470	ELLA	92	34	31	86'	1903	BF 259 - SCRAPPED 1936
PD 471	KATHLEEN	93	35	31	86. 1'	1903	SUNK BY SUBMARINE OFF START POINT 3.6.15
BF 34	FRIGATE BIRD	84	30	32	82. 1'	1905	BCK 68 - SUNK OFF MARSA SCIROCCO 11.3.18
PD 70	HONEY BEE	84	31	32	82. 1'	1905	KY 214 - SCRAPPED 1937
PD 96	HOPE	90	33	31	82'	1906	SCRAPPED 1951
BF 355	EBENEZER	83	36	32	82'	1906	INS 196, HALLMARK BCK 232 - SCRAPPED 1951
PD 122	OLIVE	89	33	31	86. 2'	1906	BCK 141 - SCRAPPED DECEMBER 1952
PD 506	ALERT	96	41	36	88. 4'	1907	BF 70 - SCRAPPED 1938
BF 710	HOLLY	90	37	33	86. 2'	1907	WRECKED AT BUCKIE 1921
PD 517	PROTECT ME	88	37	32	86. 5'	1908	SCRAPPED MARCH 1951
PD 513	FRAGRANT	94	40	32	86. 3'	1908	SCRAPPED 7.12.52
PD 519	LUPINA	88	37	32	86. 4'	1908	SCRAPPED 11.12.52
BCK 35	ROSE III	88	38	33	86. 4'	1908	WRECKED AT STRONSAY 1933
FR 263	TYRIE	93	39	34	86'	1908	BF 68, PD 77 - SCRAPPED MARCH 1951
FR 264	PITBLAE	93	39	34	86'	1908	PD 12, INS 357, GUIDE US PD 63 - SCRAPPED 1950
FR 274	ABERDOUR	93	39	34	86. 1'	1908	PD 26 SCRAPPED 1946
KY 283	GUERDON	89	39	33	86. 5'	1908	SOLD TO CAPETOWN 1920
INS 21	COVESEA	94	37	37	86. 4'	1909	DELIVERER BF 67 - SCRAPPED NOVEMBER 1950
BCK 49	REGENT BIRD	88	37	37	86. 5'	1909	BF 73 - SCRAPPED FEBRUARY 1951
BCK 46	BERYL II	88	37	27	86. 5'	1909	SCRAPPED JUNE 1951
INS 127	DEVOTION	88	37	37	86. 5'	1910	PD 113 - SCRAPPED NOVEMBER 1950
BCK 60	FORELOCK	89	37	39	86. 3'	1910	BCK 127 - SCRAPPED MAY 1952
BCK 87	LIZZIE FLETT	88	37	39	86. 4'	1910	SCRAPPED NOVEMBER 1950
INS 240	VALE OF MORAY	89	38	38	86. 8'	1911	PL 43, STEPHENS FR 292, DEVOTION PD 217 - TO NORWAY 31.7.54

ME 156	MARE	92	38	31	86'	1911	BCK 416 - LT 362
KY 116	COREOPSIS	88	39	39	86. 4'	1911	BCK 433 - SCRAPPED APRIL 1951
BCK 125	MINT	96	41	37	86. 5'	1912	LT 690, BCK 64, LT 98 - SUNK IRISH SEA 1948
BCK 127	SURMOUNT	96	41	37	86. 5'	1912	LT 994, M 231 - SCRAPPED 1954
BCK 157	POSEIDON	96	40	35	84. 4'	1912	LT 105, PD 12 - SCRAPPED 1954
KY 140	PLOUGH	95	40	39	86. 3'	1912	SOLD TO CAPETOWN, 1922
YH 730	OCEAN REWARD	95	35	42	86. 3'	1912	SUNK OFF DOVER 28.5.40
YH 345	OCEAN FISHER	96	38	34	86'	1913	MINED NORTH SEA 16.6.18
BF 19	RESPLENDENT	100	42	35	88'	1914	R 192 - SCRAPPED 1953
YH 725	OCEAN RAMBLER	96	37	34	86. 4'	1914	SCRAPPED 1955
INS 382	BRIGHTON O' THE NORTH	98	41	36	88'	1914	PD 389 - SCRAPPED 13.12.52
YH 6	CHESTNUT	107	42	35	88. 6'	1914	ADMIRALTY NAME MAIDA - MINED EAST COAST 16.3.40
KY 16	REFLORESCO	123	52	42	90'	1924	FEACO LT 201 - CONVERTED TO MOTOR 1955 - TO GHANA 1967
KY 293	WILLIAM WILSON	118	51	35	90. 2'	1929	M 90, SH 66 - TO SALVAGE WORK 1963
YH 29	OCEAN LIFEBUOY	131	56	39	94. 3'	1929	DEELITE - CONVERTED TO MOTOR 1958 - SCRAPPED 1973
YH 28	OCEAN SUNLIGHT	131	56	39	94. 3'	1929	MINED OFF NEWHAVEN 13.6.40
YH 84	OCEAN LUX	125	55	39	94. 3'	1930	DEELUX - CONVERTED TO MOTOR 1958 - SCRAPPED 1975
YH 88	OCEAN VIM	125	55	39	94. 3'	1930	SALLY McCABE - CONVERTED TO MOTOR 1958 - SCRAPPED 1976
KY 322	WILSON LINE	116	49	36	94. 2'	1932	YH 105 - CONVERTED TO MOTOR 1959 - SOLD TO GREECE 1975. THIS WAS THE LAST STEAM DRIFTER TO BE BUILT IN THE U.K.

BUSY BEE PD 95 - Built of steel by A. Hall & Co. of Aberdeen 1903 as BUSY BEE PD 479. Became BCK 444 then PD 95 - scrapped 1950. Shown here leaving Peterhead ca 1947. Courtesy of Aberdeen Libraries - Benzie Collection.

REFLORESCO KY 16 - Built of steel by A. Hall & Co. Ltd., Aberdeen 1924. Seen barking gear at Hartlepools ca 1930s after a great line trip. Later became FEACO LT207 and was converted to motor 1955 and sold to Ghana 1967. Courtesy of Scottish Fisheries Museum.

FEACO LT 207 - Ex REFLORESCO KY 16 after conversion to motor 1955. Seen here leaving Aberdeen for a herring boxing trip ca 1956. Courtesy of Scottish Fisheries Museum.

BRIGHTON O' THE NORTH PD 389 - Built of steel by A. Hall & Co. Ltd. Aberdeen 1914 as INS 382. Became PD 389, shown as PD 389 ca 1948. Courtesy of Scottish Fisheries Museum.

WILSON LINE KY 322 - Built of steel by A. Hall & Co. Ltd. of Aberdeen 1932. Became YH 105, was converted to motor 1959 and sold to Greece 1975, was the last Steam Drifter to be built in U.K. Shown here at Aberdeen ca 1954 after having been sold to Gt. Yarmouth. Courtesy of Scottish Fisheries Museum.

ANNEX V   STEEL DRIFTERS
CALEDON SHIP BUILDING & ENGINEERING COMPANY LIMITED - DUNDEE

REG NO	NAME	G.R.T.	N.T.	H.P.	LENGTH	YR BUILT	HISTORY
PD 182	GOOD TIDINGS	98	38	32	87. 1'	1907	SCRAPPED 1936
PD 217	FERTILE	96	38	32	87. 1'	1907	LY 37, PD 169, AR 1, LT 233
PD 322	DUTIFUL	98	38	32	87. 1'	1907	SOLD AS HERRING CARRIER
PD 334	DAISY	98	38	32	87. 1'	1907	SCRAPPED 1950
YH 7	KING HERRING	100	37	32	87. 1'	1909	LT 401
LT 1136	CYCLAMEN	94	39	35	87. 2'	1911	SCRAPPED 1957

REG NO	NAME	G.R.T.	N.T.	H.P.	LENGTH	YR BUILT	HISTORY
A428	CHARITY	102	40	26	90. 4'	1901	INS 40 - DISAPPEARED BETWEEN GREAT YARMOUTH AND POOLE 24.10.15
BF 1321	ROBIN	86	32	25	81. 2'	1903	SUNK NORTH SEA 1924
BF 1269	LIBERTY	86	33	30	81. 5'	1903	SCRAPPED 1938
INS 557	SUBLIME	86	33	30	81. 2'	1903	BF 446 - SCRAPPED 1951
BF 1459	SUCCESS	88	34	27	81. 2'	1904	BCK 324 - SCRAPPED 1936
BF 1444	WHITE LILY	87	33	27	81. 4'	1904	BCK 146, INS 190 - SCRAPPED 1937
BF 1474	VIOLET	86	36	27	86. 8'	1904	SCRAPPED 1937
BF 1513	RESEARCH	89	36	30	81. 4'	1904	SUNK BY SUBMARINE OFF OUTER SKERRIES 23. 6.15
BF 1515	CHOICE	89	33	25	81. 4'	1904	LOST 1910
BF 1512	LIVONIA	89	36	30	81. 4'	1904	BCK 172 - LOST SOUTH MINCH 1934
BF 1501	FRUITFUL	89	38	30	81. 4'	1904	BCK 194 - SCRAPPED 1936
BF 1528	LADYSMITH	89	36	30	81. 4'	1904	DISAPPEARED OFF MILFORD HAVEN 27.12.15
BF 1568	UNITY	88	35	30	81. 7'	1904	SCRAPPED 1936
BF 32	VICTORY	88	32	25	81. 4'	1905	BCK 427
PD 132	GUIDING STAR	93	34	26	84'	1906	SCRAPPED 1950
PD 120	SPARKLING STAR	90	34	25	81. 1'	1906	BF 91 - SCRAPPED 1938
PD 116	MARY STEPHEN	89	34	25	81. 1'	1906	NELLIE MORRISON, BF 13BCK 40 - SCRAPPED 1937
BF 172	DILIGENCE	85	33	27	81. 3'	1906	KY 164, BK 296, BF 511 - SCRAPPED 1936
FR 169	QUEEN	93	34	26	84'	1906	YH 83, R 143, BCK 249 - SCRAPPED 1937
FR 200	CHILDREN'S TRUST	95	40	26	83. 3'	1907	PD 35 - SCRAPPED 1937
FR 211	PHILORTH	100	39	35	86. 5'	1907	SANK BETWEEN SYRIA AND MALTA 24.2.19
FR 235	EXCEL	103	43	36	86. 5'	1907	R 373, LT 70 - SCRAPPED 1937
FR 237	MORNING STAR	97	41	28	86'	1907	MINED OFF BRINDISI 8.1.16
BF 927	CAMPERDOWN	91	33	28	84. 1'	1907	KY 150, BCK 423 - INS 54 - SCRAPPED 1937
INS 401	GLENGYNACK	91	41	26	84'	1907	ROSEISLE FR 357 - SCRAPPED 1951
PD 207	GRATEFUL	107	41	38	89. 2'	1907	INS 322, INVER B 659, CLOVERDALE BF 170 - SCRAPPED APRIL 1951
A 166	ISCO	100	42	28	86. 1'	1907	INS 210, ABIDING BCK 449 - SCRAPPED 1937
BF 766	TREASURE	96	41	26	84'	1907	BCK 204 - SH 112 -GY 92 - R 37 - SCRAPPED 1949
BF 756	MIGNONETTE	96	37	26	83. 7'	1907	SCRAPPED 1937
PD 315	MAGGIE	96	37	26	84'	1907	BF 424 - SCRAPPED 1936
BF 511	PROTECT	98	41	26	86'	1907	MINED OFF DOVER 16.3.17
BF 1028	SUPPORT	100	42	27	86. 1'	1907	BF 181 - SCRAPPED 1935
PD 512	KATE BAIRD	98	37	28	84'	1908	MORMOND HILL FR 584 -HL.61 - HELEN BOWIE BCK 432 - SUNK NORTH SEA 1934
FR 270	DAISY II	100	42	28	86'	1908	BCK 164, PD 92 - SCRAPPED 1950
FR 272	ERASTUS	100	42	28	86'	1908	PD 121 - SCRAPPED 1950
FR 271	CLARION	100	42	28	86. 4'	1908	BF 95, CRAIGLYNNE, INS 231 - SCRAPPED 1938
FR 268	FAIR ISLE	97	41	28	84'	1908	SCRAPPED 1937
FR 308	BROCH	90	38	28	84'	1908	SCRAPPED 1938
FR 310	JEANNIE ROBERTSON	93	39	28	86'	1908	THAINS BCK 220 - SCRAPPED 1950
PD 525	VERDURE	97	41	28	84'	1908	FR 557 - SCRAPPED1937
FR 298	ST COMBS	90	38	28	84'	1908	BF 27, FR 367, GY 11, OCEAN SEARCHER FR 75 - SCRAPPED 1953
FR 296	PHINGASK	97	41	28	84'	1908	HEATHERVALE BF 225 - SCRAPPED 1938

REG NO	NAME	G.R.T.	N.T.	H.P.	LENGTH	YR BUILT	HISTORY
BCK 40	MAGNET III	92	39	28	86'	1908	GREAT HOPE LT 697, BRAES O' ENZIE, BCK 28 - SCRAPPED 1938
BCK 50	CRAIGBO	94	30	40	86'	1909	SOLD AS SALVAGE VESSEL 1945
FR 44	ARDLAW	94	40	28	86'	1909	BCK 79 - SCRAPPED 1938
INS 50	G. M. B.	93	39	28	86	1909	FD 422, LINDUSTRIE BF 73 - SCRAPPED 1938
BCK 69	BRAES O' BUCKIE	84	35	28	81'	1910	PD 276 - SCRAPPED 1952
INS 118	HEATHERY BRAE	90	37	28	86'	1910	BF 105, FR 41, M 170, TO SALVAGE 1952 - SUNK 1953
INS 115	COULLARD BANK	91	37	31	84. 4'	1910	BCK 144 - SCRAPPED 1952
INS 126	MAGGIE GAULT	91	38	33	86'	1910	BCK 100 - SCRAPPED 1952
INS 148	ORD HILL	90	37	33	86. 1'	1910	WESTHAVEN FR 542 - SCRAPPED 1952
INS 149	WHINNY KNOWE	91	38	31	85. 8'	1910	STRATHBEG FR 387 - SCRAPPED 1951
INS 248	NORTHERN SCOT	90	38	31	84'	1911	A 225, FR 14, PD 151 - SCRAPPED 1952
BF 328	SPEEDWELL V	92	38	40	86'	1911	WRECKED OFF GREENORE POINT 1916
BF 388	FANNY MAIR	84	35	28	81. 2'	1911	CRANNOCH - SCRAPPED 1950
BF 390	BETSY SLATER	84	35	28	81. 2'	1911	SCRAPPED 1951
INS 256	BELLE O' MORAY	83	35	28	81'	1911	BF 348, PD 115 - SCRAPPED 1952
INS 224	MAID O' MORAY	84	35	28	81. 2'	1911	HEATHERY RIDGE BF 233, INS 150, MAID OF MORAY, WEALTH OF THE OCEAN FR 280 - SCRAPPED 1951
KY 134	ANDRINA	92	38	43	86'	1911	PD 599, ROSSARD FR 27, PD 382 - SCRAPPED MAY 1952
LT 1118	IMPREGNABLE	108	48	42	86. 4'	1911	SCRAPPED 1957
BCK 157	POSEIDON	96	40	35	86.4'	1912	PD 12 - CEASED FISHING 1954
BF 495	THREE KINGS	98	41	34	86'	1912	LT 517 - SCRAPPED 1946
BF 496	SWIFTWING	98	41	34	86'	1912	LT 657 - SCRAPPED 1946
BF 425	ADORATION	93	38	42	85. 8'	1912	PD 141, BK 57 - SCRAPPED 1954
BF 484	UBERTY	93	39	42	86'	1912	R 219 - BOMBED AND SUNK OFF LOWESTOFT 1941
ME 195	SOUTH ESK	93	39	30	86'	1912	MINED OFF AUSKERRY SOUND 1917
LT 1175	YOUNG SID	100	45	25	86'	1912	SUNK OF MORAY FIRTH 1940
LT 1175	YOUNG SID	100	45	25	86'	1912	SANK OFF MORAY FIRTH 1940
LT 1187	S. D. J.	100	46	25	87. 2'	1912	
LT 1176	LANNER	103	43	42	89. 7'	1912	
LT 1191	FEASIBLE	103	46	25	86'	1913	R 157, LT 122
YH 708	JOHN ROBERT	89	37	28	81'	1913	MINED OFF CAPE KARADASS 1919
ME 224	NORTH ESK	100	42	30	86. 1'	1913	BCK 66, CONVERTED TO MOTOR COASTER SHAPINSAY - WRECKED 1966
LT 136	MICHAELMAS DAISY	99	43	25	86. 1'	1913	MINED OFF SANTA MARIA DI LEUCA 1916
BCK 181	QUARRY KNOWE	98	41	43	87. 8'	1914	SUNK BY AUSTRIAN CRUISERS OFF FANO ISLAND ADRIATIC 1917
BCK 185	PRIME	101	41	42	87. 8'	1914	A 572, LT 77 - SCRAPPED 1961
BCK 102	MILL O' BUCKIE	99	41	42	86'	1914	R 129 - SCRAPPED 1957
LT 345	PRIMEVERE	100	44	25	86. 1'	1914	SCRAPPED 1960
LT 336	WIVENHOE	100	42	25	86'	1914	COASTBREEZE - SCRAPPED 1957
LT 437	HOLLYDALE	99	42	25	86. 1'	1914	SH 354, LT 1204, FR 86, PECHEUR LT 228 - SCRAPPED 1956
LT 469	D. H. S.	100	46	25	86. 2'	1915	DEWY ROSE FR 187 - LOST 1944 O.H.M.S.
LT 746	MARGARET HIDE	161	68	56	103. 5'	1920	SCRAPPED 1955
LT 1215	ARTHUR GOULBY	162	68	56	103. 8'	1921	SARAH HIDE LT 1157 - SCRAPPED 1955

PHINGASK FR 296 - Built of steel by Torry Shipbuilding Co. (J. Duthie) of Aberdeen 1908.
Became HEATHERVALE BF 225 - scrapped 1938.

MARGARET HIDE LT 746 - Built by J. Duthie of Aberdeen 1920. Entering Lowestoft ca 1948. Scrapped 1955.
Note ventilators forward of funnel denoting stoke hold is at forward end of boiler.

ANNEX V   JOSEPH T. ELTRINGHAM & Co. - SOUTH SHIELDS   STEEL DRIFTERS

REG NO	NAME	G.R.T.	N.T.	H.P.	LENGTH	YR BUILT	HISTORY
SD 61	ELLA	92	34	22	80'	1901	WK 709 - TO SPAIN 1920
SD 62	FLORA	92	34	22	80'	1901	WK 719 - TO SPAIN 1920
SSS 2	NORTH TYNE	79	28	35	80'	1904	VESPER STAR LT 94, BCK 439 - SCRAPPED 1936
SN	SOUTH TYNE	79	28	35	80'	1904	ML 83 - M 60
LT 1048	TEST	91	39	30	82. 4'	1907	REDCAR MH 61, MORAY DALE INS 61 - SCRAPPED 1935
INS 405	UBEROUS	97	42	20	86'	1907	M 87 - SCRAPPED 1950

ELLA WK 709 at Wick ca 1910 - Built by J. T. Eltringham of South Shields 1901 as ELLA SD61. Sold to Spain 1920.
Courtesy of Scottish Fisheries Museum.

ANNEX V PHILIP & SON - DARTMOUTH, DEVON STEEL DRIFTERS

REG NO	NAME	G.R.T.	N.T.	H.P.	LENGTH	YR BUILT	HISTORY
LT 317	ZOE	65	34	24	76. 6'	1901	WK 653 - SCRAPPED 1934
LT 987	INTERNOS	90	34	25	80. 2'	1903	INS 32 - SCRAPPED 1936
LT 977	COMMERCE	63	34	25	86. 5'	1903	CONSTANCY BF 373 - SCRAPPED 1932
LT 522	SEAFLOWER	80	40	21	84'	1906	WY 246
LT 1066	TRY AGAIN	97	41	34	87. 4'	1907	
LT 1168	SEDULOUS	100	42	35	88. 8'	1912	YH 2, INS 3, LT 56, CONVERTED TO MOTOR - SCRAPPED 1969

HALL, RUSSELL & COMPANY LIMITED - ABERDEEN STEEL DRIFTERS

REG NO	NAME	G.R.T.	N.T.	H.P.	LENGTH	YR BUILT	HISTORY
PD 509	LEBANON	106	45	45	90. 1'	1907	A441 - SUNK BY SUBMARINE OFF MUCKLE FLUGGA 1915
PD 138	EXPERT	100	39	38	86. 3'	1907	SCRAPPED 1950
PD 144	GUIDE ME II	100	37	38	86. 3'	1907	SUNK OFF MUGLINS 1918
PD 145	JEANNIES	100	39	38	86. 1'	1907	SCRAPPED 1951
PD 149	PEGGY	100	39	38	86. 3'	1907	SCRAPPED 1938
PD 176	ROSEBUD	100	39	38	86. 3'	1907	SCRAPPED 1952
PD 368	ENTERPRISE	100	36	41	86. 2'	1907	LOST 1921
PD 378	INDUSTRY	100	36	41	86. 2'	1907	SCRAPPED 1945
BF 965	KIMBERLEY	102	39	38	86. 5'	1907	PD 399, KY 102 - SCRAPPED 1937
FR 220	OCEANIC	99	40	38	86. 3'	1907	BCK 428, FR 10 - SCRAPPED 1936
FR 221	PITULLIE	99	40	38	86. 4'	1907	EXCELSA BF 14 - SCRAPPED 1936
ME 167	SWIFT	101	39	41	86. 5'	1907	BCK 240 - SCRAPPED 1937
PD 526	THE BRAE	77	37	34	82. 4'	1908	SCRAPPED 1937
PD 527	STAR OF BETHLEHEM	77	37	34	82. 4'	1908	SUNK BY SUBMARINE OFF THE OUTER SKERRIES 1915
BF 236	LASS O' DOUNE	92	33	41	86'	1910	1920 - 1945 - PILOT CUTTER, LASS O' DOUNE SA 116 - WRECKED SOUTH COAST 1947
BF 251	LOCH CRAIG	91	35	41	86. 1'	1910	SCRAPPED 1937

INDUSTRY PD 378 - Built of steel by Hall, Russell & Co. Ltd. Aberdeen 1907. Scrapped 1945.
Shown leaving Lowestoft ca 1910. Courtesy of Scottish Fisheries Museum.

PEGGY PD 149 ca 1909 - Built of steel by Hall, Russell & Co. of Aberdeen 1907. Scrapped 1938.
Courtesy of Scottish Fisheries Museum.

ANNEX V   STEEL DRIFTERS
LARNE SHIPBUILDING COMPANY LIMITED - LARNE, COUNTY ANTRIM

REG NO	NAME	G.R.T.	N.T.	H.P.	LENGTH	YR BUILT	HISTORY
PD 520	PRINCIPAL	91	33	39	87. 2'	1908	SCRAPPED 1951

R. COCK - APPLEDORE, DEVON   STEEL DRIFTERS

REG NO	NAME	G.R.T.	N.T.	H.P.	LENGTH	YR BUILT	HISTORY
YH 999	PROVIDER	99	35	25	86. 6'	1907	LT 42, R 19
YH 358	KIPPER	92	32	30	87'	1908	LT 1111 - SCRAPPED 1938

DUNDEE SHIPBUILDING COMPANY LIMITED - DUNDEE   STEEL DRIFTERS

REG NO	NAME	G.R.T.	N.T.	H.P.	LENGTH	YR BUILT	HISTORY
PD 363	BLUEBELL	94	35	37	86'	1907	OPHIRLAND BF 131 - SCRAPPED 1938
PD 362	DAFFODIL	94	35	37	86'	1907	SCRAPPED 1946
PD 183	IVY	94	36	30	86'	1907	SOLD TO PORTUGAL 1920
PD 203	ELIZABETH	94	35	30	86'	1907	SUNK BY SUBMARINE OFF OUTER SKERRIES 1915
PD 213	NELLIE REID	94	35	37	86'	1907	INS 362, BF 72, FR 841, COLLIEBURN PD 73, ALACRITAS FR 85, PD 91 - SCRAPPED 1938
PD 202	ANNIE	94	35	30	86'	1907	FR 420 - WRECKED OFF ENOS 1917
PD 386	VIVID	94	35	30	86'	1907	ELGAR PD 386 - SCRAPPED 1936
PD 410	WINCHESTER	94	35	30	86'	1907	WRECKED WEST COAST OF SCOTLAND 1933
PD 197	LOTTIE LEASK	94	35	30	86'	1907	SN 184 - SUNK BY SUBMARINE OFF SASENO ISLANDS 1915
PD 357	BRITANNIA	94	35	37	86'	1907	SOLD TO TYNE PILOTAGE, SOUTH SHIELDS 1921
BF 919	ONWARD	94	35	39	86'	1907	SCRAPPED 1950
BF 765	CORMORANT	94	35	37	86'	1907	SCRAPPED 1936
KY 217	MAGDALEN	94	35	37	86'	1907	LOST 1922
ME 38	CELURCA	94	40	38	86. 2'	1916	BCK 41, INVERCAIRN FR 305, LT 110 - SCRAPPED 1956

STEEL DRIFTERS   RITCHIE, GRAHAM & MILNE - WHITEINCH, GLASGOW

REG NO	NAME	G.R.T.	N.T.	H.P.	LENGTH	YR BUILT	HISTORY
BF 1277	HYSSOP	88	32	20	80'	1903	INS 77 - SCRAPPED 1937

STEEL DRIFTERS   SCOTT OF BOWLING - DUMBARTON

REG NO	NAME	G.R.T.	N.T.	H.P.	LENGTH	YR BUILT	HISTORY
GY 906	DON PEDRO	67	31	15	72'	1914	YH 441, INS 59 - SCRAPPED 1929

STEEL DRIFTERS
R AND W. HAWTHORN LESLIE & Co.,LTD. - HEPBURN ON TYNE

REG NO	NAME	G.R.T.	N.T.	H.P.	LENGTH	YR BUILT	HISTORY
SN 254	NELLIE	109	40	39	93. 6'	1898	
SN 255	T.W.MOULD	109	17	45	91	1898	
SN 258	RHODESIA	110	41	33	93. 5'	1898	
SN 259	VALENTIA	110	41	33	93. 5'	1898	YH 60

ANNEX V   COOK WELTON & GEMMELL LIMITED - HULL   STEEL DRIFTERS

REG NO	NAME	G.R.T.	N.T.	H.P.	LENGTH	YR BUILT	HISTORY
H 528	SHIELDS	72	30	17	76'	1901	SCRAPPED 1924
H 529	GRIMSBY	72	30	17	76'	1901	YH 444, LT 913 - SCRAPPED 1924

GEORGE COOPER OF HULL   STEEL DRIFTERS

REG NO	NAME	G.R.T.	N.T.	H.P.	LENGTH	YR BUILT	HISTORY
BF 1402	EARN	80	37	20	78. 4'	1903	EARNMORE - SCRAPPED 1933
BF 1396	WALLFLOWER	80	37	20	78. 4'	1903	WRECKED NEAR MALLAIG 1914

STEEL DRIFTERS
GOOLE SHIPBUILDING & REPAIRING COMPANY LIMITED - GOOLE - YORKS

REG NO	NAME	G.R.T.	N.T.	H.P.	LENGTH	YR BUILT	HISTORY
LT 390	LORD RODNEY	104	45	44	88'	1928	LT 79, A 50, CONVERTED TO MOTOR 1958 - SCRAPPED 1976
LT 183	LORD COLLINGWOOD	116	51	30	92. 3'	1930	CONVERTED TO MOTOR - SCRAPPED 1970
LT 181	LORD KEITH	116	51	30	92. 3'	1930	CONVERTED TO MOTOR 1957 - TO GREECE 1975
LT 246	NEVES	122	62	36	94. 1'	1931	FELLOWSHIP - CONVERTED TO MOTOR 1955 - SOLD TO GREECE 1975

NEVES LT 246 - Built of steel 1931 by Goole Shipbuilding & Repairing Co. Ltd. Goole, later renamed FELLOWSHIP LT 246. Converted to motor 1955. Sold to Greece 1975. Courtesy of Port of Lowestoft Research Society.

STEEL DRIFTERS   J. DUTHIE & COMPANY LIMITED - MONTROSE

REG NO	NAME	G.R.T.	N.T.	H.P.	LENGTH	YR BUILT	HISTORY
A 59	WHITE QUEEN	126	49	34	92.85'	1897	BUILT AS YACHT,TO FISHING 1899, KY 94 - SCRAPPED 1934
A 8	ROSLIN	128	52	35	95.4'	1899	SUNK BY SUBMARINE GUNFIRE 24.7.15
PD 389	ROSE	77	37	20	79.1'	1900	SOLD TO LIVERPOOL AS A BARGE
PD 390	THISTLE	77	37	20	79.1'	1900	SOLD AS A LIGHTER

WHITE QUEEN KY 94 - Built of steel by J. Duthie & Co. Ltd. Montrose 1897 as a pleasure craft. Converted to fishing 1899 as A 59 then KY 94. Scrapped 1934. Shown in Gt. Yarmouth River. Courtesy of Scottish Fisheries Museum.

ANNEX V GIBBS - GALMPTON, DEVON STEEL DRIFTERS

REG NO	NAME	G.R.T.	N.T.	H.P.	LENGTH	YR BUILT	HISTORY
SN 343	URSULA	72	44	20	80' 1"	1902	
SN 350	NELLY	75	26	20	80'	1903	

COCHRANE & SONS LIMITED - SELBY, YORKS STEEL DRIFTERS

REG NO	NAME	G.R.T.	N.T.	H.P.	LENGTH	YR BUILT	HISTORY
BF 1345	BLOEMFONTEIN	87	35	26	82'	1903	BCK 151 - SCRAPPED 1936
LT 998	SELBY	75	32	20	78. 8'	1903	PD 123 - SUNK BY AUSTRIAN CRUISERS OFF FANO ISLAND, ADRIATIC 15.5.17
YH 709	THE CROWN	80	29	20	82'	1904	
BF 886	VINE	95	36	40	86'	1907	BCK 412 - SCRAPPED 1937
PD 217	CITY OF LONDON	88	32	32	84'	1907	YH 301, GY 1346, PD 45, YH 57 OCEAN RANGER, BCK 45, FR 149, TRV AT ANSTRUTHER W.W. II - SCRAPPED 1951
PD 228	CITY OF EDINBURGH	88	32	32	84'	1907	YH 311, GY 1350, PD 49 - LATER RESEARCH VESSEL
PD 239	CITY OF HULL	88	32	32	84'	1907	YH 185, GY 1351
PD 224	CITY OF PERTH	88	32	32	84'	1907	YH 203, GY 1348
PD 263	CITY OF LIVERPOOL	88	32	32	84'	1907	YH 244 - MINED OFF SOUTH FORELAND 31.7.18
PD 286	CITY OF GLASGOW	88	32	32	84'	1907	YH 204, GY 1347
PD 296	CITY OF BELFAST	88	32	32	84'	1907	YH 208
PD 299	CITY OF ABERDEEN	88	32	32	84'	1907	ATTAIN BCK 453 - SCRAPPED 1949
LT 1046	LORD CHARLES BERESFORD	81	29	30	82'	1907	BCK 265 - SCRAPPED 1937
LT 1047	LORD CLAUDE HAMILTON	81	29	30	82'	1907	BCK 345 - SCRAPPED 1937

REG NO	NAME	G.R.T.	N.T.	H.P.	LENGTH	YR BUILT	HISTORY
H 950	FRASERBURGH	83	36	32	82'	1907	FR 950, PD 20, A. J. BUCHAN FR 70 - TO SALVAGE AT STRANRAER 1940 - SR1- MALTA 1947
LT 63	SUSSEX COUNTY	83	40	32	84. 2'	1908	
LT 103	NORFOLK COUNTY	83	35	32	84. 2'	1908	
BCK 67	SCOTCH GIRL	76	32	30	80. 1'	1910	TRANSCEND BCK 67, PD 69 - SCRAPPED NOVEMBER 1950
LT 750	SUPERNAL	83	35	32	83.2'	1910	GOLDEN MILLER LT 750 - SCRAPPED 1956
LT 623	LORD LEITRUM	78	36	28	80. 1'	1910	TRIPP M 62, WEST NEUK INS 539, BF 375 - SCRAPPED 3.51
LT	INCENTIVE	83	35	32	83.3'	1910	MISSING PRESUMED LOST 1915
LT 677	TORBAY II	83	35	32	83. 2'	1910	YH 103 - BOMBED OFF DOVER 1.11.40
LT 661	WISHFUL	83	35	32	83. 2'	1910	WY 247
LT 593	GOLDEN RING	83	35	32	83. 2'	1910	
LT 770	BEACON STAR	99	45	25	88'	1911	LOST ENGLISH CHANNEL 1937
LT 1158	CONSTANT STAR	98	43	35	88'	1911	PD 38 - CEASED FISHING DECEMBER 1954
LT 1141	LORD HALDANE	91	40	30	84'	1911	SUNK BRISTOL CHANNEL 12.9.40
LT 1143	LORD WENLOCK	91	40	30	84'	1911	CONVERTED TO MOTOR - TO GHANA 1963
LT 1129	KENT COUNTY	86	39	32	84'	1911	MINED OFF CROSS SAND, LOWESTOFT 8.12.16
LT 1124	E. W. B.	95	42	35	87'	1911	SCRAPPED IN BELGIUM 1955
LT 1116	PARAMOUNT	95	42	35	87'	1911	R 193
LT 1166	EAGER	102	47	35	88'	1912	CONVERTED TO MOTOR, FD 50, TO GHANA 1963 - SANK 1972
LT 1179	SILVER LINE	92	40	33	84. 4'	1912	SH 50
LT 1177	PLOUGH BOY	102	47	35	88'	1912	
LT 1173	HILDA AND ERNEST	102	47	35	88'	1912	BOY NAT R 116, AVAILABLE LT 1298, BCK 440, FR 167 - SCRAPPED 1952
YH 245	R. R. S.	159	73	25	110' 1'	1913	
YH 50	ENGLISH ROSE	188	82	25	115. 1'	1914	
H 404	ADELIA	97	35	20	85. 1'	1922	* SOLD TO BELGIUM GY 294, SCATTAN, LT 8 DICKETA - SCRAPPED 1959
H 477	TELIA	97	35	20/42	85. 1'	1922	* SOLD TO BELGIUM, RE-ENGINED, PEACE WAVE LT 47 - SCRAPPED 1955
H 478	OLEARIA	97	35	20/45	85. 1'	1922	* SOLD TO BELGIUM
H 421	COLUTEA	97	35	20	85. 1'	1922	* SOLD TO BELGIUM, ALCOR, LT 140
H 425	BIOTA	97	35	20	85. 1'	1922	* SOLD TO BELGIUM THEN CICERO LT 141
H 495	AREA	97	35	20	85. 1'	1922	* SOLD TO FRANCE
H 504	EXTENSION	97	35	20	85. 1'	1922	* SOLD TO FRANCE
H 471	MYRICA	97	35	20	85. 1'	1922	* SOLD TO ICELAND
H 496	BERBERIS	97	35	20	85. 1'	1922	* SOLD TO BELGIUM
H 435	DEUTZIA	97	35	20	85. 1'	1922	* SOLD TO BELGIUM
H 469	FORSYTHIA	97	35	20	85. 1'	1922	* SOLD TO BELGIUM
H 498	COLEUS	97	35	20	85. 1'	1922	* SOLD TO BELGIUM
H 551	SILENE	97	35	20	85. 1'	1922	* SOLD TO BELGIUM THEN TO ICELAND 1927
H 804	RIBES	97	34	20	85. 1'	1922	* SOLD TO BELGIUM
YH 69	A. ROSE	208	100	46	120. 1'	1924	SOLD TO NORWAY 1946
YH 141	PLAYMATES	96	41	27	88. 5'	1925	LT 180 - LOST OFF LAND'S END 1950
LT 222	FAIRBREEZE	96	41	27	88. 5'	1925	YH 65 - SUNK OFF DUNKIRK 1.6.40

FR 123	SHEPHERD LAD	98	45	43	87'	1925	LT 7 - SCRAPPED 1960
LT 240	MARINUS	96	41	27	88. 5'	1925	JUSTIFIED LT 240 - MINED OFF MALTA 6.6.42
LT 224	JUSTIFIER	97	42	27	88. 5'	1925	SCRAPPED 1958
LT 211	LORD BARHAM	97	42	27	88. 5'	1925	LEASED TO POLAND 1946, LT 55 ON RETURN - SCRAPPED 1960
LT 215	LORD HOOD	96	41	27	86. 5'	1925	LEASED TO POLAND 1946, LT 20 ON RETURN - SCRAPPED 1960
LT 344	LORD ANSON	100	42	27	88. 5'	1927	SCRAPPED 1957
LT 238	STERNUS	95	41	25	88. 5'	1927	CONVERTED TO MOTOR 1954, SWIFTWING LT 238, HL 147 - SCRAPPED 1970
LT 323	FAITHFUL STAR	98	44	35	88. 5'	1927	CONVERTED TO MOTOR 1952 - WRECKED ORFORD NESS 1957
LT 324	ONE ACCORD	99	43	35	88'	1927	CONVERTED TO MOTOR 1960 - SCRAPPED 1970
YH 392	HILDA COOPER	127	55	46	94. 3'	1928	CONVERTED TO MOTOR 1957, SPECIOUS - SCRAPPED 1968
YH 370	D'ARCY COOPER	127	55	46	94. 3'	1928	BOMBED OFF HARWICH 9.3.41
LT 381	LAURUS	98	41	43	88'	1928	LAUNCHED AS MOTOR VESSEL BUT SOON CONVERTED TO STEAM, SILVER CREST LT 46 - SCRAPPED 1960
LT 403	COMRADES	114	51	50	92'	1928	CONVERTED TO MOTOR 1955 SCRAPPED 1970
LT 201	QUIET WATERS	117	53	35	94. 1'	1931	PEACEFUL STAR LT 201 A 61 - CONVERTED TO MOTOR 1961
LT 235	SILVER SEAS	117	53	35	94. 1'	1931	CONVERTED TO MOTOR 1960, A 65 - SCRAPPED 1971
							* THESE VESSELS WERE FITTED WITH ENGINES AND BOILERS TAKEN FROM SCRAPPED WOODEN STANDARD DRIFTERS BUILT IN CANADA

A. ROSE YH 69 - Built of steel by Cochrane & Sons Ltd. Selby 1924. Probably the largest Steam Drifter ever built at 120.1' O.L. Note unusual position of steam capstan immediately in front of wheelhouse, this was moved to the normal position some time later. Courtesy of Port of Lowestoft Research Society.

LORD WENLOCK LT 1143 - Built by Cochrane & Sons Ltd Selby 1911show after conversion to Motor ca 1960.
Courtesy of Port of Lowestoft Research Society.

ANNEX V   STEEL DRIFTERS
FELLOWS & COMPANY LIMITED - SOUTH TOWN - GREAT YARMOUTH

REG NO	NAME	G.R.T.	N.T.	H.P.	LENGTH	YR BUILT	HISTORY
YH 380	CLAUDIAN	63	33	15	75'	1899	CONVERTED TO MOTOR 1914 THEN BACK TO STEAM 1915, LT 587
YH 447	TOGO	76	26	28	80. 3'	1905	LT 609, YH 248, LT 69, CONVERTED TO MOTOR 1936 - SCRAPPED 1964
BCK 15	PROMOTIVE	78	32	30	82. 5'	1908	MINED IN LOCH EWE 23.12.39
LT 361	RULER OF THE SEAS	86	28	31	84. 8'	1909	KIDDAW LT 361 - SCRAPPED 1951
YH 217	FRONS OLIVAE	98	34	28	87. 1'	1912	MINED OFF ELBOW BUOY 12.10.15
YH 370	COPIOUS	100	45	33	88'	1913	MINED OFF GREAT YARMOUTH 3.11.14
YH 42	CAISTER CASTLE	109	52	33	92'	1914	R 120
YH 73	OLIVAE	107	51	30	92'	1915	R 212, LT 1297 - SCRAPPED 1956
YH 73	ROSE HILDA	116	50	33	92. 3'	1930	CONVERTED TO MOTOR 1954, DAWN WATERS LT 90 - SCRAPPED 1970

KIDDAW LT 361 - Built of steel 1909 by Fellows & Co. of Southtown, Gt. Yarmouth as RULER OF THE SEAS LT 361.
Scrapped 1951. Courtesy of Port of Lowestoft Research Society.

OLIVAE LT 1297 - Built of steel by Fellows & Co. Ltd. Southtown, Gt. Yarmouth 1915. Was originally OLIVAE YH 73, R 212 before LT 1297. Scrapped 1936. Courtesy of Port of Lowestoft Research Society.

ANNEX V   STEEL DRIFTERS
SELBY SHIPBUILDING & ENGINEERING COMPANY LIMITED - SELBY - YORKS

REG NO	NAME	G.R.T.	N.T.	H.P.	LENGTH	YR BUILT	HISTORY
LT 981	JOE CHAMBERLAIN	79	27	26	77. 5'	1903	
LT 982	LORD MILNER	79	27	26	77. 5'	1903	
LT 1000	UNDAUNTED	79	35	18	77. 5'	1903	FR 382 SCRAPPED 1924
LT 1003	CORONET	79	38	20	77. 5'	1903	FR 11, PD 125 - SCRAPPED 1936
INS 546	FORTITUDE	86	31	32	80. 4'	1903	SUNK MORAY FIRTH 1924
INS 548	CARMI	86	31	32	80. 4'	1903	BF 256, LT 567 - SCRAPPED 1925
PD 472	BETSY	86	31	32	80. 4'	1903	SCRAPPED 1936
PD 473	W. H. LEASK	86	31	32	80. 4'	1903	BCK 108 - SCRAPPED 1938

STEEL DRIFTERS
CRABTREE & COMPANY LIMITED - SOUTHTOWN, GREAT YARMOUTH

REG NO	NAME	G.R.T.	N.T.	H.P.	LENGTH	YR BUILT	HISTORY
LT 1008	ALBATROSS	76	36	28	78'	1903	FR 478 - LOST 15.2.19
YH 853	PROGRESS	72	31	28	79. 8'	1904	JOE MUDD YH 853, HARVEST MOON R 148 - SUNK AS BLOCKSHIP 9.9.40
LT 442	KESTREL	75	36	31	79. 4'	1906	YH 187, R 7 - BOMBED OFF LUNDY LIGHT 28 3. 41
LT 552	FRIENDS	81	41	31	82. 4'	1906	SCRAPPED 1937
LT 1082	REAPER	90	38	31	84. 4'	1907	SCRAPPED 1938
LT 1068	DRAKE	90	38	31	84'	1907	RETRIEVE LK 56 - SCRAPPED 1937
LT 1055	LIBERTY	88	37	31	84'	1907	INS 46, LUSTRE GEM BF 69 - SCRAPPED 1936
LT 1096	RETRIEVER	90	38	31	84. 1'	1907	KY 34, SCORE HEAD LT 120 - SCRAPPED 1951
LT 59	DEWEY	84	37	31	84. 1'	1908	SUNK OFF ROYAL SOVEREIGN LIGHT VESSEL 12.8.17
LT 117	LORD CROMER	84	37	30	84. 1'	1908	LOST OFF OBAN 1930
LT 66	MAJESTY	84	39	31	84. 2'	1908	BF 174 - TO NORWAY 1946
LT 53	ROOKE	84	37	43	84. 2'	1909	SUNK OFF DEAL 3.8.16

CRABTREE & COMPANY LIMITED - SOUTHTOWN, GREAT YARMOUTH (CONTINUED)

REG NO	NAME	G.R.T.	N.T.	H.P.	LENGTH	YR BUILT	HISTORY
BCK 51	LASSIE II	88	29	31	82'	1909	BF 492 - SCRAPPED 1937
LT 655	SILVER QUEEN	84	38	32	84. 4'	1910	SUNK BY GERMAN DESTROYERS OFF DOVER 15.2.18
LT 741	ARCADY	85	39	31	82. 8'	1910	SCRAPPED 1951
LT 1125	ACCEPTABLE	82	37	32	84. 5'	1911	R 78, LT 1291 - SCRAPPED 1954
LT 1134	SHIPMATES	82	37	32	84. 4'	1911	BOMBED OFF DOVER 14.11.40
LT 756	BUCKLER	81	37	32	84. 4'	1911	SCRAPPED 1954
LT 1120	PRESENT HELP	82	37	32	84. 5'	1911	SCRAPPED 1953
YH 987	G. M. H.	88	42	32	84'	1911	LOCARNO LT 275 - SCRAPPED 1953
LT 758	VERA CREINA	80	35	32	83. 1'	1911	SCRAPPED 1955
LT 1121	EYRIE	84	35	25	84.5	1911	MINED OFF OUTER DOWSING 2.9.14
LT 1150	MERRY SPINNER	84	37	32	83. 1'	1911	TOUCHWOOD, MARINUS - TO NORWAY 1945
SM 325	BOY DANIEL	83	37	33	82. 8'	1912	REPAY LT 273 - SCRAPPED 1938
YH 665	FRED SALMON	102	46	35	89'	1912	OCEAN PLOUGH BK 417, STRIVE LT 133 - SCRAPPED 1952
YH 295	GIRL KATHLEEN	95	40	34	86'	1913	UNITED BOYS LT 53 - TO NORWAY 1946
LT 111	LOYAL STAR	95	40	34	86'	1913	R 246 - SCRAPPED 1953
LT 203	JOHN AND NORAH	95	40	34	86'	1913	VISCERIA GY 214 - SCRAPPED 1954
YH 779	TWIDDLER	99	42	33	87. 5'	1913	SUNK BY SUBMARINE OFF COQUET ISLAND 2.8.16
LT 62	GLEN HEATHER	95	40	34	85. 7'	1913	SCRAPPED 1948
LT 227	RECLAIM	95	40	34	86. 2'	1913	LOST 1937
LT 237	VERITY	100	47	35	87. 5'	1913	TO HOLLAND 1937
LT 102	CAMPANULA	95	40	34	86'	1913	LOST 1930
LT 276	GIRL GRACIE	95	40	35	86. 2'	1913	SUNK BY AUSTRIAN CRUISERS OFF FANO ISLAND, ADRIATIC 15.5.17
YH 29	OCREAN CREST II	99	42	33	87. 5'	1914	SUNK OFF SMITH'S KNOLL 1919
LT 420	GIRL MARGARET	99	42	35	87. 2'	1914	SCRAPPED 1947
YH 973	FLOANDI	99	42	33	87. 5'	1914	SOLD TO FRANCE 1926
LT 395	GARRIGIL	99	42	33	86. 8'	1914	R 267
YH 473	ADELE	100	43	33	86. 8'	1915	PW 3, LT 19 - SCRAPPED 1957
LT 137	BOY PHILLIP	128	56	39	92. 5'	1930	LATANIA GY 44, CONVERTED TO MOTOR 1957 - SCRAPPED 1970
LT 106	KENT COUNTY	128	52	39	92. 3'	1930	DUBLIN PILOT CUTTER - INISFAIL

STEEL DRIFTERS   RICHARD'S IRONWORKS - LOWESTOFT

REG NO	NAME	G.R.T.	N.T.	H.P.	LENGTH	YR BUILT	HISTORY
LT 253	MERBREEZE	120	53	28	93. 8'	1931	CONVERTED TO MOTOR 1959, LT 365 - SCRAPPED 1976 - LAST STEAM DRIFTER TO BE BUILT IN ENGLAND

STEEL DRIFTERS   COCHRANE & COOPER - BEVERLEY, YORKS

REG NO	NAME	G.R.T.	N.T.	H.P.	LENGTH	YR BUILT	HISTORY
LT 149	LORD ROBERTS	72	39	17	75. 1'	1900	
LT 150	GENERAL BULLER	72	39	17	75. 1'	1900	SUNK BY SUBMARINE OFF SUMBURGH HEAD 2.7.17
LT 151	GENERAL WHITE	72	39	17	75. 1'	1900	
LT 152	BADEN POWELL	72	39	17	75. 1'	1900	

WOOD, SKINNER & Co. - BILL QUAY ON TYNE STEEL DRIFTERS

REG NO	NAME	G.R.T.	N.T.	H.P.	LENGTH	YR BUILT	HISTORY
SN 210	ROSE	96	34	33	91. 4'	1896	LT 1754
HL 50	ST. HILDA	99	34	36	91. 6'	1897	SUNK BY SUBMARINE OFF SCARBOROUGH 25. 9. 16
SN 250	MERCIA	108	40	31	94'	1898	TO FRANCE 1912
HL 54	ST. MARY	99	36	36	91. 4'	1898	

STEEL DRIFTERS

KING'S LYNN SHIPBUILDING COMPANY LIMITED - KING'S LYNN

REG NO	NAME	G.R.T.	N.T.	H.P.	LENGTH	YR BUILT	HISTORY
YH 89	LYDIA EVA	139	64	41	95'	1930	SOLD TO AIR MINISTRY - WATCHMOOR - NOW OWNED BY MARITIME TRUST AND PRESERVED AT GT. YARMOUTH

STEEL DRIFTERS

LINERS AND TRAWLERS WHICH BECAME DRIFTERS - NOT INCLUDED PREVIOUSLY

REG NO	NAME	I/S	G.R.T.	N.T.	H.P.	LENGTH	YR BUILT	BUILDER	HISTORY
A 819	KITTY	S	135	49	50	96. 6'	1897	A. HALL ABERDEEN	SH 290, YH 250
A 782	CRAIGIEVAR	S	112	44	45	90. 3'	1896	A. HALL ABERDEEN	OCEAN'S SHIELD, LT 386
A 791	BRILLIANT STAR	S	108	49	45	96. 6'	1896	A. HALL ABERDEEN	SH 46
A 769	FRIGATE BIRD	S	99	40	40	87'	1895	HALL RUSSELL ABERDEEN	TO FRANCE 1926
A 424	LAPWING	S	124	47	45	96'	1896	HALL RUSSELL ABERDEEN	GOLDEN THOUGHT LT 110
A 770	BETTY INGLIS	S	109	44	45	90'	1895	HALL RUSSELL ABERDEEN	KY 14, A 445, BF 349 - SCRAPPED 1946
A 903	EVA	S	88	34	30	86. 5'	1893	A. HALL ABERDEEN	KY 109, HERMONA GY 4
FR 755	MORMOND	S	73		55	110'	1898	HALL RUSSELL ABERDEEN	A 293 - WRECKED NEAR DUNCANSBY HEAD 1916
A 798	CHINGKIANG	S	120	48	45	96. 3'	1896	A. HALL ABERDEEN	SOLD TO BANFF - SUNK BY SUB-MARINE OFF BUCHAN NESS 12.4.17
A 860	NORTH CAPE	S	122	46	50	95. 1'	1889	HALL RUSSELL ABERDEEN	SOLD TO PORTUGAL, RETURNED AS A560, GYII54, FR 239, B3 - HERRING CARRIER SCRAPPED 1925
A 747	NORTH AMERICAN	I	97	39	40	86. 7'	1894	HALL RUSSELL ABERDEEN	PD 485, HAZELDENE, BCK 104 - SCRAPPED 1938
A 746	NORTH BRITON	I	97	39	40	86. 7'	1894	HALL RUSSELL ABERDEEN	PD 487 - SCRAPPED CA 1950
ME 226	KITTY	S	181	47	55	105'	1898	COOK, WELTON & GEMMEL - HULL	SUNK BY SUBMARINE OFF ST. ABB'S HEAD 9.5.17
SH 903	CYGNET	I	105	46	40	94. 6'	1883	ELTRINGHAM SOUTH SHIELDS	ME 186 - SCRAPPED 1936

STEEL DRIFTERS
LINERS AND TRAWLERS WHICH BECAME DRIFTERS NOT INCLUDED PREVIOUSLY (CONTINUED)

REG NO	NAME	I/S	G.R.T.	N.T.	H.P.	LENGTH	YR BUILT	BUILDER	HISTORY
BN 187	KIRTON	I	125	51	35	92. 2'	1886	COCHRANE & COOPER - BEVERLEY	GN 42 - TO GREECE 1923
GN 300	RECTOR	I	112	47	44	88'	1891	COOK, WELTON & GEMMELL - HULL	CECIL RHODES, PD 458, YH 757 YH 328, PD 458 - SCRAPPED 1922
SN 59	CHANCELLOR	I	81	30	27	80'	1899	ELTRINGHAM SOUTH SHIELDS	PD 379 - SUNK 1913
PD 502	NORMAN	I	120	47	43	87. 4'	1894	COOK, WELTON & GEMMELL - HULL	GW 20, AS HERRING CARRIER - SCRAPPED 1950
SSS 7	ELLA	I	113	45	45	93'	1891	ELTRINGHAM SOUTH SHIELDS	BF 337, GOLDEN MONARCH, A 406, EVENING STAR - SUNK OFF MAY ISLAND 9.5.27
GY 620	LILLIAN	I	110	49	35	89. 7'	1894	COCHRANE & COOPER - BEVERLEY	BF 473, A 603 - SUNK BY SUBMARINE OFF GIRDLENESS 12.5.17
SN 56	PREMIER	I	89	40	'40	86'	1889	ELTRINGHAM SOUTH SHIELDS	BF 696 - SUNK BY SUBMARINE OFF SKYE 7.1.18
H 120	MAJESTIC	I	152	61	50	105. 3'	1890	COCHRANE & COOPER - BEVERLEY	FD 180, H 444, BF 478, GY 1054, SUNFLAME YH 229 - SCRAPPED 1926
GY 746	UNICORN	I	124	46	40	90. 6'	1895	EDWARDS NORTH SHIELDS	INS 249 - TO MILFORD HAVEN 1920
GY 45	BRAVO	I	137	44	45	93. 5'	1896	EARLES HULL	INS 516, A 305 - SANK OFF FAEROE 1927
GY 635	BLACKBIRD	I	136	45	45	94'	1894	EARLES HULL	INS 571 - SOLD TO NORWAY
GY 44	OWL	I	117	41	30	90. 7'	1896	EDWARDS NORTH SHIELDS	FR 249, A 618, LT 405 - SCRAPPED 1935
SN 92	CROWN PRINCE	I	110	44	40	93'	1890	ELTRINGHAM SOUTH SHIELDS	FR 180, A 369 - SUNK BY SUBMARINE OFF GIRDLENESS 12.4.17

I = IRON

S = STEEL

Part II

Admiralty Steam Drifters - Built During World War I (1914 - 1918)

At the start of World War I, the Admiralty did not possess any steam drifters and it was necessary to requisition privately owned drifters for minor war duties, thus relieving larger vessels, mainly trawlers, of these duties. It was thus decided during 1917, owing to the perceived usefulness of the requisitioned drifters and the need to incorporate the resources of smaller shipyards into the war effort, to construct a number of steel and wooden drifters to a standard design.

Steam drifters had evolved principally as herring catchers using drift-nets and were eminently suitable for that purpose. Thus the basic design was well proven as a sea-kindly versatile fishing vessel. The designs submitted by Alex Hall & Co. of Aberdeen (for steel drifters) and J. Chambers & Co. Limited of Lowestoft (for wooden ones) were chosen by the Admiralty out of all designs submitted for consideration. The drawings were modified somewhat by the Director of Naval Construction to equip the drifters for naval service and all were built to comply with rules of Lloyds and other shipping Agencies (1).

Unknown steel standard drifter alongside a battleship. Probably between the wars.
Courtesy of Scottish Fisheries Museum.

It is generally accepted in Scotland (2) that the steel standard design was based on the "Brighton O' the North" INS 382 built Alex Hall & Co., Aberdeen during 1914. Although some 2 feet longer (registered length) than standard design, she was regarded in fishing communities as a beautiful, well proportioned drifter. Similarly "Boy Roy" LT 1167 is reputed to be the basic design for wooden standards. She was designed and built by the prolific drifter builder, J. Chambers & Co. Limited of Lowestoft (who built approx. over 200 drifters between 1904 and 1927). I have no personal knowledge of "Boy Roy" (unlike "Brighton O' the North") as she was lost off Dunkirk on 28th May 1940.

Each builder of standard drifters, although using the same design, drawings and specifications, managed to incorporate a degree of individuality mainly in the wheelhouse and casing area. These individual features were quickly recognised within the fishing industry (after the war) and those who made informed studies of standard drifters could generally tell the builder after a cursory glance at a vessel.

All standard drifters, wooden and steel, were fitted with the same type of "triple expansion" engines and boilers designed by William Beardmore & Co. of Coatbridge. Despite the use of identical machinery, not all vessels achieved the same top speed with some being faster than others. Indeed the design speed was 9 knots but average speed on trials only reached 8.9 knots. (see Annex A)

The average cost of a wooden standard was £11,500 whilst steel standards cost somewhat less at £10,800 on average. In all 123 steel and 89 wooden drifters were completed for the Admiralty and 48 steel and 21 wooden ones were cancelled. Of the 69 cancellations, four steel and seven wooden drifters were completed privately by various builders and sold direct mainly to the fishing industry. In addition two steel and 11 wooden non-standard drifters were completed for the Admiralty. These vessels were all purchased while on the "stocks" during 1917 having been ordered privately for the fishing industry. The two steel ones were about six feet longer than their standard counterpart and all the wooden ones were about the same length (3).

Two standard drifters entering Gt. Yarmouth ca 1930. Left EUNELMA PD 102 (steel), Right REFRACTION FR 243 (wooden). Courtesy of Scottish Fisheries Museum.

It should be noted that whilst the steel standards were all within inches of the design length, wooden ones ranged from 84' to 90' between perpendiculars but those cancelled then completed privately showed the larger variation in length. All wooden standards were built with "tumblehome" sterns as per design except three built by Fellows & Co. of Great Yarmouth with "counter" sterns similar to the sterns of steel standards.

In addition 100 wooden standards (CD 1 - 100) were built in Canada during 1917 to 1919 to the general design of those built in the U.K. They were all fitted with "Compound" engines instead of the "triple expansion" ones fitted in the U.K. as per the specifications shown at Annex A. As far as is known only four served in the Royal navy. It is also known that five (CD 54, 86, 87, 88 and 93) were lost during passages across the North Atlantic to the U.K. during 1920. The fate of the crews is not known but apparently three fleets of CD drifters sailed across the Atlantic during 1920. (4) I have not found any evidence that any Canadian built standards were bought and used in the UK fishing industry.

However the boilers and engines of these vessels, after being reconditioned, were installed in newly built steel hulls (three from Cook, Welton & Gemmell of Beverley, Yorks, and 12 from Cochranes of Selby, Yorks). During 1922/23 with the original wooden hulls being broken up. Standard drifters proved to be first class herring drifters and most fished successfully until early 1950s when age and economics caught up with them. They were used for seine-netting, long-lining and trawling from various ports mainly between herring seasons. The steel standards proved to be rather more versatile than the wooden ones. They made first class great-line vessels operating as far afield as Rockall and around the Faeroe Islands as well as the North Sea grounds. Generally these steel standards used as liners retained their "cross" (thwartship) bunkers in front of their boiler whereas those vessels concerned mainly with herring fishing incorporated the "cross" bunkers into the fish hold. The reason for the liners retaining the "cross" bunkers was to enable as much coal as possible to be stowed below decks even although the length of a great-line trip particularly to the more distant grounds meant that a deck cargo of coal was necessary. This amount of coal was usually burnt whilst steaming to the fishing grounds and made space for the deck cargo to be stowed below in the bunkers before fishing started. A considerable number of steel standards were used as trawlers mainly from Great Yarmouth, Lowestoft and other English ports during seasons and times when herring fishing was out of season or unremunerative. They were most successful operating as trawlers in the relatively shallow waters of the Southern North Sea, Bristol Channel and Irish Sea. Wooden standard drifters were used as seine-netters particularly in the Moray Firth immediately prior to the evolution of custom built seiners.

All standard drifters, except those built in Canada, received names by the Admiralty relating to natural meteorological phenomena.

Notes on Part II

Reg. No.   PORT LETTERS AND NUMBERS AS PER FISHING BOAT REGISTER.

G.T.   GROSS TONS.

N.T.   NET TONS.

H.P.   NOMINAL HORSEPOWER.

W.W. I   WORLD WAR I 1914 - 1918.

W.W. II   WORLD WAR II 1939 - 1945.

H.M.D.   HIS MAJESTY'S DRIFTER.

R.N.   ROYAL NAVY.

U.K.   UNITED KINGDOM.

T.R.V.   TORPEDO RECOVERY VESSEL.

1.   These comments are based on information contained in an article in SHIP'S MONTHLY, OCTOBER 1983 By JOHN LAMBERT.

2.   According to Hawkins - THE OCEAN FLEET. "Ocean Reward" YH 730, also built by A. Hall & Co. of Aberdeen during 1912, was used as a role model but as both "Brighton O' the North" and "Ocean Reward" were from the same design with "Brighton O' the North" being 2' longer, Hawkin's is probably correct.

3.   SEE BRITISH WARSHIPS 1914 - 1919 By DITHAR AND COLLEDGE.

Annex A.   ADMIRALTY SPECIFICATIONS FOR DRIFTERS.
            As per John Lambert, Ship's Monthly - October 1983.

DRIFTER DATA

Item	Steel Drifter	Wooden Drifter
Moulded dimensions	86ft x 18ft x 10ft 6in	86ft x 19ft x 10ft 4.5in
Extreme length & breadth	93ft 3in x 18ft 10in	94ft 3in x 19ft 11in
Light displacement	148 tons	133 tons
Light draft forward (mean)	4ft 3in (7ft 4.5in)	4ft 0in (7ft 1in)
Light draft aft	10ft 6in	10ft 2in
Load displacement	199.5 tons	175 tons
Load draft forward (mean)	6ft 2.5in (8ft 10in)	5ft 7in (8ft 3.5in)
Load draft aft	11ft 5.5in	11ft 0in
Dead-weight	51.5 tons	42 tons
Gross steel & iron	69.5 tons	17 tons
Weight of main machinery	42 tons	42 tons
Coal capacity	37 tons	35 tons
Feed water	5.5 tons	5.5 tons
Fresh water	2.75 tons	2.75 tons

Machinery - Design of Messrs W. Beardmore & Co. of Coatbridge used in both types (parent).

Diameter of cylinders	9.5in, 15.5in, 26in
Stroke	18"
Revolutions	140
Design ihp	270
NHP	42
Designed speed of vessel	9 knots
Average speed on trials	8.9 knots
Condensing surface	275 sq ft
Boiler - length & diameter	9ft 6in x 10ft
Working pressure	180 lbs/sq in
Number of furnaces (plain)	2
Diameter of furnaces (external)	3ft 2in
Heating surface	810 sq ft
Grate surface	30.5 sq ft

BUILDERS OF ADMIRALTY DRIFTERS

STEEL		Numbers Built	
		Standard	**Non Standard**
Pg 118	I. J. ABDELA & MITCHELL LIMITED, QUEENSFERRY, CHESTER	2	
112	AILSA SHIPBUILDING COMPANY LIMITED, TROON	2	
112	BROWN'S DRYDOCK & SHIPBUILDING COMPANY, HULL	1	
117	J. W. BROOKE & COMPANY LIMITED, LOWESTOFT	18	
118	J. CHAMBERS LIMITED, LOWESTOFT	3	
118	CHRICHTON THOMSON, KING'S LYNN	2	
116	COLBY BROTHERS, LOWESTOFT	14	
113	J. DUTHIE, TORRY SHIPBUILDING COMPANY, ABERDEEN	7	
111	FELLOWS & COMPANY, GREAT YARMOUTH	-	2
110	ALEX HALL & COMPANY LIMITED, ABERDEEN	35	
111	LEA SHIPBUILDING COMPANY LIMITED, CANNING TOWN, LONDON	2	
111	J. LEWIS & SONS, ABERDEEN	12	
115	OUSE SHIPBUILDING COMPANY, HOOK, GOOLE, YORKSHIRE	10	
118	ISAAC PIMBLOTT & SONS, NORTHWICH	2	
114	ROSE STREET FOUNDRY & ENGINEERING COMPANY LIMITED, INVERNESS	4	
112	SCOTT & SONS, BOWLING, DUMBARTONSHIRE	2	
117	W. H. WARREN, NEW HOLLAND, LINCOLNSHIRE	2	
114	J. S. WATSON, GAINSBROUGH, LINCOLNSHIRE	4	
111	WEBSTER & BICKERTON LIMITED, GOOLE, YORKSHIRE	5*	
TOTAL	* Includes 4 completed after cancellation	127	2
WOODEN			
123	CLAPSON & SONS, BARTON ON HUMBER	2	
121, 122	J. CHAMBERS LIMITED, LOWESTOFT	18*	
120	COLBY BROTHERS, LOWESTOFT	25*	1
123	COURTNEY, LYMINGTON, HAMPSHIRE	2	
126	R. DUNSTON LIMITED, THORNE, YORKSHIRE	2	
123	FELLOWS & COMPANY LIMITED, GREAT YARMOUTH	3	3
125, 126	J. & G. FORBES, SANDHAVEN & FRASERBURGH	3	
125	HERD & MACKENZIE, FINDOCHTY	3	
124	JONES, BUCKIE SLIP & SHIPYARD LIMITED, BUCKIE	2	
125	KITTO & SONS, PORTLETHEN, CORNWALL	1	
124	G. INNES, MACDUFF	3	1
125	W. NOBLE & COMPANY, FRASERBURGH	2	
121	RICHARDS IRONWORKS, LOWESTOFT	6*	4
123	ROSE STREET FOUNDRY & ENGINEERING COMPANY LIMITED INVERNESS	2	
123	ROUTH & WADDINGTON, WINTERINGHAM, WILTSHIRE	1	
118	G. T. SMITH & COMPANY, RYE, SUSSEX	2	
126	G. SMITH JR., BUCKIE	3	
123	W. & G. STEPHEN, BANFF	3	1
124	STEVENSON & ASHER, BANFF	4	
123	W. WOOD & SONS, LOSSIEMOUTH	1	
TOTAL	* Includes 7 completed after cancellation	96	12

STEEL ADMIRALTY DRIFTERS
BUILDER
ALEX HALL & Co. LTD. - ABERDEEN

Admiralty Name	G.T.	N.T.	H.P.	Length	Completon Date	HISTORY
EDDY	96	36	42	86.2'	1918	R.N. 1918 - 42 LOST OFF MALTA 26.5.42
FAIRWIND	96	41	42	86.2'	1918	HMD ATTENTIVE, HAWTHORNBANK GN 67, M 237, LT 231, BK 163, TO FRANCE, JACKETA LT 237 - SCRAPPED 1956
FALLING STAR	96	41	42	86.2'	1918	FALLING STAR LT 633, BETTY BODIE BCK 400, PD 304 - SCRAPPED 17.12.52
FLICKER	96	38	42	86.2'	1918	RN 1918 - 35, MARY WATT FR 217, SEA REAPER, PD 396, KY 245 - SCRAPPED 30.4.55
FRESHET	96	35	42	86.2'	1918	JEAN PATERSON A 382, XMAS ROSE FR 531 - MINED THAMES ESTUARY 11.40
FROTH	96	38	42	86.2'	1918	FLORENCE PRITCHARD LL120, MANX PRINCESS, DO 91, EUNICE & NELLIE BCK 118, PD 309 - SCRAPPED 17/12/52
GLITTER	96	41	42	86.2	1918	HMD RALEIGH 1918 - 45, OCEAN RALEIGH PD 139, (LAST PD DRIFTER) - SCRAPPED 30.4.55
GLOW	96	41	42	86.2'	1918	GLOW LT 688 - TO NORWAY 1946
GUST	96	38	42	86.2'	1918	R 347 BURNHAVEN, PD 591, BCK 73, LT 164 - SCRAPPED 1955
HALO	96	41	42	86.2'	1918	RN 1918 - 46, HALO SA 121
HARMATTAN	96	41	42	86.2'	1918	RN 1918 - 46, HARMATTAN PD 399, WELLSPRING - SCRAPPED 12.52
HORIZON	96	41	42	86.2'	1918	RN 1918 - 45, HAMNAVOE FR 123, AMARANTH, YH 117 - SCRAPPED 1956
ICEFLOE	96	41	42	86.2'	1918	ICEFLOE LT 733, INS 477, SUNNY BIRD BCK 68, PD 86, A 571, LT 305 - SCRAPPED 1957
ICEPACK	96	41	42	86.2'	1918	ICEPACK LT 1247, ACCORD PD 90, OCEAN SUNBEAM YH 344 - SCRAPPED 1956
ICICLE	96	35	34	86.2'	1918	MILDRED W. RAWSON LL 82, JUNE ROSE PD 592 - SCRAPPED 7.7.54
LEVANTER	96	41	42	86.2'	1918	RN 1918 - 27, WRECKED OFF PETERHEAD 1927
SANDSTORM	96	35	42	86.2'	1918	SANDSTORM A 381, GLENBRECK A 381, RIVER EYE BK 3, OLDEN TIMES BK 3, SEASON'S GIFT LT 127 - SCRAPPED 1954
SEABREEZE	96	41	42	86.2'	1918	RN 1918 - 46, SAPPHIRE STONE BF 117 - SOLD TO FAEROE ISLANDS 31.7.54
SUNDOWN	96	41	42	86.2'	1918	RN 1918 - 39, WRECKED OFF SHETLAND 30.8.39
GALE	96	41	42	86.2'	1919	OCEAN LOVER YH 107, PD 157 - SANK OFF PETERHEAD 1948
PAMPEREO	96	41	42	86.2'	1919	EDALBA YH 218, ACORN KY 194, LT 31 - SOLD TO CANADA 1954 - SCRAPPED 1975
PHOSPHOROUS	96	41	42	86.2'	1919	OCEAN SPRITE YH 56, PD 94, ENDED UP AS A "BARKING SHIP" AT FRASERBURGH - SCRAPPED 12/52
THUNDERCLAP	96	41	42	86.2'	1919	ZENA & ELLA BCK 321, MACE KY 224, GDY 113 , LT 35 - SCRAPPED 1955
TIDALWAVE	96	41	42	86.2'	1919	TIDAL WAVE BF 604, SOPHIE S. SUMMERS PD 379, NORMAN WILSON KY 228 - SCRAPPED 1956
TYPHOON	96	41	42	86.2'	1919	OCEAN LASSIE YH 78, LOST W.W.II 4.6.40 - MINED OF HARWICH
WATERFALL	96	41	42	86.2'	1919	HOMOCEA YH 214, STRENUOUS LT 112, CONVERTED TO MOTOR - SCRAPPED 1963
WATERSHED	96	41	42	86'2'	1919	WATERSHED LT 628, SALVIAN GY 1302, TO FRANCE 1923, BACK 1924
						CONVALLARIA BF 51 LT 247, BF 497 - SCRAPPED 1954
WATERSMEET	96	41	42	86'.2'	1919	GEORGE BAKER YH 210, LT 1253 - SCRAPPED 1955
WAVELET	96	41	42	86.2'	1919	OCEAN DAWN YH 47 - TO BELGUIM FOR SCRAP 1955
WHIRLPOOL	96	41	42	86.2'	1919	RN 1919 - 47, WHIRLPOOL SA 114 - SCRAPPED 1956

Admiralty Name	G.T.	N.T.	H.P.	Length	Completon Date	HISTORY
WHITE HORSES	96	41	42	86.2'	1919	BENACHIE A 301, FR 15, A 568 - SCRAPPED 10.52
WINDWARD	96	41	42	86.2'	1919	BCK 349, COULET HEAD PD 454 , FR 537, SCARLET THREAD PD 57 KY 197 - SCRAPPED 3.5.52
LASHER	96	41	42	86.2'	1920	LASHER KY 25, BF 79,GOLDEN RING LT 408 - SCRAPPED 1957
WINDFALL	96	41	42	86.2'	1920	WINDFALL INS 189, SY 567 - SCRAPPED 12.54

MARIGOLD PD 124 - Standard Steel Drifter built by A. Hall & Co. Ltd. Aberdeen for Admiralty 1918 as ICEBERG. Became ICEBERG LT 662, MARIGOLD INS 478, PD 81, A 573, PD 124, scrapped ca 1952. Shown leaving Peterhead ca 1947. Courtesy of Aberdeen Libraries - Benzie Collection.

ACORN KY 194 - Steel Standard Drifter built by A. Hall & Co. Ltd. Aberdeen 1919 for Admiralty as PAMPERO. Became EDALBA YH 218, ACORN KY 194 LT 31. Sold to Canada 1954 - scrapped 1975. Shown entering Gt. Yarmouth setting up nets ca 1938. Courtesy of Scottish Fisheries Museum.

STEEL ADMIRALTY DRIFTERS
BUILDER   LEA SHIPBUILDING - CANNING TOWN, LONDON

Admiralty Name	G.T.	N.T.	H.P.	Length	Completion Date	HISTORY
WHIRLBLAST	96	41	42	86.2'	1920	STELLA AURORA KY 45, FR 54, ABIDING FRIEND LT 116, JACKEVE LT 116 - SCRAPPED 1955
WHITE CLOUD	96	41	42	86.2'	1920	ADMIRAL STARTIN LH 304, GY 376, FISHER LAD BF 204 TO NORWAY 1947

FELLOWS & Co. GREAT YARMOUTH

NON STANDARD						
Admiralty Name	G.T.	N.T.	H.P.	Length	Completion Date	HISTORY
DAYSPRING	108	39	44	92.4'	1917	FD 377, LT 1295, CASTLEBAY PD 101, HAZELGLEN BCK 145, CONVERTED TO MOTOR VESSEL, TO FLEETWOOD, 6.57 - SCRAPPED 1983
ELEPHANTA	107	51	43	92.1'	1919	BYNG LT 632, SCRAPPED 1955

WEBSTER & BICKERTON LTD. GOOLE, YORKSHIRE

Admiralty Name	G.T.	N.T.	H.P.	Length	Completion Date	HISTORY
SUNSHINE	96	41	42	86.2'	1918	HMD BILLOW 1935, CRAIGROY, FR 251, BF 81 - SCRAPPED 12.54
SUNSET	96	41	42	86.2'	1918	RN 1918 - 43, SUNK OFF MALTA 7.43
SEAFOG	96	41	42	86.2'	1918	SEAFOG LT 710, SELNIUS GY 1330, B 5101 (FRANCE) PRIMORDIAL INS 81, FR 200 - SCRAPPED OCT. 1952
SNOWFLAKE	96	37	34	86.2'	1919	CSD, SN 46, MARY HERD FR 24, A 570 - SCRAPPED 10.52
CLOUDBANK	95	41	20	86.2'	1921	H 464, ARABIS - SOLD TO BELGIUM (COMPLETED AS FV AFTER CANCELLATION)

STEEL ADMIRALTY DRIFTERS
BUILDER   J. LEWIS & SONS - ABERDEEN

HMD Admiralty Name	G.T.	N.T.	H.P.	Length	Completion Date	HISTORY
INDIAN SUMMER	97	41	34	85.8'	1918	RN 1918 - 47, T.R.V. AT ANSTRUTHER W.W.II, INDIAN SUMMER A 342 - SCRAPPED 11.12.52
LANDFALL	97	41	42	85.8'	1918	RN 1918 - 46, SOLD TO EGYPT
LEEWARD	97	41	34	85.8'	1918	RN 1918 - 47, BETTY DUTHIE FR 207, LUSTRE PD 201 - SCRAPPED 12.54
LULL	97	43	34	85.8'	1918	LULL B 38, EUNELMA BCK 438, MYRTLE LEAF PD 102, MARSHALL PAK LT 200 - SCRAPPED 1956
LUNAR BOW	97	41	34	85.8'	1918	RN 1918 - 46, LUNAR BOW PD 245 - SOLD TO FAEROES 31.7.54
MIRAGE	97	42	34	85.8'	1918	THORNTREE GN 73, KY 33, MARY & JANE BK 271, JACKORA LT 129 - SCRAPPED 1955
MIST	97	41	42	85.8'	1918	RN 1918 - 46, CONVERTED TO MOTOR 1933, JAMES JOHNSTON BF 101, CAIRNMOR PD 375, WELCOME BOYS LT 293 - SCRAPPED 1966
MOONBEAM	97	42	43	85.8'	1918	SKIMMER GY 21 - SOLD TO SPAIN
MOONSHINE	97	41	42	85.8'	1918	RN 1918 - 24 - SOLD TO HONG KONG 1926
MURK	97	38	34	85.8'	1918	GIRL'S FRIEND LT 171, TRUST PD 243, SCRAPPED 12.54
SNOWDRIFT	97	42	43	85.8'	1918	FIFENESS A 522, KY 27, GEORGE G. BAIRD PD 256 - SCRAPPED 10.54
SUNBURST	97	42	43	85.8'	1918	BOY ANDREW BF 592, LOST W.W.II, IN COLLISION WITH ST. ROGNVALD OFF INCHKEITH, FIRTH OF FORTH 9.11.41

INDIAN SUMMER A 343 - entering Gt. Yarmouth ca 1948. Scrapped 1952. Built by J. Lewis & Sons Aberdeen 1918. Served in Royal Navy 1918 - 1947, was a Torpedo Recovery Drifter at Anstruther during World War II. Courtesy of Scottish Fisheries Museum.

STEEL ADMIRALTY DRIFTERS

BUILDER   AILSA SHIPBUILDING CO. LTD. - TROON

HMD Admiralty Name	G.T.	N.T.	H.P.	Length	Completion Date	HISTORY
CLEARING	98	41	34	86.5'	1919	CLEARING PD 179, VERNAL BF 525, PD 239 - SCRAPPED 12.54
COLD BLAST	98	41	34	86.7'	1919	COLDBLAST PD 195, ELSIE BRUCE BF 531 - TO PILOT BOAT AT CARDIFF 1937

BROWN'S DRY DOCK & SHIPBUILDING CO. LTD., HULL, YORKS

HMD Admiralty Name	G.T.	N.T.	H.P.	Length	Completion Date	HISTORY
CHIMERA	95	40	42	86.2'	1920	J.R.MITCHELL PD 443, TWINKLING STAR PD 443, KY 347, MERCHANT VENTURER M 49 - SCRAPPED 1960

SCOTT & SON'S, BOWLING, DUMBARTONSHIRE

HMD Admiralty Name	G.T.	N.T.	H.P.	Length	Completion Date	HISTORY
UNDERTOW	96	42	42	86.2'	1919	UNDERTOW BCK 368, LH 297, SPES MELIOR KY 19, PD 397 - SCRAPPED 12.52
WAFT	96	41	42	86.2'	1919	GENIUS BCK 358, FR 299, MERCHANT VALOUR M 46 - LOST 1956

TWINKLING STAR KY 347 - Steel Standard Drifter built by Brown's Dry Dock & Shipbuilding Co., Hull for Admiralty as CHIMERA 1920. Became J. R. MITCHELL PD 443, TWINKLING STAR PD 443 KY 347, MERCHANT VENTURER M 49. Scrapped 1960. Shown entering Gt. Yarmouth ca 1938. Courtesy of Scottish Fisheries Museum.

SPES MELIOR KY 19 - Steel Standard Drifter built by Scott & Sons, Bowling 1919 as UNDERTOW. Became UNDER-
TOW BCK 368, LH 297, SPES MELIOR KY 19, PD 397. Scrapped 1952. Shown leaving Anstruther Harbour ca 1935.
Courtesy of Scottish Fisheries Museum.

STEEL ADMIRALTY DRIFTERS
BUILDER   J.DUTHIE, TORRY SHIPBUILDING Co. - ABERDEEN

HMD Admiralty Name	G.T.	N.T.	H.P.	Length	Completion Date	HISTORY
CALM	96	35	42	86'	1918	JOHN HEDLEY SN 35, PRE-EMINENT INS 55, FR 173, YH 91 - SCRAPPED 1956
CLOUD	96	40	42	86'	1918	RN 1918 - 46, CORNUCOPIA FR 129, PROTECT ME PD 209 - SCRAPPED 31.7.54
COLD SNAP	96	41	42	86'	1918	RN 1918-46, COLDSNAP A222, WHITEHILL PD 390, SCRAPPED 31.7.54
CRESCENT MOON	96	41	42	86'	1918	RN 1918 - 46, SOLD TO WAR DEPARTMENT
DAWN	96	41	42	86'	1918	DAWN LT 32, PL 97, JANE WRIGHT PL 97
DAYBREAK	96	41	42	86'	1918	RALPH HALL CAINE DO 90, YH 447, ALLOCHY FR 124, LT 109 - SCRAPPED 1956
DUSK	96	41	42	86'	1918	DUSK PZ 139, COSMEA KY 21, CORIEDALIS KY 21 - SCRAPPED 31.1.57

COSMEA KY 21 - Steel Standard Drifter built by Torry Shipbuilding Co. (J. Duthie) Aberdeen 1918 for Admiralty as
DUSK. Became DUSK PZ 139, COSMEA KY 21, CORIEDALIS KY21. Scrapped 1957. Shown leaving Gt. Yarmouth
ca 1930s. Courtesy of Scottish Fisheries Museum.

STEEL ADMIRALTY DRIFTERS
BUILDER   ROSE STREET FOUNDRY & ENGINEERING CO. LTD. - INVERNESS

HMD Admiralty Name	G.T.	N.T.	H.P.	Length	Completion Date	HISTORY
NEBULA	97	41	42	86.3'	1918	NACRE A 410, SEA TOILER BCK 14, CALLIOPSIS KY 223, LT 92 - SCRAPPED 1955
NORTHERN LIGHTS	98	43	42	86.2'	1919	SUNNYSIDE GIRL LT 415 - TO NORWAY 1946
NEW MOON	95	40	42	86.2'	1920	THE MILNES PD 202, UGIEVALE PD 202 - SCRAPPED 1952
OZONE	95	40	42	86.1'	1920	GIRL GEORGIA LK 152, MARY WEST FR 61 - WRECKED WEST COAST OF SCOTLAND 1925

J. S. WATSON - GAINSBOROUGH, LINCS

HMD Admiralty Name	G.T.	N.T.	H.P.	Length	Completion Date	HISTORY
CONFLAGRATION	96	37	42	86.1'	1919	CONFLAGRATION M 158, MADELINE JEANNE, LT 620, SOLD TO FRANCE, BACK TO ENGLAND AS JACKLYN LT 327, SCRAPPED 1955
CYCLONE	96	37	42	86.1'	1919	BLUSTER LT737, SERGIUS GY 657, TO FRANCE, BACK TO SCOTLAND AS HELEN WEST, BF 84, FERTILITY PD 147 - SCRAPPED 1952
FLAFF	96	40	43	86.1'	1920	FLAFF BCK 359, RIVER UGIE CARGO BOAT, NELLIE GARDNER BF 74 - WRECKED OFF SHETLAND 1935
FLOW	95	38	43	86.1'	1920	FLOW GN 84, GY 18, BCK 436, PD 291 - SCRAPPED 1952

CALLIOPSIS KY 223 - Steel Standard Drifter built by Rose Street Foundry & Engineering Co. Ltd., Inverness 1918 for Admiralty as NEBULA. Became NACRE A 410, SEA TOILER BCK 14, CALLIOPSIS KY 223, LT 92. Scrapped 1955. Shown leaving Anstruther Harbour ca 1930s. Courtesy of Scottish Fisheries Museum.

NELLIE GARDNER BF 74 - Steel Standard Drifter built by J. S. Watson, Gainsborough, Lincs. 1920 for Admiralty as FLAFF. Became FLAFF BCK 359, RIVER UGIE (cargo boat), NELLIE GARDNER BF 74. Wrecked off Shetland 1935. Shown entering Lowestoft ca 1930s. Courtesy of Scottish Fisheries Museum.

STEEL ADMIRALTY DRIFTERS
BUILDER   OUSE SHIP BUILDING CO. - HOOK, GOOLE, YORKS

HMD Admiralty Name	G.T.	N.T.	H.P.	Length	Completion Date	HISTORY
BRINE	96	41	42	86.2'	1918	BRINE A 388, GY 85, BCK 246 - SOLD TO ROYAL NAVY 1938
CASCADE	96	41	43	86.2'	1918	RN 1918 - 1945, ILLUSTRIOUS PD 187, SCRAPPED 1955
CATSPAW	96	41	42	86.2'	1918	RN 1918 - 19 - FOUNDERED IN KATTEGAT, 1919
DEW	96	41	42	86.2'	1918	DEW A 361, MOYRA INS 586, OLIVE TREE FR 321, CALM WATERS LT 407 - SCRAPPED 1955
GROUNDSWELL	96	37	42	86.2'	1919	ELIENESS A 638, TRUSTY STAR LT 1259 - LOST W.W.II OFF MALTA 1942
ICEFIELD	96	37	43	86.2'	1919	JESSIE WATSON, ANSTER BELLE, CAMPANULA MEMORIA, ALL KY 52, UNITY BCK 109, OCEAN UNITY YH 293 - SCRAPPED 1955
RAINBAND	96	37	42	86.2'	1919	CRAIGLEA LH 270, INS 540, YH 81 - SCRAPPED 1955
NEAPTIDE	96	37	42	86.2'	1920	A 504, SMILING THRU, LT 1274 - LOST 1924
SCINTILLA	96	37	42	86.2'	1920	ASPARAGUS LH 248, INCENTIVE, BK446, MARY SWANSTON BK 446 TO DENMARK 1947
RADIATION	96	37	42	86.2'	1920	RADIATION KY 185, AGNES GARDNER KY 185, PD 395, SCRAPPED 1952

ILLUSTRIOUS PD 187 - Steel Standard Drifter built by Ouse Shipbuilding Co. Hook, Goole, Yorks for Admiralty 1918 as CASCADE. Served in Royal Navy 1918 - 1945. Became ILLUSTRIOUS PD 187. Scrapped 1955. Shown entering Gt. Yarmouth ca 1948. Courtesy of Scottish Fisheries Museum.

STEEL ADMIRALTY DRIFTERS
BUILDER   COLBY BROTHERS - LOWESTOFT

HMD Admiralty Name	G.T.	N.T.	H.P.	Length	Completion Date	HISTORY
BLIZZARD	96	35	34	86.1'	1918	SATINSTONE H 585, HARVEST GLEANER FR 73, BF 484 SUNK OFF EAST COAST 1940
FLASH	96	37	34	86.1'	1918	A. J. A. FD 379, GY 309 - SOLD TO SPAIN 1929
NODE	96	35	34	86.1'	1918	TIGER'S EYE H 577, GY 60, LOSSIE INS 125, GOLDEN VIEW FR 44, PD 23 - TO NORWAY 1954
NOONTIDE	95	41	34	86.1'	1918	RN 1918 - 46, KY 6, KY 163, YH 33 - SCRAPPED AT CHARLESTON 1960
OVERFALL.	97	42	43	86..1'	1918	BF 590, LT 76 - SCRAPPED 1960
FUMAROLE	96	40	34	86.1'	1919	RN 1919 - 47, PD 367 - SCRAPPED 1952
FUME	96	41	34	86.1'	1919	LT 534, SOLD TO FRANCE - SAINT PIERRE
GALAXY	96	41	34	86.1'	1919	LT 417, SOLD TO CAPETOWN SOUTH AFRICA
GLOSS	96	41	34	86.1'	1919	LT 568, SOLD TO FRANCE, RETURNED AS MURIELLE LT 269, MINED OFF MORECAMBE - Lt. VESSEL 1941
GULF STREAM	95	40	34	86.1'	1919	LT 601,SN 42, JENNY IRVIN , EUSTACHIUSZ GDY 112 (POLAND), JENNY IRVIN SN 21, LT 57 - SCRAPPED 1955
HIGH TIDE	95	42	43	86.1'	1919	LT 700, BF 571, SOLD TO FRANCE - LOST OFF NORTH WALES 1945
QUICKSAND	96	42	34	86.1'	1919	A 394, PD 7, EPHRATAH PD 170, M 292 - SCRAPPED 1950
GREEN SEA	95	40	34	86.1'	1920	GLADYS & VIOLET A 639, RIANT INS 301 - LOST OFF GIGHA 1940
LAND BREEZE	94	40	34	86.1'	1920	A 315, LT 1296 - SCRAPPED 1955

*FUMAROLE PD 367 - Steel Standard Drifter built by Colby Bros. Lowestoft 1919 for Admiralty as FUMAROLE.
Served in Royal Navy 1919 - 1947. Became PD 367. Scrapped 1952. Shown entering Gt. Yarmouth ca 1948.
Courtesy of Scottish Fisheries Museum.*

STEEL ADMIRALTY DRIFTERS
BUILDER   J.W.BROOKE & Co. LTD. - LOWESTOFT

HMD Admiralty Name	G.T.	N.T.	H.P.	Length	Completion Date	HISTORY
SHOWER	97	42	30	86.1'	1918	RN 1918 - 46, A 11 - SCRAPPED 1952
SHEEN	96	41	42	86.1'	1918	RN 1918 - 46, GOOD TIDINGS PD 246, SUMMER ROSE - SCRAPPED 1955
SLEET	97	39	27	86.1'	1918	SN 47, EYEDALE BK 5, CONSOLATION, FAIR HAVEN PD 75, KY 173, SCRAPPED 1955
SPECTRUM	97	41	42	86.1'	1918	R 343, "WK 217, BF 196, PD 73 - SCRAPPED 1952
FORK LIGHTNING	97	39	45	86'.1'	1918	RAMSEY BAY FD 378, LT 1290 - SCRAPPED 1955
BLARE	96	41	42	86.1'	1919	MAY BIRD LT 449 - SOLD TO SPAIN
GREY SEA	98	41	42	86.1'	1919	BM 211, LT 1279, BCK 184, ROSEBAY PD 65,A 379, BF 69, YH 78 - SCRAPPED 1961
BLUE HAZE	97	41	42	86.1'	1919	LT 564, JEAN BAIRD PD 1 - SCRAPPED 1954, T.R.V. AT ANSTRUTHER W.W.II
BOW WAVE	97	41	42	86.1'	1919	LT 589, LILIUM PD 67 - SCRAPPED 1952, T.R.V. AT ANSTRUTHER W.W.II
BREAKER	96	41	42	86.1'	1919	KATHLEEN LT 673
BROIL	96	41	42	86.1'	1919	LT 610, BF 572, M.A. WEST FR 240 - LOST OFF NORFOLK 1941
BUBBLE	96	41	42	86.1'	1919	LT 734, UNICITY R 22 - SANK OFF BLYTH 1942
LOW TIDE	96	41	42	8.1'	1919	LT 725, SEAWARD GY 1301, ECAULT, MARY FLEET INS 137, LOYAL FRIEND LT 126 - SCRAPPED 1956
WILLIWAW	96	41	42	86.1'	1920	BM 207, MORAY ROSE INS 101, PD 97 - SCRAPPED 1952
MOONSET	95	40	42	86.1'	1920	FLORA TAYLOR PD 444, LT 239 - SCRAPPED 1954
THE FOLLOWING WERE CANCELLED THEN COMPLETED BY BUILDER						
OCEAN SWELL	96	44	29	86.1'	1920	LT 1210, YH 471 - SCRAPPED 1954
OUTLINE	96	44	37	86.1'	1920	INSPIRATION LT 1211, NORBREEZE , LT 316 - SCRAPPED 1955
PUFF	96	44	29	86.1'	1920	LT 1106, GOWAN HILL FR 39 - LOST OFF GREENOCK 1941

W. H. WARREN - NEW HOLLAND, LINCS.

HMD Admiralty Name	G.T.	N.T.	H.P.	Length	Completion Date	HISTORY
WINDRISE	97	38	43	86'	1920	CASSIOPEIA KY 14, LT 86, PD 34 - SANK OFF PETERHEAD S - 52.
WINDSHIFT	97	38	43	86'	1920	QUIET WATERS A 291 ,PD 589 , GIRL PATRICIA FR 237 - WRECKED FRASERBURGH BEACH 1932

STEEL ADMIRALTY DRIFTERS
BUILDER   I. J. ABDELA AND MITCHELL LTD., QUEENSFERRY, CHESTER

HMD Amiralty Name	G.T.	N.T.	H.P.	Length	Completion Date	HISTORY
FOAM	95	39	42	86.1'	1920	STARWORTH LH 288, MENAT, KY 232, PLOUGH - SUNK IN ENGLISH CHANNEL 1948
FOGBREAK	95	39	42	86.1'	1920	CRAIGHALL LH 273, SPES AUREA KY 81, LT 72, PD 58 - SCRAPPED 12.54.

CHRICTON THOMSON, KINGS LYNN

HMD Amiralty Name	G.T.	N.T.	H.P.	Length	Completion Date	HISTORY
MELODY	97	41	42	86.8'	1921	ROSE DUNCAN A 666, BCK 122, SH 105, LORD DUNCAN, LT 273 - SCRAPPED 1954
MORN	97	41	42	86.4'	1921	HOMEFINDER LH 282, BENE VERTAT KY 20, DEFENSOR KY 208, PD 185, SOLD TO BELGIUM 31.7.54 FOR SCRAPPING

J. CHAMBERS LTD., LOWESTOFT

HMD Amiralty Name	G.T.	N.T.	H.P.	Length	Completion Date	HISTORY
CURRENT	96	41	42	86.2'	1919	CURRENT SN 43, COPIOUS KY 175, OCEAN HUNTER YH 296, LT 322 - SCRAPPED 1955
DISTANCE	96	41	42	86.2'	1920	LEONARD BOYLE SN 45, DUNDARG FR 212, EXCEL IV, BK 260, LT 171, TRV AT ANSTRUTHER W.W. II, - SCRAPPED 1955
DRIZZLE	96	35	42	86.2'	1920	PILOT STAR LT 1060, KY 48, FR 106, PD 200, SCRAPPED 12.52

ISSAC PIMBLOTT & SONS, NORWICH

HMD Amiralty Name	G.T.	N.T.	H.P.	Length	Completion Date	HISTORY
SPURT	96	41	42	86.5'	1920	CRAIGENTINNY LH 261, GY 89, PD 185, PL 63, FR 567, SCRAPPED
STERN WAVE	96	43	34	86.5'	1920	CRAIGLEITH LH 255, SUMMER ROSE PD 594, LOST OF SUNDERLAND 13.10.40

BENE VERT KY 20 - Steel Standard Drifter built by Chrichton Thomson, Kings Lynn for Admiralty 1921 as MORN.
Became HOMEFINDER LH 282, BENEVERTAT KY 20, DEFENSOR KY 208, PD 185.
Sold to Belgium for scrapping 1954. Shown entering Gt. Yarmouth ca 1930s. Courtesy of Scottish Fisheries Museum.

PILOT STAR FR 106 - Steel Standard Drifter built by J. Chambers Ltd. Lowestoft for Admiralty 1920 as DRIZZLE. Became PILOT STAR LT 1060, KY 48, FR 106, PD 200. Scrapped 1952. Shown leaving Fraserburgh ca 1948. Courtesy of Scottish Fisheries Museum.

CRAIGENTINNY FR 567 - Steel Standard Drifter built by Isaac Pimblott & Sons, Norwich for Admiralty 1920 as SPURT. Became CRAIGENTINNY LH 261, GY 89, PD 185, PL 63, FR 567. Scrapped ca 1950s. Shown leaving Fraserburgh ca 1948. Courtesy of Scottish Fisheries Museum.

WOODEN STANDARD ADMIRALTY DRIFTERS
BUILDER   COLBY BROTHERS - OULTON BROAD, LOWESTOFT

HMD Amiralty Name	G.T.	N.T.	H.P.	Length	Completon Date	HISTORY
BACKWASH	99	43	34	87.7'	1918	GY 1299, WILLIAM C. FARROW H 664, MORVEN HILL WK 83 - SCRAPPED 1946
BLACKFROST	100	35	34	87.6	1918	RN 1918 - 1929, RENAMED COLUMBINE, TIMOR GY 152, MILLWATER FR 81 - SCRAPPED 1948
BLACKNIGHT	96	35	42	87.6'	1918	BLACKNIGHT GY 188
BLUE SKY	96	35	34	87.5'	1918	RN 1918 - 22, FOUNDERED THAMES ESTUARY 6.22
BOREALIS	98	34	34	87.9'	1918	BRASH GY 119 - LOST 1925
CIRRUS	97	41	43	87.6'	1918	RN 1918 - 26, TRAVELER'S JOY PD 123 - SCRAPPED 1939
CUMULUS	97	41	43	87.5'	1918	BOY JERMYN GY 105 - SCRAPPED 1939
RAINSTORM	97	35	34	87.5'	1918	RAINSTORM LO 527
RISING SEA	97	36	34	87.5'	1918	RISING SEA, LO 526, BCK 110 - SCRAPPED 1950
RUNNEL	97	36	42	87.5'	1918	RUNNEL GY 1226, LH132 SCRAPPED 1940
SILHOUETTE	97	42	44	87.5'	1918	RN 1918 - 31, HONORIA EVELYN FD 165 - SCRAPPED 1937
REVERBERATION	97	41	36	87.5'	1918	REVERBERATION LT 369, SCRAPPED 1947
SHIMMER	97	34	34	86'.8'	1919	SHIMMER LO 524 SCRAPPED 1935
SET WEATHER	97	41	39	87.4'	1919	SET WEATHER R 96, TANKERTON TOWERS R 96 - SUNK OFF ST. GOVENS LIGHT 9.5.41
SCUD	97	41	34	87.5'	1919	FLEURBAIX LT 422 - SCRAPPED 1939
SCOUR	98	35	34	87'5"	1919	CHEVIOTDALE SN 54, BK 427 - SCRAPPED 1942
SCEND	97	41	34	87.5'	1919	GIRL HAZEL PZ 179, WILLIAM WOLVEN PH - LOST 1925
SHADE	96	41	34	87.7'	1920	SHADE GY 186
SIROCCO	97	41	34	87.6'	1920	RENAMED DOUBLE TIDE 1920, CAT'S EYE H 316 - LOST 1941
TIDAL RANGE	97	41	34	87.1'	1920	TIDAL RANGE GY 403 - SCRAPPED 1948
TWINKLE	97	41	34	87.6'	1920	RENAMED CLOUDARCH, CLOUDARCH GY 187 - SCRAPPED 1947
SHOOTING STARS	97	41	34	87.5'	1918	RN 1918 - 29 SHOOTING STARS BCK 57 - SCRAPPED 12.48 (NON STANDARD)
CANCELLED WOODEN STANDARD DRIFTERS COMPLETED BY COLBY BROTHERS						
VOLUME	100	43	44	89'.9'	1919	GO AHEAD LT 534, LOST W.W.II 18.11.40 - SUNK OF SHEERNESS
WINDHOWL	100	42	28	89.9'	1919	HARNSER LT 627 - TO NORWAY 1940
WINDWAIL	113	48	44	90'	1919	RENAMED PLUMER 1919, PLUMER LT 596 - SCRAPPED 1947
NO. 75 (YARD NO:)	100	48	33	90'	1920	SILVER WAVE LT 724 - SOLD TO SPAIN 1923 (CADIZ)

WOODEN STANDARD ADMIRALTY DRIFTERS
BUILDER   RICHARDS IRONWORKS - LOWESTOFT

HMD Admiralty Name	G.T.	N.T.	H.P.	Length	Completon Date	HISTORY
MIDNIGHT SUN	96	41	43	88'	1918	RN 1918 - 29, SCRAPPED 1930
NADIR	99	42	43	88'	1918	SALPA, RESEARCH VESSEL
NIGHTFALL	94	41	43	88	1918	NIGHTFALL H 317
NIMBUS	98	36	42	87.9'	1918	GIRL BELLA GY 1292, JETSAM GY 1292 - LOST 1924 NORTH SEA
ALL ABOVE FOUR VESSELS WERE NON STANDARD						
HAILSTORM	98	42	43	87.2'	1918	GIRL LIZZIE, GOSSWATER LK 173 - TO SALVAGE WORK 12.52
HEATWAVE	98	34	43	87.7'	1918	HEATWAVE GY 1296
HURRICANE	99	42	43	87.8'	1919	CHARDE R 90 - SUNK OFF PORTSMOUTH AFTER COLLISION 21.6.40
MISTRAL	99	42	43	87.8'	1919	GOLDEN LINE LT 619 - SCRAPPED 1948
MOONLIGHT	93	45	25	87.4'	1919	CARRY ON LT 553, COMPLETED AFTER CANCELLATION, SUNK OFF SHEERNESS - MINED 17.12.40
MOONRISE	92	44	25	88'	1920	MOONRISE LT 1003, ASCENDANT YH 35, COMPLETED AFTER CANCELLATION - TO NORWAY 1939

GOSSA WATER LK 173 - Wooden Standard Drifter built by Richards Ironworks, Lowestoft for Admiralty 1918 as HAILSTORM. Became GIRL LIZZIE LK 173, GOSSA WATER LK 173 converted to Salvage work 1952. Shown entering Lerwick with 260 crans of herring on board ca 1948. Courtesy of D. Georgeson, Shetland.

WOODEN STANDARD ADMIRALTY DRIFTERS
BUILDER   J.CHAMBERS LTD - LOWESTOFT

HMD Admiralty Name	G.T.	N.T.	H.P.	Length	Completon Date	HISTORY
AFTERGLOW	99	40	34	86.5	1918	SOLD TO FALKLAND ISLANDS AT PORT RICHARD 1981
AIRPOCKET	99	38	42	86.3'	1918	RENAMED AMBITIOUS 1919, CINERARIA KY 76, GY 51, AMBITIOUS
ANTICYCLONE	99	40	42	86.5'	1918	RN 1918 - 31, SOLD ABROAD - SCRAPPED 1942
ASTRAL	99	41	42	86.4'	1918	FOUNDERED ON PASSAGE TO GRIMSBY 1921
ATMOSPHERE	100	44	42	86.6'	1918	GY 1298, H 798, GY 45 - LOST 1929 OFF FLAMBOROUGH

WOODEN STANDARD ADMIRALTY DRIFTERS
BUILDER   J.CHAMBERS LTD - LOWESTOFT (CONTINUED)

HMD Admiralty Name	G.T.	N.T.	H.P.	Length	Completion Date	HISTORY
AVALANCHE	99	43	43	86.4'	1918	LOCHALSH INS 221, MOSTLY HERRING CARRIER - SCRAPPED 1938
SQUALL	100	42	42	86.2'	1918	BCK 399, GOLDEN FEATHER FR 11 - SCRAPPED 1936
STORMCENTRE	99	43	42	86.4'	1918	BD 6 ,"GY876 NORTHHAVEN, PD164 - SCRAPPED 1952
SWIRL	99	39	42	87'	1919	GY189 - SCRAPPED 1948
SUNLIGHT	98	35	34	86.3'	1919	HANNAH TAYLOR GY1193, SNOWSTORM - SCRAPPED 1935
TIDERIP	100	42	42	87'	1919	KENTISH BELLE R94 - SANK AFTER COLLISION 1923
SURGE	99	42	42	86.7'	1919	LT487 , RESURGE YH21 - SCRAPPED 1947
FLOTSAM	100	43	42	86.4'	1919	LT592, GY137 CRAIGROY FR 27 - LOST 1932
FLECK	99	42	42	86.2'	1919	LT599, M240
FIRELIGHT	99	42	42	86.3'	1919	LT726, JUST REWARD - SCRAPPED 1943
FLURRY	100	43	42	86.4'	1920	INS252, GLEAM ON PD37 - SCRAPPED 1950
THE FOLLOWING WERE COMPLETED AFTER CANCELLATION						
FLOODTIDE	88	37	30	83.6'	1920	MARJORIE GRACE LT491, YOUNG CHARLIE YH40 - SUNK OFF NEWLYN 1926
FLUTTER	88	37	30	83.5'	1920	GOLDEN SUNBEAM YH277 - SUNK OFF DUNGENESS 1943

GLEAM ON PD 37 - Wooden Standard Drifter built by J. Chambers Ltd. Lowestoft for Admiralty 1920 as FLURRY.
Became FLURRY INS 252, GLEAM ON PD 37. Scrapped 1950. Shown leaving Gt. Yarmouth ca 1948.
Courtesy of Scottish Fisheries Museum.

WOODEN STANDARD ADMIRALTY DRIFTERS
BUILDER   FELLOWS & CO. LTD. - YARMOUTH

HMD Admiralty Name	G.T.	N.T.	H.P.	Length	Completion Date	HISTORY
ETESIAN	94	38	42	86.3'	1918	ETESIAN BS26, INS575, M. H. STEPHEN FR17, SY 789 - SCRAPPED 1950
DAYLIGHT	94	38	42	86.5'	1918	RENAMED H.M.D. TRADEWIND, TRADEWIND BF575, HMD MONSOON WWII 1943 - 45 - SCRAPPED 1950
FIREBALL	95	39	42	86'	1920	MAVISON INS186, HOLLYDALE FR171, BF70 - SCRAPPED 1950
THE ABOVE THREE VESSELS WERE THE ONLY WOOD STANDARDS WITHOUT "TUMBLEHOME" STERNS							
NON- STANDARD VESSELS						
DARKNESS	95	40	42	86.8'	1918	HMD COLUMBINE, SEA HOLLY PD158, TAKEN OVER WHILST ON STOCKS - LOST NORTH EAST ATLANTIC 5.9.44
NO. 299 (YARD NO:)	100	43	29	86'	1921	NEWPORT PILOT CUTTER - BELLE VIEW

CLAPSON & SONS - BARTON ON HUMBER

HMD Admiralty Name	G.T.	N.T.	H.P.	Length	Completon Date	HISTORY
FOGBANK	95	41	42	86.5'	1920	DYKER LASSIE KY75 - SCRAPPED 1924, ENGINE BOILER BUILT INTO REFLORESCO KY16
FOUNTAIN	95	40	42	86.5'	1920	WHITENIGHT GY88

ROUTH - WADDINGHAM, WINTERINGHAM, WILTS

HMD Admiralty Name	G.T.	N.T.	H.P.	Length	Completon Date	HISTORY
SWELL	92	39	42	86'	1920	SILVERNIGHT GY138

COURTNEY, LYMINGTON, HAMPSHIRE (LATER BERTHON BOAT CO. LTD.)

HMD Admiralty Name	G.T.	N.T.	H.P.	Length	Completion Date	HISTORY
LOP	96	40	43	87'	1920	GREYNIGHT GY141 - SUNK 2.6.40
MAELSTROM	96	38	25	87'	1920	MAELSTROM GY15, FAIR HAVEN PD214 - LOST W.W.II 5.9.44 NORTH EAST ATLANTIC

ROSE STREET FOUNDRY & ENGINEERING CO. LTD., INVERNESS

HMD Admiralty Name	G.T.	N.T.	H.P.	Length	Completion Date	HISTORY
TROPIC	91	40	42	85.9'	1919	DUNDEE PILOT CUTTER 1922 - 47, JOHN PLENDERLEITH
THAW	93	43	42	85.9'	1920	THAW INS176, OLIVE LEAF PD196 - SCRAPPED 4.52

W. WOOD & SON, LOSSIEMOUTH

HMD Admiralty Name	G.T.	N.T.	H.P.	Length	Completon Date	HISTORY
FLUSH	97	41	42	87.4'	1920	FLUSH INS177, KY184, FD43 - SCRAPPED 1952

W. & G. STEPHEN - BANFF

HMD Admiralty Name	G.T.	N.T.	H.P.	Length	Completion Date	HISTORY
RED SKY	94	41	42	87.4'	1918	RED SKY BCK387, PD25 - CONVERTED TO SALVAGE VESSEL 1947
REFRACTION	93	41	42	87.4'	1919	REFRACTION BCK350, BF412, FR243, YH111 - SCRAPPED 1954
RIME	93	40	34	86.8'	1919	RIME PD166, BF 440 - SCRAPPED 1947
RAY	86	40	27	88'	1917	COMMANDEERED ON STOCKS RN 1917-27, NON STANDARD. MARGARET FRANCIS LH188 - LOST OFF BELHELVIE 12.37

WOODEN STANDARD ADMIRALTY DRIFTERS

BUILDER
G. INNES - MACDUFF

HMD Admiralty Name	G.T.	N.T.	H.P.	Length	Completion Date	HISTORY
SHEETLIGHTNING	92	33	42	85.8'	1918	ROSEACRE BF479, PD99 - SCRAPPED 1948
ST. ELMO'S LIGHT	94	40	42	86.8'	1919	BCK354, SWEET PROMISE PD385 - TO SALVAGE VESSEL 1950
THUNDERBOLT	97	41	43	87'	1920	INA ADAM KY42, MIDNIGHT SUN GY 7, GREEN PASTURES PD39, FR 72 - SCRAPPED 1950
IRIDESCENCE	94	40	42	83	1917	COMMANDEERED ON STOCKS, RN 1917-26, THEN SOLD, NON - STANDARD

STEVENSON & ASHER - BANFF

HMD Admiralty Name	G.T.	N.T.	H.P.	Length	Completion Date	HISTORY
SHADOW	95	34	43	86.5'	1918	PILOT US WK177, PD219 - SCRAPPED 1950
STORMWRACK	95	31	42	86'.3'	1918	RN 1918 - 27, PERILIA FR110 - SCRAPPED 1950
STARLIGHT	94	41	42	86.2'	1919	STARLIGHT RAYS KY68, PD21 - SCRAPPED 1949
SUNRISE	94	41	46	86.9'	1919	RENAMED TAALHINA, TAALHINA LT621,SCANIA, TILLY DUFF FR190 - SCRAPPED 1947

JONES' BUCKIE SLIP & SHIPYARD LTD. - BUCKIE

HMD Admiralty Name	G.T.	N.T.	H.P.	Length	Completion Date	HISTORY
IMBAT	92	33	45	87.1'	1918	IMBAT BCK384, PD105 - SUNK AT SCAPA FLOW 4.2.41
ICEBLINK	94	40	43	87'	1920	STAR DIVINE PD377 - SUNK KYLE OF LOCHALSH NARROWS 2.39

G.SMITH, JR. - BUCKIE

HMD Admiralty Name	G.T.	N.T.	H.P.	Length	Completion Date	HISTORY
PACKICE	94	40	42	86.7'	1918	PACKICE INS314, MURRAY CLAN INS314, UTILISE PD17 - SCRAPPED 1952
RIFT	94	40	42	87.6'	1920	DOORIE BRAES INS344 - SCRAPPED 1946
PHASE	96	40	34	87'	1920	PHASE PD197, INS301, BCK91 - SCRAPPED 1951

STARLIGHT RAYS PD 21 - Wooden Standard Drifter built by Stevenson & Asher, Banff for Admiralty 1919 as STARLIGHT. Became STARLIGHT RAYS KY 68, PD 21. Scrapped 1949. Shown entering Gt. Yarmouth ca 1947. Courtesy of Scottish Fisheries Museum.

UTILISE PD 17 - Wooden Standard Drifter built by G. Smith, Jr., Buckie for Admiralty 1918 as PACKICE. Became PACKICE INS 314, MURRAY CLAN INS 314, UTILISE PD 17. Scrapped 1952. Shown entering Peterhead ca 1947. Courtesy of Scottish Fisheries Museum.

WOODEN STANDARD ADMIRALTY DRIFTERS
BUILDER   HERD & MCKENZIE - FINDOCHTY

HMD Admiralty Name	G.T.	N.T.	H.P.	Length	Completion Date	HISTORY
SOLSTICE	98	43	43	87'	1918	SOLSTICE INS276, BF140 - SCRAPPED 1950
SILT	100	43	43	87'	1919	ROSE VALLEY INS94 - LOST W.W.II 16.12.43 AT SCAPA FLOW
SUNSPOT	100	42	34	87' .6'	1920	SUNSPOT INS317, MARY JOHNSTON BF15 - SCRAPPED 2.51

W. NOBLE & CO. - FRASERBURGH

HMD Admiralty Name	G.T.	N.T.	H.P.	Length	Completion Date	HISTORY
MACKEREL SKY	92	33	43	87.6'	1919	DRAINIE INS365, HEADWAY FR37 - SCRAPPED 1951
MILKY WAY	92	39	42	86.9'	1919	MILKY WAY BF336, BOYDS FR294 - SCRAPPED 1951

KITTO & SONS - PORTLETHEN, CORNWALL

HMD Admiralty Name	G.T.	N.T.	H.P.	Length	Completion Date	HISTORY
WILL O'THE WISP	96	35	34	85.9'	1920	WATERWAY - SOLD TO FRANCE

J. & G. FORBES - SANDHAVEN & FRASERBURGH

HMD Admiralty Name	G.T.	N.T.	H.P.	Length	Completion Date	HISTORY
FAIRWEATHER	93	39	42	86.5'	1918	FAIRWEATHER KY47, PD603 - SCRAPPED 1948
FIERY CROSS	93	36	43	86.4'	1918	FIRCROFT GY242 - SCRAPPED 1948
FIRMAMENT	93	39	43	86.5'	1918	FR 242, FOXGLOVE PD593 - SCRAPPED 1939
FLAME	92	40	42	86.5'	1918	UBEROUS KY62, PD249 - LOST W.W.II 11.1.41 OFF LONDONDERRY
FULL MOON	93	39	42	86.5'	1918	RN 1918-29, ROSEHAUGH INS20, BF98 - SCRAPPED 1950
GLEAM	92	39	43	87.1'	1919	DOUGALS BK247, REIDS PD189 - SCRAPPED 1947
GLOAMING	93	39	42	87.1'	1919	RN 1919 - 21 WRECKED OFF LIZARD 3.21 - SALVED AND SOLD 1922
GREEK FIRE	93	39	42	86.5'	1920	FR 89 PARADIGM , BK147 - SCRAPPED 11.51
GLACIER	96	40	42	87.1'	1918	BF 203, GIRL JOEY LK166, SILVER SKY PD41 - SCRAPPED 1951
GLINT	95	40	42	86.9'	1919	GLINT BCK352, PROSPECTS AHEAD KY74, PD596 - LOST OFF GREAT YARMOUTH 1949
GREY SKY	96	41	43	86.9'	1920	GREY SKY LK168, STAR OF BUCHAN FR3 - WRECKED OFF STORNOWAY 1940

WOODEN STANDARD ADMIRALTY DRIFTERS
BUILDER   J. & G. FORBES - SANDHAVEN & FRASERBURGH (CONTINUED)

HMD Admiralty Name	G.T.	N.T.	H.P.	Length	Completion Date	HISTORY
HULLS COMMANDEERED ON STOCKS AT SANDHAVEN - NON STANDARD						
FLAT CALM	94	39	43	86.5'	1918	RN 1918-1930, ROWAN TREE BF199 - LOST W.W.II 21.11.41 OFF LOWESTOFT
FOGBOW	94	39	43	87.8'	1918	FERTILE VALE BF52, FR103 - LOST W.W.II 17.7.41 - OFF TAY ESTUARY

UBEROUS KY 62 - Wooden Standard Drifter built by J. & G. Forbes, Sandhaven for Admiralty 1918 as FLAME.
Became UBEROUS KY 62, PD 249, lost off Londonderry January 1941. Shown in Anstruther Harbour ca 1930.
Courtesy of Scottish Fisheries Museum.

WOODEN ADMIRALTY DRIFTERS
BUILDER   R. DUNSTAN LTD. - THORNE, YORKS

HMD Admiralty Name	G.T.	N.T.	H.P.	Length	Completion Date	HISTORY
SPATE	96	32	43	86.6'	1919	SPATE H 326, MARGUERITA M11
SPLASH	96	34	43	86.6'	1920	RN HMD SPACE 1920, SPACE H 293, BELOVAR GY 410 - LOST 1928

G.T.SMITH & CO., RYE, SUSSEX

HMD Admiralty Name	G.T.	N.T.	H.P.	Length	Completion Date	HISTORY
DOLDRUM	94	40	42	86.8'	1920	BEATRICE EVES LT 291, GLOAMIN FR 96, HERRING CARRIER WRECKED LOCH BOISDALE 1948
VAPOUR	95	39	42	87'	1920	VAPOUR LT 1088, XMAS EVE BF 86, FR 68 - SCRAPPED 1951

VAPOUR LT 1088 - Wooden Standard Drifter built by G. T. Smith & Co. Rye, Sussex for Admiralty 1920 as VAPOUR.
Became VAPOUR LT 1088, XMAS EVE BF 86, FR 68. Scrapped 1951. Shown in Lowestoft ca early 1920's.
Courtesy of Scottish Fisheries Museum.

<u>Acknowledgements</u>

A number of persons have, over the years, been involved in the compilation of this list of Steam Drifters and I inherited a basic list before starting this project. I believe that the compilation was begun by Captain Buchan of Peterhead and was added to by the late David Smith of Cellardyke, the late Alec Stevenson of St Monans along with Henry Findlay of Anstruther.

Grateful thanks to the following:

Alistair Parket of Perth provided valuable assistance in filling in gaps in the details from his extensive records of Scottish Fishing Vessels.

Kate Newlands, sometime curator of the Scottish Fisheries Museum and Dr. Robert Prescott of St. Andrews University for very helpful suggestions to the first draft.

Sandy Mackie and John Doig for producing prints of all the photographs used.

Malcolm Stockdale of Grimsby for information on English drifters and their builders.

Sid Durrant of Kessingland for some photographs.

The Port of Lowestoft Research Society for providing some photographs.

Mrs. Margaret Sutherland for extremely valuable computer assistance.

Mrs. Chris Pringle for the typing work.

Linda Fitzpatrick for reading and correcting the proofs.

The Board of Trustees of the Scottish Fisheries Museum for their encouragement and agreement to publish the book.

Lastly but certainly not least, David Smith of Anstruther for his enthusiasm and encouragement.

James Tarvit